The Europeanization of Cinema

The Europeanization of Cinema

Interzones and Imaginative Communities

RANDALL HALLE

UNIVERSITY OF ILLINOIS PRESS
Urbana, Chicago, and Springfield

Manufactured in the United States of America
1 2 3 4 5 C P 5 4 3 2 1

This book is printed on acid-free paper.

Library of Congress Cataloging-in-Publication Data
Halle, Randall.
The Europeanization of cinema : interzones and imaginative communities / Randall Halle.
pages cm
Includes bibliographical references and index.
ISBN 978-0-252-03845-7 (hardback)
ISBN 978-0-252-07995-5 (paper)
ISBN 978-0-252-09633-4 (ebook)
1. Motion pictures—Europe—History. 2. Space and time in motion pictures.
I. Title.
PN1993.5.E8H34 2014
791.43'094—dc23 2013047792

Contents

Acknowledgments

Major research for this book was conducted while I was a Fulbright Scholar. I benefited greatly from the generosity of that grant and the time it afforded.

Many people have given much appreciated feedback on various parts of the project along the way. I would especially like to thank Savaş Arslan, David Bathrick, Daniela Berghahn, Paul Cooke, John Davidson, Kristin Dickenson, Tobias Ebbrecht, Friederike Eigler, Janina Falkowska, Veronika Fuechtner, Deniz Göktürk, David Gramling, Sabine Hake, Ewa Hauser, Todd Kontje, Priscilla Layne, Venkat Mani, Barbara Mennel, Tobias Nagl, Mary Rhiel, Katrin Sieg, Jill Smith, Ayça Tunç, and Astrid Weigert.

The University of Pittsburgh has offered me a great intellectual home and my colleagues have been a great support and important interlocutors. The programs in German Studies, Film Studies, Cultural Studies, European Studies, Global Studies, and the Humanities Center have variously offered important venues in which I could benefit from the exchange of ideas. I want to thank Susan Andrade, Jonathan Arac, Daniel Balderston, Suzanna Crage, Nancy Condee, Sabine von Dirke, Pinar Emiralioğlu, Lucy Fischer, Jane Feuer, Lina Insana, Marcia Landy, John Lyon, Colin MacCabe, Barbara McCloskey, Clark Muenzer, Volodia Padunov, Alberta Sbragia, Terry Smith, and Gregor Thum. I appreciate very much N. John Cooper's generous support of the book; valuable leave time allowed me to bring it to completion.

I am grateful to the students in my seminars for the opportunity to develop ideas with them. The conversations with Yvonne Franke along the way helped clarify many ideas and I am happy she is now a colleague in the profession.

Sabine Penak and Rita Bakacs have graciously offered their insights and insider knowledge.

I am grateful to Nancy Albright for her careful engagement with the text. Danny Nasset has been an exceptional editor.

Most of all I want to thank Mohammed Bamyeh, who was there.

The Europeanization of Cinema

Introduction

The Idea of Bridges and the Image of Roads: Culture and Space

Traveling along the Oder-Neisse rivers that form the border between Germany and Poland, one confronts a series of ruins, bridge supports standing on the banks and in the water of the rivers, with the spans that once stretched over them missing. The retreating forces of the Third Reich blew up these bridges to hinder the advance of the Soviet army. This measure may have served a purpose in the Spring of 1945 when the water was higher, but in the summer weather much of the Neisse dwindles to a level where it is possible simply to step broadly from sandbar to sandbar without having to get even the hem of long pants wet. These rivers did not serve as barriers historically, certainly not borders; rather, they tended to function as transportation routes that allowed trade to flourish and cities to grow up on either side of the banks. The question one confronts when traveling along the banks of the Oder and Neisse rivers is not what made this a border. There is an easy and obvious answer to that question: the decision of state power declared these rivers a border. The more interesting question really is what was it that obstructed for decades the understanding of these banks of the rivers as actually belonging together.

Certainly when one travels along the banks now, there is a plethora of new bridges, some small pedestrian bridges, some large enough to bear double-rig long-haul semis laden with materials of all kinds. Some of the bridges are structured with border-crossing lanes, evidencing architecturally that they were built between 1990 and 2007—the period after the fall of the Wall and before the entry of Poland into the Schengen Area. Some of the bridges simply span the river with no sign of restriction or control, maybe a Polish flag on the one side and a German on the other and a European on both. Clearly, such bridges were built after 2007 and evidence a new European architecture. They are built for the freedom of movement afforded to members of the EU.

Most of the bridges span the river to link cities. There are a few notable exceptions such as the crossing point of the E40, the longest highway in Europe, which stretches from the coast of France to the edge of China. In considering the centrality of cities to the bridges, one has a sense that for the divided cities along the border—Frankfurt/Słubice, Guben/Gubin, Bad Muskau/Łęknica, Görlitz/Zgorzelec, and so on—they are overcoming not just the physical but also ideational obstructions that hindered the spanning of the rivers since the end of World War II. The ruins of bridges along the way, however, tend to be in the middle of fields, or in spots where there is a city on only one side. Historically, many of these towns, especially those now on the German side, spanned the banks of the river to the other side. In many instances the other side simply no longer exists, dismantled by the same state powers that once declared it a border. The Polish side of the river is riddled with flagstones of forgotten streets and foundations of demolished buildings. These ruins thus bear witness to a distinction of sides, a continuing sense that for those who live on either side, there is nothing on the immediate other side that merits (re)building what once connected.

Traveling along the Oder-Neisse border, one has a sense of the relationship of the ideational and the material. It is not the bridges that spanned the rivers, but rather the idea that both sides stand in connection to each other that formed the bridges. The idea of bridging precedes the spanning of the two sides. The awareness of a need or desire to connect compels the material association. Yet also it is not just the idea of a bridge as such that gave rise to these bits of architecture but rather an understanding of how the two sides belong together that gave them specific form. One-lane, two-lane, multilane; with or without guardhouse; with or without ornamentation—these are not any bridges. Each of these bridges instantiates the kinds of material needs and ideational connections that operate in the moment of their construction, destruction, and/or reconstruction.

Moreover, the ideational connection does not require a bridge to be drawn; the sense of contact can derive from relations not bound up in immediate proximity. Consider that in 2009 starting from the Kottbusser Tor and stretching over the Dresdener Strasse, to the Oranienplatz in Berlin Kreuzberg, the home to Germany's most populous Turkish community, the photographer Uta Langkafel installed twenty large-format, broad-panorama, color photos of the stretches of highway between Berlin and Istanbul, the stretches of highway that famously many of the *Gastarbeiter* (guest worker families) traveled in order to spend holidays in Turkey. These trips are legendary: autos packed full with families, luggage, food, and gifts, often traveling for three days straight through to get to their destinations. The trip covered all of central Europe stretching from Germany and Austria to Czechoslovakia and Hungary, through all the republics of the former Yugoslavia, into Greece, Rumania, and Bulgaria, arriving via various highways at the border of Turkey. Long lines marked the border-crossings made during the midst of the Cold War.

The photos appear without comment all at about the same level, parallel to the house numbers on the street. They can be passed by with little notice, or just taken for decoration without understanding the nature of the journey. The installation of the photos in this neighborhood, spread out between two large and busy squares, nevertheless invites consideration from those who traveled the route and from those who did not. Langkafel keeps the photos largely free of individuals and seeks instead to consider them as projection surfaces of the journey. The memories and desires of first-generation migrants who visited their points of departure play a significant role, but so do those of the second and third generation, who began to experience the trips as holiday visits to often distant and extended family. For those who did not make the journey, for those without "a migrant background," the contemporary politically correct appellation to describe the children of the *Gastarbeiter*, the series sets up a possibility of attachment, least of all to the locations and the route. Rather, it sets of the possibility of an attachment to those who did make the journey. The trip to Istanbul becomes thus a part of the communal experience of all those living in Kreuzberg and all those passing by the installation—with or without migrant background.

The cities Ljubljana, Beograd, Niš, Skopje, and Sofia appear in the photos as central transit points along the route. Langkafel notes that the cities were not tourist sites in themselves; rather, they were spots along the way of journey of forty or more hours. Hence the photos are taken from roads and bypasses. The photos bespeak a journey spanning a distance like a bridge, from Berlin to another place located across a much greater distance than the stretch of the Oder and Neisse, yet ideationally more proximate, more connected. Here the photos and the installation form a different kind of bridge. Where the blasted bridges mark a lack of connection between people living often not more than fifty meters apart, the photos portray an imaginative communal connection across eighteen hundred kilometers of space. The expanse is spanned by the ideational relationship. Beyond the typical movement in Berlin's urban landscape, the installation positions the "spectators," typically pedestrians, in a multiplied multivalent space.

Toward the Interzone

The bridge as cultural metaphor has served as an all too frequent trope, and the bridge as an expanse between cultures or as an experience of being between cultures has received much insightful criticism. Leslie Adelson has importantly critiqued the imposition of the bridge metaphor, identifying how dominant discourse has historically excluded migrants by locating them in a condition between two places.[1] Such "in-betweenism" keeps individuals in a status as foreign, outsider, between two cultures and therefore belonging to none. Adelson encourages us to look beyond "between." This is an important critical point, yet by taking up the bridge here, I am not seeking to develop that trope. Rather, I am interested in acknowledging that

1. This is a common trope not limited to exclusionary politics; the trope is common in Turkey, offering a sense of purpose and even pride in being a culture and state that bridges Europe and Asia. Likewise, the historic communities of ethnic Germans that once resided throughout Central Europe all the way down to regions in contemporary Turkey understood themselves in this very same bridging role.

2. The problem with in-betweenism is fundamentally that it perceives the bridge as a nonspace between point A and B. I am interested in this study in exploring how this space of spanning is indeed a very real and material place. Even if we largely want only to get to the other side on these journeys, Ljubljana, Beograd, Niš, Skopje, and Sofia exist, the roads exist, the architecture of the bridges is unique, and this space of spanning is a *zone* with its own particular dynamic. Moreover, this type of connecting zone needs our direct and specific attention because it is increasingly a significant space of geopolitical relations. It plays especially a key role in the cultural dynamic of Europeanization, how the European imaginative community is being formed.

The bridge discussed here is not a sign of a connection between two ontological realms; rather, it is a marker of a space of becoming, of *interzones*. The nature of the interzone calls for investigation, but immediately the two examples display a dynamic of the interzone. These examples indicate two different experiences of space in Europe, two different experiences of proximity and commonality: the Polish-German is spatially close yet understood only haltingly as a common place, while the Turkish-German is geographically distant, certainly not contiguous, but understood as connected and even continuous. The interzone thus is an experience not limited to geographic cartographic proximity but rather an ideational space, a sense of being somewhere that unites two places, if even only transitionally or temporarily. For questions of globalization or specifically of Europeanization, this ideational connecting space is important because it is seldom if ever the case that people experience themselves as European. Europe is not a meta-identity. Europe is a space of transit crisscrossing and connecting A and B. Europe is not experienced as a totality but rather as that moment of productive transit in the interzone.

Ulrich Beck, central figure in considering processes of globalization, especially in Europe, wrote about the transformations underway, "What has previously lain hidden is thus becoming visible: namely, that there are not one but *many* Europes—a Europe of nations, a Europe of regions, a Europe of civilizations, a Europe of Christianities, and so on."[2] He unearths different ways in which individuals imagine their interdependence. Beck does presume a common or general space, the expanse of Europe stretching from the Atlantic to some point east, but he recognizes that Europe is not limited to the eastern border of the EU. This vagary of where Europe ends forces us to attend to how this Europe is a new space, a multiple fractured and heterogeneous space that operates according to terms distinct from the nation-state and in need of better more thorough consideration. We need to account for a condition that is not either/or, either national or European, either regional or civilizational, either Christian or Muslim; rather, we need to account for a condition that opens the possibilities of a here and now. My proposition is that transnationalism in Europe is *not* leading to a cultural space unified along the same model of the nation-state. Hence I draw on the understanding of zone and the possibility it offers.

Imaginings of the Zone

Zone certainly has an important prehistory in a world divided into time zones and temperate zones. Famously, Guillaume Apollinaire published his classic of surrealist modernist poetry with the title "Zone" in 1913 at the advent of the great European bloodletting:

> À la fin tu es las de ce monde ancien
>
> Bergère ô tour Eiffel le troupeau des ponts bêle ce matin
>
> Tu en as assez de vivre dans l'antiquité grecque et romaine
>
> Ici même les automobiles ont l'air d'être anciennes
> La religion seule est restée toute neuve la religion
> Est restée simple comme les hangars de Port-Aviation
>
> Seul en Europe tu n'es pas antique ô Christianisme
> L'Européen le plus moderne c'est vous Pape Pie X

Et toi que les fenêtres observent la honte te retient
D'entrer dans une église et de t'y confesser ce matin
Tu lis les prospectus les catalogues les affiches qui chantent tout haut
Voilà la poésie ce matin et pour la prose il y a les journaux
Il y a les livraisons à 25 centimes pleines d'aventures policières
Portraits des grands hommes et mille titres divers

J'ai vu ce matin une rue dont j'ai oublié le nom[3]
[. . .]

Hans-Robert Jauss described the poem as the programmatic lyrical production that, in contrast to the ambiguity of the "countless theoretical manifestos of the period," actually "marked the threshold to a new wave of modernism, which would henceforth be characterized by the concept of the avant-garde."[4] In it the Eiffel Tower is a shepherdess who stands above a world of rapidly altering time, in which even the most modern of transportation, the auto, has already become antique and the most antique of human experience, religion, has become the height of modernity. She, symbol of industrial modern design, is tired of, even fed up with, all this antiquity at her feet. "Zone" is at once a space but also slang for a walk, to bum about, the actions perhaps of a flaneur. Thus the lyric voice speaks to you as they traverses and leaps rapidly across private and public spaces, across Paris and across France and Europe and the globe. The verbs slip from present to past to future, leaping likewise in time. "Zone" is a space of contrast, old and new, modern and antique, here and there, now and then, you and I, and a she that is coexistent in the poem but unstable and fracturing, at times blood-soaked and cut-throated, at times sublimely beautiful in a ray of light.

The poem observes something of the experience of the world that is new, modern, and needing a transformation of form and technique to find expression. "Zone" designates the space of this experience and the ability to traverse. In vastly different realms of discourse, the word comes into use to demarcate this modern spatial temporal experience. It is not so much Harvey's famous space-time compression but rather a warping and folding of space and time. The world of zones is not smaller as such but that which was once distant is proximate and that which was once primitive is now coeval, while exactly that which is down the street or seated across in the same bus is distant and from another time.

In their discussions of postmodern models of communication, literary scholars Ellen Berry and Mikhail Epstein speak of a contemporary transcultural "zone of fuzziness and interference" that challenges historic models of discreet identity, like the nation-state model.[5] Considering the Russian critical tradition that influences Epstein and Berry, we could look back to Mikhail Bakhtin who employed zone in his discussion of the challenge heteroglossia presents to authoritative discourse; he described a "contact zone, which results in semantic and emotionally expressive (intonational) changes."[6] The term *contact zone* that Bakhtin deployed there was, of course, a transformation of a linguistic understanding of what happens when relations develop between speakers of differing languages, such as the trade relations on the East African coast that developed between Arabic- and Bantu-speaking merchants among others. The contact zone is the place out of which pidgins, creoles, and eventually new means of communication arise.

Bakhtin was considering the possibility of multiple language systems within an already existing linguistic frame; the contact zone of empire and nation, of aristocrat and plebian, of Stalinist bureaucrats and formalist poets. Drawing from the use of contact zone in the Saussurean/structuralist direction of linguistics, Mary Louise Pratt underscored the aspect of power in zone. Her discussion of contact zone considered "the space of colonial encounters, the space in which peoples geographically and historically separated come into contact with each other and establish ongoing relations, usually involving conditions of coercion, radical inequality, and intractable conflict."[7] For Pratt, the contact zone is "often synonymous with 'colonial frontier.'"[8] Pratt concentrates in her discussion of zones on the contact between peoples who were geographically and historically brought into intersection by colonial activity.

Sheila Petty took up the term in her work *Contact Zones* in which she considers Black diasporic cinema as exemplifying a "not-here/not-there" condition of the contemporary globalized world.[9] Petty notes that this condition has actually characterized the experience of people of African descent who survived the Middle Passage across the Atlantic. The book attends to the experience of the Black diaspora, attaining a broad sweep across the Atlantic, not just an African American experience.

Aihwa Ong similarly considers zones as a matter of material-economic contact but by contrast discusses zones as a question of "graduated sovereignty" within a particular terrain of long historic inhabitation. She notes "these zones, which do not necessarily follow political borders, often contain ethnically marked class groupings, which in practice are subjected to regimes of rights and obligations that are different from those in other zones."[10] For Ong, zones can be noncontiguous; the spatial and temporal quality of a zone does not need to map out onto a standard grid. Rather, multiple zones can fill the same territory, the same street, while a single zone can describe relations in disparate points across the globe. Likewise, while coeval a radically different sense of history and time can infuse conterminous zones.

Germany was of course divided into occupation zones after World War II. In 1947 the British and American occupation forces formed their zones into an administrative unit known as *Bizonia*, and in March of 1948 the addition of the French-occupied territory resulted in the creation of *Trizonia*. This administrative precursor to the West German state intensified growing Cold War tensions with the Soviet occupying forces. The experience of living in these various contested and conflictual zones resulted in a certain creativity and led Karl Berbuer famously to write the song "Wir sind die Eingeborenen von Trizonesian" ["We Are the Natives of Trizonia"] (1948), which became a great hit in the 1949 Carnival festivities. It humorously described life in "Trizonia" a world of new political orders. The lyrics began noting that the old days are gone and now "a small pile of diplomats is responsible for today's grand politics. They create zones and alter ." The song helped as a parody of the tense conditions that surrounded the final division of Germany in that year and was so popular that it competed for a while as an alternative national anthem for West Germany. We could understand Trizonia as designating a condition more inchoate and complex than the clear relations that resulted with the constitution of the two states, the Federal Republic and the Democratic Republic of Germany. And while the creation of the two states may have resulted in a certain geopolitical clarity defined by two sides, the popularity of Trizonia bespeaks a human ability to imagine relations in a much more complex fashion than just (two) state borders.

The term *zone* did not disappear from German culture; at that point of the founding of the two states, the term *interzone* became codified and designated a new and concrete experience. The train that traveled from the FRG to the GDR was designated for instance as the *Interzonenzug*, the interzonal train. The term *interzone*, we can recognize, develops then as a specific and localized term of contact and transfer. Much later, in 1990, video artist Franz John recorded his famous *Interzone* project in which he traveled the length of the death strip that had constituted the, by that time, defunct but still largely intact *Mauer*. Passing between the Wall that once divided Berlin, he filmed this old space of surveillance and threat drawing on the term *interzone* to designate this space between the two barriers that constituted the Wall. At the same time William S. Burroughs drew on the term as title for a late literary collection, which, among other things, reflected on his experiences in Tangiers in the 1950s but also, typically, his countercultural drug and sexual experiences.[11] In 1997 Kevin Mumford published a detailed study of the black/white sex districts in Chicago under the title *interzone*. Here the term demarcated a kind of illicit and liminal interracial space.

The Interzonal Space

In all these works, then, the term *zone* describes a material ideational relationship that occupies a complex and contested space. A zone designates a relationship in which language and culture cannot describe easy and clear categories. Language is, in the broadest sense, communication, in which discreet linguistic units of "proper" standard grammar hold little meaning and rather give way to a localist vernacular born out of a necessity to interact across whatever barrier. Culture is not the sum of attitudes, customs, and beliefs that distinguishes one group of people from another; nor is it is transmitted, through language, material objects, ritual, institutions, and art, from one generation to the next; nor is it that which distinguishes as highly civilized particular subjects from the rest. *Culture is a fluid, transforming possibility of interaction arising out of the contact of peoples with differing and varying interests. Culture thus happens in zones; it is that possibility that raises the distinctions between groups of people and changes from generation to generation at such a pace that it undermines institutions and destabilizes rituals.* These aspects of zone are fundamental to the understanding of interzone developed in this study.

The interzone is a material and a psychical terrain and it designates a space in which divergent communities of people actually come in contact. What we recognize in these historic approaches is that the interzone was largely ignored by or off the map of the general public. The Interzonal Train was not a stable place, but a transient experience. At times, though, something could emerge out of the interzone itself: a localized space of a substantial kind of self-determination that can even contravene state authority and distant interests.

In the contemporary period, the interzonal possibilities expand because of the withdrawal of the nation-state from the singular privileged organizing position it had acquired over especially geopolitical definitions of space. Europe is of primary importance for the contemporary consideration of the interzone in that the European Union constitutes itself precisely as a space designed to eliminate state borders. However—and this is why we need to consider a term like *interzone*—reconsidering the last two decades, we can note that the lifting of state borders in the EU has resulted in the proliferation of mental borders. The free flow of people, goods, and services fostered by a Europe without borders has actually resulted in the dynamic production of distinctions based on class, region, ethnicity, religion, education, locality, dialect, and so on. In contradistinction to the celebrations of freedom of movement, increased mobility has not generated a condition in which people move without borders and boundaries; rather, the distinctions of solidarity and community have become located more firmly in the cognitive maps of the roughly five hundred million inhabitants of the EU. Simultaneously and without paradox, the proliferation of communities has expanded experiences of contact and cohabitation. The Europe I speak of is thus not to be reduced to a cartographic space; rather, it is a process. Europeanization promotes border-crossings *and* the proliferation of imaginative communities. Europe, inasmuch as it is a space, is an interzonal terrain.

Culture and/of Europeanization

To this date the questions of culture in the European Union, or even the culture of the European Union, have been underexamined. The European Union Studies Association—the premier scholarly and professional association focusing on the European Union, the ongoing integration process, and transatlantic relations, founded in 1988, with members on all continents—has an executive committee that consists exclusively of social scientists, almost all political scientists. The biennial conference has not, in its more than a decade of meetings, had a panel devoted to culture. At the annual International Conference for Europeanists organized by the Council for European Studies, an entity founded at my home institution, the question of culture has rarely appeared. On the very few panels and papers where it has appeared, culture has been discussed from a social scientific perspective: the culture of social movements, health care convergence, crisis management in institutions, Muslim culture clash.

Culture in the European Union or even the larger question of European culture has not been a central subject for humanists who have largely been trained in national models of studies, i.e., German Studies, French Studies, Italian Studies, Russian Studies, and so forth. These models have roots in the nineteenth-century period of nation-building and continue to train students with a nation-specific focus. Even Comparative Literature as a discipline traces its roots to this period and relies on models of comparativity based in national traditions, i.e., the French, German, and Russian novel. National models influence the approaches in the newer studies: e.g., Film Studies, Cultural Studies, or Gender Studies, because their practitioners come from positions with a national focus: e.g., German Film Studies, Italian Cultural Studies, or Gender in Poland. It is understandable and one cannot do everything; however, it is important that we attend to the developments of culture on a European level.

In my own home discipline of German Studies, decades ago the German Academic Exchange funded centers of German and European Studies. Deutsche Welle, the central German international news outlet shifted its orientation from German language programming to a largely English-language–based "made in

Germany" strategy. The German economy is understood as the motor of Europe; the German government dominates the policy of the Euro zone; and the German state understands a necessity to bail out not just regions of the former East Germany but countries in the EU. It is not an easy process, but Germany is not the state it was when founded in 1871, 1919, 1948, or 1991. Germany exists in a state of interdependence in the EU and beyond. France, likewise, and Italy, the Benelux, Poland, the other Central European states, most of Scandinavia, and so on exist now in a state of associated sovereignty and semiautonomy. Even if it is not recognized yet in the studies of Europe's cultures, EU subsidiarity has transformed the basic conditions of legitimacy, autonomy, and accountability through which the national communities were once imagined. The European condition of interdependence that orients the states of Europe needs to be taken into account in investigations of the cultures of Europe. If we do not, we run the risk of watching our objects of study move away from us. Our models of approach will become anachronistic.

In truth, though a certain privileging of the nation-state continues to obtain in political and social science, a neo-Hegelianism infuses the models of approach in the social sciences as well. The nation-state typically remains understood as the most important organizing factor of political organization and cultural production. Europe is approached as a next-order level of cognitive abstraction, beyond the local and national, frequently described as too distant and alienated to allow for strong cognitive maps of social relationships to develop.[12] This neo-Hegelianism is extensive, infusing the work of prominent commentators as varied as Jürgen Habermas, Étienne Balibar, Jacques Derridas, Fredric Jameson, and Ulrich Beck, resulting in an idealist analysis that negates the actual material, political, or cultural potentials of European transnational organization.

The New Realism

In the 1990s some social scientists focusing on the EU did begin a descriptive and comparative project frequently described as "institutional realism." Foundational for this direction was the work collected by Alberta Sbragia in *Europolitics: Institutions and Policymaking in the "new" European Community* and developed further by scholars such as Gary Marks, Stephen Leibfried, Paul Pierson, and Wolfgang and Sylvia Streeck.[13] This approach focused not on grand politics but on unremarkable processes such as the creation of a common milk policy, and in doing so it recognized in European transnational union not a deficiency vis-à-vis the nation-state, but a positive new form of political union. The realists suggested that contrary to the homogenizing imperatives of the nation-state, transnational union operates through a form of divergence and variation: *the fundamentally new European condition of multilateral associated sovereignty and national semisovereignty*.

The interzones project I describe here extends this realist strategy by attending to culture. Cultural union is of course one of the three central goals of Europeanization identified for the EU and the quality that actually distinguishes it the most from other globalist projects. In the world, many free-trade agreements exist that strive for the lifting of restrictions on the movement of goods, services, and peoples. The quest for political union is less common but not unknown: the League of Nations, the United Arab Republic, or the United Nations offered models that preceded the EU. The quest for cultural union marks the European project as distinctive. Cultural union is the expansive project. Cultural union here is not simply a macromodel of the culture of the nation-state—and that is the point of the interzone. It is something else, an open terrain, a field not delimited by borders but by traversal. Inasmuch as the institutional realists have tried to appreciate the new political possibilities inherent in the European Union, rather than simply compare it to known models of political organization, we need to consider ways to appreciate the new cultural possibilities rather than simply assess them in light of familiar models.

Europe Is . . .

Europe is what Europe is. The European Union is not a common collective of more than five hundred million people. The European Union is not Europe. Europe is not bound by clear borders. In the West, Europe extends to include Greenland and Iceland. Canada is part of a European commonwealth. North and South America as with the rest of the entire colonized world, which is to say the rest of the world, have been reshaped by European powers and shaped by European ideas. To the East the Urals and the Bosporus do not mark geological barriers between two continents. The gap between Europe and Asia is not like the gap between Australia and Asia. It is not even like the gap between Australia and New Zealand. Rather, the Urals and Bosporus belong to discourses that distinguish geopolitical collectives through cartographic lines that do not and cannot bespeak the reality of the people who live on and cross those lines. For the people who commute across the Bosporus on a daily basis, who travel by boat or who brave the constant traffic jams on the massive bridges that span the busy waterway below, the experience of traveling from Asia to Europe is less cumbersome than for those who travel from the European side of Atatürk

International airport to any point in the European Union. The barrier between the Schengen space of free travel in the EU and the space outside is a stronger abjecting apparatus than the discourse of continents.

The EU is not a perfect union. Europe is not a union at all. Europe is an idea that may inspire union. The EU is a weak union inspired by the idea of Europe and the idea of Europe is an idea constantly changed by the ideals with which it is imbued. Europe is filled with imaginative communities that compete with each other, motivate collectives, establish complex connectivities, and unsettle the simplest experience of neighborliness with the people next door. The EU is a decentralized and weak union that compels not one form of connection; rather, it multiplies connections; it compels connectivity, contact, commerce, correlation, communication. Europe is not a perfect union; it is a terrain of possibilities connected as interzones.

The interzone is not a perfect union; it is really not a union at all. It is a tentative communication that can double space and shift time, bind distant places, and give separated individuals a sense of possible community. Union, perfect or weak, does not happen because of a treaty or by decree. An apparatus of governance may organize peoples but that is no guarantee that the organization conveys a sense of union. Material-economic connections, contrary to Marx's assessment, do not result in unified identities. If union happens, weak or strong, perfect or imperfect, it transpires in a process that proceeds through a drawing in and together. It proceeds through interzones.

Cinema Is . . .

Cinema, the moving image experienced collectively, has been the privileged medium for the imagining of communities.[14] Print culture compelled those processes we describe as modernization. However the solitary pleasures of reading did not bring the reader into a public experience. Cinema arose with modern mass society and the moving image, experienced collectively, has brought spectators together not just to view imaginary worlds but to experience themselves as an audience. The audience is a community of the imagined, a transformation of a mass into a society at least for the duration. The much-vaunted death of cinema is nonsense. The black box of cinema is a historical form, one that will not entirely disappear, but clearly the new modes of producing and reproducing the moving image only expand and extend our ability to experience collectively. The current changes in the cinematic apparatus do not remove cinema from the world experience; rather, they make our experience of the world ever more cinematic. Our world is cinematic and our collectives are moving images.

The cinematic apparatus repeatedly and uniquely proves capable of imagining collectivities and of acting as a bridge to bring people together in new ways. Recall that after the great bloodletting of World War I, in 1921 the first "export" from Germany to the United States was *Das Kabinett des Doktor Caligari* (Wiene, 1920). Already in 1922 leading film producers from former antagonistic sides in Europe began considering the Film Europe project as a combining of resources on a European level.[15] Egyptian cinema, Indian Cinema, and Nigerian Cinema serve important roles in forming supraregional collectivities and uniting populations in diaspora. It goes without saying that Hollywood enjoys global success. Central to this ability of the cinematic apparatus has been the need to expand spectatorship in order to offset the cost of production. The more grandiose the imaginative project was, the higher the expense, and the broader the appeal necessary to draw in spectators. This may be changing. Recent film projects like *Iron Sky* (Vourensola, 2012) have developed crowd-sourced funding techniques as part of the production. Interestingly such projects simultaneously realize a grand film project *and* build a new form of enthusiastic spectator base.

Cinema has this ability universally, but the cinematic apparatus takes on a special form in the EU, a result of historical legacy, intentional transformations, and serendipitous developments out of ongoing experiments. The need for national cinemas to reach out beyond national boundaries meets the goal of cultural unification at the level of European governance. This combination has reorganized audiovisual production and fostered new imaginings of collectivities across the continent and beyond. The "problem" of European cultural union for the EU though is that European culture is not bound by the Schengen borders. There is a quasi-inside and -outside formed within the European cinematic apparatus. To foster cultural union means that the apparatus of governance is confronted by the promiscuity of cultural intercourse. Internally, inside the Schengen zone, we find free love. However "outside," the catholic potential of European culture confounds EU goals. European producers partner not just with each other but with colleagues in the United States, in India, in China, in North Africa, in sub-Saharan Africa, and so on.

Political union is easy to limit. Economic union can be defined by free-trade agreements. Cultural union has an ideational quality that is more difficult to control. Consider the mobility of European belonging. Algeria was once a part of the departmental system of France. Up until the Algerian War, the region was European. Ceuta and Melila on the coast of Morocco are in the territory of the EU. Up until the 1950s Turkey was considered a part of Europe. With the labor migration of the period, especially to Germany, Turkey shifted ideationally and politically to the outside of the European community. South Africa, the subcontinent, the ruling elite of much of East, West, and Central Africa was educated and trained in European elite settings; Australia, New Zealand, Hong Kong, Macau, the Falklands, hold fast to their Europeanness; the lists of world literature and world cinema are dominated by European works, the tug and push of mass migration: I reiterate, Europe has shaped the world. What part of the globe does not participate in European culture? What part of the globe does European union not affect?

European Film: Industry, Culture, and National Cinema

What is European film? How does European film differ from national film? The question of European film is increasingly a point of consideration. There has been great advance in the study of transnational film, although the national mode of production has remained frequently the primary mode of analysis. Important collections on European cinema like those Wendy Everett, Jill Forbes, Sarah Street, Elizabeth Ezra, or Mary Wood brought forward have offered historical overview but pursued precisely a set of national case studies to find specificity.[16] An influential and productive collection like Thomas Elsaesser's *European Cinema* draws together essays largely focused on single films. The contextualization the essays offer to those films sets them in a European context that has varying degrees of profile vis-à-vis Hollywood production. Like the other works mentioned here, European film has the potential to become thus a sum of national counter-cinematic practices. From Everett's volume through to Elsaesser, these scholars express deep critical concern over the success of European cinema's struggle against Hollywood.

Mike Wayne is less concerned about the contrast of Europe/Hollywood. With his book *The Politics of Contemporary European Cinema*, he offered a very solid overview of the dynamics of cinema production in Europe from the silent period to the present.[17] He sought to position national cinemas in international dynamics; his attention, however, was addressed at very broad dynamics in globalization and contains only marginal considerations of the mode of production initiated by the EU. In *European Film Industries*, by contrast, Anne Jäckel offered a thorough investigation starting with early Film Europe projects but focusing mainly on the interlocking mechanisms of the modes of film production in the contemporary EU.[18] Jäckel pays less attention to the contrast with Hollywood and instead details a lively dynamic film industry developing within the EU. In these works the question is less one of counter-cinematic practice and competition with Hollywood; rather, it is a broad engagement with industrial viability taking high and popular cultural film into account.

As response to the focus on art cinema, a few scholars have brought important attention to what this form really is and what role it plays in Europe. This work challenges some of the presumptions expressed in work on European cinema. While at the University of Rochester Mark Betz and I overlapped in our interests in European cinema.[19] His project *Beyond the Subtitle* brought high relief to the contours of European art cinema and revealed, through careful considerations of classics of film study critical investigation, how those films had emerged in a European condition of coproduction.[20] Betz challenged assumptions of language and interrogated how perceptions of national authenticity were actually misperceptions of the complexity of production. Rosalind Galt and Karl Schoonover extended this work to consider the problem of art cinema globally.[21] Katrin Sieg undertook an important comparative project considering the potentials of not just European cinema but also European theater.[22] Her work revealed that the effect of Europeanization extends throughout various modes of cultural production including the stage.

Rosalind Galt's own investigation of the new European cinema, *Redrawing the Map*, continues to stand out as a project that sought to apprehend the broad terrain of European production. This is a question with which a number of scholars have struggled. Remapping European space is a common goal in the attempts to apprehend transnational transformations to cinema in Europe.[23] In my work on *the transnational aesthetic*, I considered extensively this move from a national to a transnational mode of production in Europe.[24] In that work as well as with the work of my colleagues mentioned here I have become concerned by a neo-Hegelian presumption that infuses our approaches.

In the contemporary era transnational film now proceeds out of an already existent national film industry. And it is important to underscore that the European Union is not a United States of Europe in which the national federation supersedes the states. This assumption is key to the neo-Hegelianism in our work. Just as the EU operates according to a transnational principle of associated sovereignty that differs largely from the model of full sovereignty in the national era, we can expect that European cinema does not replace national cinema.[25] Associated sovereignty pools "competencies in over-lapping domains of power and interest."[26] Because of its associated sovereignty, discussions of the EU cannot take place without attention to the member states. Alberta Sbragia noted already the difference between analyses of the United States where typically state policies play a minor role in comparison to federal decisions.[27] Such is not the case in Europe. We cannot simply follow national production models to a new transnational meta-level. The transnational is incumbent on the national. The EU does not supersede; rather, it sublates the nation-states so that in the new system they remain constitutive. Thus to analyze German, French, Dutch, or Polish cinema means one de facto attends to Europe, while inversely it is impossible to consider Europe without attention to specific member states, such as Poland and Germany—and especially

Germany with its role as both catalyst of the European project and its economy as the central motor for Europe.

Consider that the national film apparatus proves malleable, allowing for coproductions; it precedes its transformation into a transnational form. The stamp of a transnational aesthetic is endowed now at a later state, partly as a competitive move and partly as a way of legitimizing such a move. A pointed focus on production underscores importantly that the economic and political conditions of the governing apparatus will shape the possibilities of film production. We can consider the historical difference between film production in the United States and the Soviet Union, which is well known, but likewise distinctive are the subsidy systems that defined New Wave French, German, or Italian film, and these in turn were distinctive from the Commonwealth policies that fostered film production in Australia, Canada, and New Zealand.

Yet, too rigid a distinction of industry from culture leads only to the dead end of base/superstructure debates. The economic and political conditions of the state are cultural. And when the nation-state enters into a transnational arrangement, as in the EU, then the transformations develop expressly through a shift that is simultaneously industrial and cultural, i.e., a shift in the full apparatus of production. To be sure, the shapes that pass on the screen always lag behind economic and technological arrangements; projection cannot precede production. Nevertheless this "lag" is so negligible that it cannot serve to define the primacy of the industrial aspect of the apparatus over the projected. What it can do, however, is create the conditions under which the projected diverges from the intended, under which the image sets out in a different direction than the orientation the state had given it in the first place.

Wim Wenders: Enacting the "Europe without Borders"

Wim Wenders's *Lisbon Story* (1994) was the first film of the "Europe without borders." Wenders, whose oeuvre contains many road movies, depicted the first journey across the newly opened European "frontier." In *Lisbon Story*, the main character Phillip Winter drives from Germany to Spain to find his lost friend Friedrich Monroe. That journey takes up a significant portion of the initial sequence. Narratively it serves no function. It does not drive the plot along. Winter could have flown or been shown entering into a car or train in Germany and getting out in Portugal. The film is not just interested in jumping from location A to location B. Instead we see Winter drive this distance. The film in effect visualizes the interzone connecting A and B. And this is a significant visualization of cultural transformation; first Winter drives through the rainy north, accompanied by the sound of the car radio, in German. Windshield wipers clear dirty rain from the window on which the camera is trained. As he moves south, the film shows how he passes through vacant guard booths at now defunct border-crossings. The sun comes out. The language of the radio changes to French, and Spanish, and Arabic, and finally Portuguese. After arriving, there is no subsequent reference to this journey.

The purpose of this sequence is to represent the crossing of open borders. In portraying the interzone here, the film transforms the terrain of the plot into a European and not a national or even international relation. In most of his films, which are road films, Wenders has displayed an interest in these border-crossings and experiences of transition. But here there is a new experience, that of crossing a Europe *without* borders.

The Genre of Contact Film: *One Day in Europe*

We could list other road movies that subsequently similarly traversed a European space. But more interesting perhaps is how these films gave way to a genre of *cultural contact films* in which mobility in the EU is not represented by travel as such as much as the contact that ensues when Europeans travel. Films like *Bin ich schön?*, *Bella Martha*, *L'Auberge Espagnole*, *Lichter*, and so on narrate directly international experiences of contact and transformation. They show Europeans in contact, that is to say they imagine individuals from different parts of Europe who represent their particular national qualities coming into contact. Spaniards meet Germans, Germans meet Italians, French come in contact with Spaniards, Ukrainians bump up against Poles and Germans; in these contact films the characters are driven by diverse and often divergent motivations, and participate in often halting communication.

As contact film we can examine *One Day in Europe* (Stöhr, 2005), a film that directly reflects a relationship to the new European mode of production. It is an episode film comprised of four segments, each taking place in different cities, but all transpiring in the course of the same day. The backdrop for the story is the Champions League final soccer game between Galatasaray and Deportivo La Coruña being played in Moscow. In addition to transpiring in settings located on the "four corners" of Europe, each of the episodes has a slight time shift, ending at a slightly later point in the game. Additionally, the narratives have a common genre structure, generally comedic; and they follow in each instance a traveler who is awkwardly out of place in the local setting, not being fluent or proficient in the language or regional customs, they are either robbed or stage a robbery, actions that bring them into contact with police, bureaucracies, and kindly locals. Finally, each episode is linked by an animation of a plane flying from an outline sketch of the cityscape in which the episode took place, to the site of the next one.

The film thus constitutes the kind of cinematic European space toward which Rosalind Galt pointed in her study.[28] This space occurs on a contiguous yet divergent land mass. Each episode is an interzonal moment, depicting journey and contact, a clash of cultures in which the figures vacillate between ethnic stereotypes and surprise twists. It thus belongs to a successful strategy of European storytelling epitomized by such films as *A Couch in New York*, *L'Auberge Espangole*, *Bella Martha*, *Italian for Beginners*, and so on, in which characters who are marked by cultural presumptions meet and interact: the orderly German is frustrated by the chaotic Italian. The romantic French character is appalled by the gauche Brit, while the naive post-totalitarian Pole is exploited by the good-hearted swindling Spaniard.

In the second of the four episodes, for instance, Rocco, a German tourist in Istanbul, stands against a window overlooking the city of Istanbul. Techno music fills the frame creating this as a space in opposition to the city over which the Muezzins's calls to prayer echo. A cliché connection of Germans to Techno and Turks to Islam, or the call to prayer, structures an opposition here especially when the spaces collapse in on each other at the point that Rocco turns off his computer and we realize that the music was diegetic, a result of Rocco's tastes and lack of engagement with the reality of the culture around him. Rocco sets off to feign a robbery so that he can submit an insurance claim that will reimburse him for his journey. Comedic elements arise at this point through certain inversions of expectations drawn again from clichés. Rocco the German proves to be a conman huckster trying to scam his system, while the Turks around him prove to be upright, law-abiding, hyperorderly.

Pretending to be traumatized Rocco jumps into Celal's cab and asks to be taken to the police station so he can file a report. Celal, recognizing Rocco as a German, switches the conversation out of international tourist English into German. Celal is a Swabian dialect speaker, his "Leit" [people, or peeps] hail from around Stuttgart and his attempts to apprehend the perpetrators and aid his countryman Rocco only confound Rocco's scam. Rocco ultimately gets in over his head vis-à-vis the Turkish police and in the end has to turn to Celal to bail him out.

The director Hannes Stöhr has made a career out of a consideration of people inhabiting transformed geopolitical spaces.[29] With *One Day in Europe*, we traverse a new geopolitical expanse of Europe, although the inclusion of Russia and Turkey as locations bespeaks the broader more open terrain of cultural unification, developing an understanding of Europe that exceeds EU boundaries.

For narrative realism, the multicultural cast of the film matches its locations, while behind the scenes, the apparatus of the film likewise bespeaks a form concomitant to the narrative. The press kit for the film states: "Just like the stories related in the film, the film itself has a truly pan-European origin that, surprisingly, seems perfectly natural. The core of the film team, centered around Hannes Stöhr, producers Sigrid Hoerner and Anne Leppin, . . . is completed by four teams from Moscow, Istanbul, Galicia and Berlin. *One Day in Europe* was produced by Berlin's *moneypenny filmproduktion* in coproduction with workshop, Spain's Filmanova, ZDF—Das kleine Fernsehsepiel, and in collaboration with ARTE and Televisión de Galicia." It received MEDIA support and was eventually selected to travel as part of a European Commission–organized European Cinema Days festival that traveled a global circuit including Tunisia, Palestine, and Burma.

This film of cultural contact functions very differently in its structure, technology, and technique in comparison to Wenders's work. While the cultural logic of *One Day* imagines communities beyond the EU, the apparatus of the film brings transnational coproduction film and television funds together, developing a specific crew for each location, therewith enacting a kind of multilateral semisovereignty that parallels the political and economic structure of the EU. Although the director and core crew feel quite capable of drawing disparate and remote regions of Europe together, traveling themselves into those regions and working across cultures to produce something that is at core a transnational film, ideationally, however, the story displays a fundamental internationalism. It does not suspend interzonal conflict into a larger dialogic space; rather, it continues to imagine Europe as a space of communities in communication.

The film's episodes propose a border-crossing as a journey into the land of the other. Celal's interzonal status, a German in Turkey and a Turk in Germany, is a polyglot and multivalent cultural quality that gives the episode its comedic twist. However, this quality does not appear in the other episodes in which the characters exhibit no such fluid qualities. They are more like Rocco, strangers among indigenes. As the film imagines it, Europe is a contiguous space of relatively homogeneous cultures and languages, heterogeneous to each other, although people are on the move, traversing those spaces. The travel breaks open that homogeneity and transforms the space into one of conflict. The film, though, is a comedy and strives for a positive resolution to interzonal conflict; while it suggests that to cross borders is to be out of place, nevertheless it avoids any essentializing nationalist logics of blood and soil. Rather, as with Rocco's reliance on Celal, to be out of place is also to subject oneself to the kindness of strangers. This is not Derrida's right of hospitality; rather, in the film through their contact both enter into a mutual dynamism, opening up new possibilities of community. This basic value marks the terrain on which all the interzones are experienced. Contact with other Europeans seems always to free the travelers, but if the end of the conflict that drives the plot does not result in a sublation of the difference between the peoples the film's types represent, nevertheless in the end they all prove to be better Europeans as a result of the contact.

Although *One Day in Europe* evidences specific visual strategies to relate the European narrative, there are more extensive aesthetic developments that have emerged that on the one hand promote a Europeanization qua universalization of the film and on the other hand recede into the deeper structuring formulas of the film, and hence they do not actually and easily appear to the spectator. We can think of films, for instance, that reveal a certain *operatic quality*. Opera knows no boundaries because the specifics of the language sung recede into questions of music, intonation, performance, literacy, and so on. Likewise, the language-"heavy" European films of the 1960s and 1970s give way to films that rely on the cinematic, the potential of the image and the editing. The lack of dependence on language liberates the image from a linguistic fetter and makes it immediately more mobile. Even documentaries, as a form once dominated by the informative narrative voice, now turn to the image of masses of birds flying, "Gypsies" playing music in global diaspora, feet walking on the streets of New York, long static shots of a monastery without comment.

The innovation in European cinema does not take place on the screen explicitly. It takes place behind the screen, and this is a point we will take up extensively in the first two chapters of this study. We must not ask just what has happened on the screen and what or how does it signify. We must learn to also ask, what does it mean that what is on the screen was produced in this way or that way? What does it mean that what was on the screen is produced within a certain realm of interests? It is not possible to say that what is on the screen is determined by the conditions of production alone, but it is possible to say that knowledge about the conditions of production certainly has the ability to transform our understanding of what is on the screen.

Transnational and Prenational Cinema/Interzones of Culture

The nation-state is not the only form of social organization. There were other forms of social organization before the nation-state and there is always a plethora of communal imaginings available at any given moment. To be sure the predominance of the nation-state as a globally privileged form of political organization has made it rich in material resources and coercive potentials;

nevertheless, there are and have been other imaginative communities—and this point becomes increasingly important in the contemporary transnational era.

Europeanization is not simply the easy and immediate sublation of the nation-state into a broader and more advanced form. It is a different if not alternative imaginative community. This study fundamentally critiques this general assumption found in the discussions of transnationalism, especially those focused on the European Union that understand European transnationalism as supranationalism. Europeanization retains the nation-state and yet unleashes the potential of other forms of social organization to exist in increased significance: the local, regional, global, but also the subcultural, minoritarian, ethnic, migrant, diasporic, exiled, displaced, relocated, nongovernmental. Not just the imagined community, but rather as this study investigates, cinema offers images for various imaginative communities. Unlike print culture, which was bound immediately to linguistic and ethnic-national communities, film from its start proved capable of crossing borders and appealing to divergent communities.

This study focuses on cinema as a privileged vehicle for the representation of imaginative communities. It considers questions of spatial and temporal organization in cinema as they intersect with the socioeconomic arrangements. It explores developments of transnational Europe but it also returns to a prenational era to investigate the interzonal potential of cinema. Right from its earliest days the moving image brought the distant close and it imbued the proximate and quotidian with a potential to become exotic and to entertain. (Workers leaving a factory, a gardener spraying a lawn, blacksmiths pounding, a baby being fed, a boxing kangaroo, dancing peasants, were film themes that thrilled audiences for years.)

This study develops its analysis according to four interrelated discussions.

1. Culture is not a product of a contained coherent unity growing out of a *Geist* of a homogeneous people. In the study of culture, attention beyond state boundaries and heedfulness to similarities one finds, combined with consideration of disjunctions within presumed unities reveals that culture is a matter of *complex connectivities*, alternative imaginative communities, and interzonal potentials. Culture is alive when it is changing, when it is a result of frictional contact and conflictual struggle. Currently the study of culture is shaped and formed by the discourse of the nation that presumes homogenous peoples and interests. We need to develop autonomous approaches that bespeak the reality of the social organization of the transnational era but also the prenational imperial era. Resolutely comparative perspectives foster such approaches.

2. Cinema is a privileged vehicle for the studying of cultural shifts. Film studies generally focus on the projected image, the surface of the screen. Yet the image is only a small part of cinema. Constituting its projections, cinema is a conjunction of three often conflictual forces: technology, politics, *and* economics. As a result of the conflictual quality of these forces, cinema destabilizes easily vis-à-vis any single interest. It is not just a vehicle for political interests, nor is it for economic or aesthetic interests. Thus the high period of European nation-building before and after World War I, a period of intense restrictive cultural and linguistic orientations, could not contain cinema. From the days of its first invention, film and the moving image sought to appeal to ever-larger audiences, reaching beyond borders. Cinema is *the* mechanism of complex connectivity. The conflicts of technological, political, and economic interests generate multiple orientations in cinema. They give rise to the central concept of the study: interzones.

3. This study discusses interzones as a conflictual dialogic space. By *interzone*, I mean that geographical and cultural space that develops through border-crossing in the broadest sense. The imperial condition contended differently with territory drawing borders and presuming locality differently than the ensuing national era. Now under conditions of globalization conditions have changed again; the crossing of borders for instance is less a matter of contiguous and continuous space and more a question of discontinuous places and transfer. Through all these eras, an interzone, as a physical and ideational space, is one of transit, interaction, transformation, and contentious and contested diversity.

4. Contemporary transnational economic and political configurations in particular have accelerated the production of such interzones. Europe in particular, and especially the Europe defined by the European Union, has a central role in this study because it is the vanguard of national and transnational organization. The free flow of people, goods, and services fostered by a contemporary Europe without borders has actually resulted in the dynamic production of distinctions based on class, region, ethnicity, religion, education, locality, dialect, and so on. In contradistinction to the celebrations of freedom of movement, increased mobility has not generated a condition in which people move without borders and boundaries; rather, the distinctions of solidarity and community have become located more firmly in the cognitive maps of the roughly five hundred million inhabitants of the EU. Simultaneously and without paradox, the proliferation of communities has expanded experiences of contact and cohabitation.

The Chapters of the Book

CHAPTER 1 THE FILM APPARATUS

In the emerging field of film studies in the 1960s the question of the cinematic apparatus was a hotly discussed and debated concept. The discussion of apparatus was international (in French, *dispositif*; in German, *Dispositiv* or *Apparat*; in Dutch, *Filmapparaat*, and so on) and in many instances foundational for the establishment of film studies as a discipline. Apparatus offered a means to consider precisely the study of film as more than formal analysis of the projected image; it sought to arrive at a more comprehensive discussion of cinema. The production of the image was understood not simply as an industrial tale—who wrote the script and what studio produced the image—but as a matter of signification, social relations, modes of production, methods of projection, space of reception, and subjective effects on spectators. Indeed, the exploration of the cinematic apparatus extended the analysis of film to questions of what role film plays in the establishment and maintenance of social order. How does cinema support an existing social order and how does it support change in the social arrangements? In the 1960s, of course, the discussion of the apparatus was connected to the quest for revolutionary forms. In the 1980s, the debates around apparatus theory became bogged down by considerations of ideology and an overwhelming focus on psychoanalytic models.

In this chapter, a breaking of the hold of Althusserian and Lacanian theory allows for a return to considerations of apparatus and a reinvigoration of the basic propositions. It poses anew the question of the relationship of film to social order. Stated pointedly, this chapter explores the following questions: What is the relationship of the cinematic apparatus to the interzone? What is the apparatus of the interzone? The chapter considers the relationship of film production to the projected image, and analyzes film funding structures and how they derive from sociopolitical interests. It puts forward theoretical propositions regarding space in the visual image, the space behind the camera, and the space of the audience. The discussion here develops through the analysis of a few select contemporary films and sets up the turn to film history in the following chapter.

CHAPTER 2 INTERZONE HISTORY

The latter part of the nineteenth century when film makes its appearance is the period in which old multiethnic empires such as the Austro-Hungarian, the Russian, or the Ottoman competed with the colonial powers of France and Great Britain, and new rising powers like the German Empire for world domination. The moving image entered into the medial apparatus intimately connected to questions of nationalism and imperialism, but it was a fraught connection. As a medium, silent film was not bound explicitly to national markets. The silent moving image was more mobile and more flexible, and the film market was expansive, crossing political borders and linguistic boundaries.

This chapter focuses on the historical development of cinema from the early silent to early sound eras. It seeks to revise that history by considering closely the relationship of the cinematic apparatus to the imperial and national social configuration, and it underscores the production of interzones in those relationships. This chapter focuses on the region stretching from the Baltic to the Marmara Sea to explore the potentials and limitations of cinema.

In the imperial era, this region was commonly exposed to conflictual Germanification, Russification, and Turkification policies that set early cinema into a position of more than mass entertainment. In the era of nation-building following especially World War I, the area of Central Europe was the vanguard of geopolitical transformations. Yet inasmuch as the new states sought to dissociate themselves politically from their former imperial centers, Berlin, Vienna, and Istanbul continued to function as points of convergence for the culture industry of the entire region.

The popular mass media followed economic and ideational logics at odds with imperial *and* national bureaucratic administrative modernization, and political reform. It crossed political borders and linguistic boundaries with a fluidity that no other medium enjoyed. This chapter explores how the conflict reaches its head in new language politics of sound film and the Multiple Language Version Films (MLVF) of the first decade of sound film (1928–1938).

CHAPTER 3 CONTIGUOUS: THE GERMAN-POLISH INTERZONE

After the broad European discussion of the preceding chapter, this chapter concentrates on a specific region and German-Polish film relations in particular. World War II drew a caesura between Germany and Poland. For decades, the complex connectivity that existed in the region was broken and instead dissociation and disconnect characterized relations. This chapter explores the return of contact in a particularly fraught region or rather a region in Europe that has been understood as fraught. We can recall that it took six years after the end of World War II and two years after the founding of the Federal Republic of Germany for France and the Benelux to enter into a new trade zone with the former aggressor states of Germany and Italy. For Poland and Germany the wait was on the one hand longer, over forty years from the end of the war, and on the other hand shorter; a year after the unification of the two Germanies into the new Federal Republic Germany became Poland's largest trading partner, replacing Russia. If the German-Polish relationship is any the more fraught than the German-French, German-Dutch, or German-anybody relationship, it is an ideational question.

This chapter thus investigates not just the sundering but also the tentative conciliation of the two. It focuses on documentary film starting with the work of a few documentarists who headed east at the time of the *Wende*, the moment of the collapse of the East Block. When all were headed west, these filmmakers headed east. In bucking trends and heading east they captured images that ultimately speak more to the future of Europe. They not only documented important moments of "first contact," they literally envisioned relationships that are still developing today. In this chapter we find a set of filmmakers who have led the way in addressing a European public sphere and recognition of the Europe of interzones.

CHAPTER 4 INTERZONE DIS/CONTINUOUS: THE BORDERS OF EUROPE

Then suddenly and punctually in 2002–2003 as part of the run-up to Polish ascension to the EU a pointed transformation began. Especially the German-Polish border became a new object of filmic representation and investigation. Subsequently, this space has become a regular region of cinematic exploration, and more importantly the contacts begun during this period have led to an expansion of Polish-German coproductions in general.

This chapter explores this question: How do films structure for us a vision of space, in particular a vision of borders and the borderland? A central proposition of the chapter is that *borders are first ideational before they are spatial geographical*. Important here is that the films of 2002–2003 deployed new handheld cameras, drawing on new possibilities of the moving image to record spatial relations. This chapter thus considers how the mobility of the apparatus is not simply a matter of technological indulgence; rather, the liberated lens is an expansion of cinema's semiotic field. The liberation of the camera, the ability of the moving image to move in space is crucial here.

Cinema, the cinematic apparatus, provides an edifice whereby the imagination of spatial and geopolitical relationships come together. As an aspect of the cinematic apparatus, we can consider how visual aesthetic strategies, technological innovations, and social policy result in images with particular angles and perspectives. Choices of depth of field, establishing shot, distant or proximate frame position spectators vis-à-vis the image, but also within an entire imaginative world of affective possibilities. The camera can reveal who is with and against "us."

CHAPTER 5 "OUTSIDE" EUROPE

The previous discussion of the apparatus of European film focused on production within the boundaries of the EU. The apparatus, however, extends beyond those borders, well beyond even the ideational boundaries of Europe and this chapter explores the distinction between an "inside" and "outside" production. Within the European Union a number of programs have arisen to develop synergy with non-European filmmakers and film industries. For instance the MEDIA program alone sponsors Outside MEDIA, MEDIA MUNDUS, and coordinates with the European-Mediterranean (EUROMED) partnership. The programs entailed here aim to foster the distribution and exhibition of European films abroad, especially in the Mediterranean regions. These programs work further in harmonized and synergistic connections with other programs.

For instance, as a significant part of MEDIA, the Europa Cinema network has branched out beyond the territory of the EU. In addition to the various aspects of MEDIA it works with Eurimages, and furthermore received support from the French Ministry of Foreign Affairs to subsidize theaters in eastern Europe and from the EUROMED program to subsidize cinemas in twelve Mediterranean countries. Within the network there are now over fifteen hundred screens in forty-six countries, thereby allowing European film to reach well beyond Europe from Kabul to Ramallah, from Sao Paolo to Toronto.

This course of distribution and production does not flow only in one direction. This chapter focuses on how these programs also support the distribution and exhibition in Europe of *European cosponsored* films from those regions. European involvement supports feature films and documentaries. Stipulations placed on filmmakers vary, but often these funds are associated with a screening requirement, e.g., that they premier at Berlin, Cannes, Göteborg, or Rotterdam, or that a European national production partner must be involved. The coproduction funds thereby foster an ease of distribution in European film markets, giving rise to a complex network that reaches across the globe. Yet central to the analysis here is the question of how this network changes the orientation of storytelling. In effect, the apparatus here produces foreign films for European consumption. This chapter discusses critically how much these films represent a drawing together of disparate regions as interzone and how much they are a command performance for orientalist and neocolonial interests.

CHAPTER 6 INTERZONE XPERIMENTAL: MIGRATION AND MOVING IMAGES

Technological transformation is a central aspect to the definition of the film apparatus put forward in this study. For instance the moving image currently undergoes rapid transformations as a result of digitalization. This chapter focuses specifically on the rapid and accelerating technological transformations to film that we have witnessed in the last decade. These transformations make it actually anachronistic to speak solely of film and require the analysis of a more inclusive moving image. Moreover, this chapter notes that these transformations importantly have occurred simultaneously with the developments of globalization and transnationalism. Broadband, streaming video, networked social relationships have been central to the formation of new communities and new forms of engagement with existing social conditions. In this chapter the discussion seeks to highlight the interconnection between technology politics and economy by focusing on the question of moving-image experiments and migration. Narrative entertainment film has been the dominant object of analysis in research on portrayals of the experience of migration. This chapter focuses on the works of filmmakers who have worked in an experimental mode.

This chapter also expands our understanding of avant-garde technological experimentation. It takes up the questions of aesthetics and politics central to the definition of the avant-garde. The connection between migration and avant-garde work drawn in this chapter has been a central but overlooked part of those debates, starting with the community of exiles that gathered in Zurich during World War I to give rise to the DADA movement, through to those displaced persons who brought their audiovisual experiments to New York and beyond during the 1930s and 1940s. If those migrants largely worked on formal and theoretical questions, a contemporary group of visual artists has taken up their strategies to address specifically the experience of migration.

In the current moment where the forces of globalization have intensified patterns of mass migration, artists and artist collectives like Kutlug Ataman, Aysun Bademsoy, Ursula Biemann, Michael Brynntrup, Neco Çelik, Harun Farocki, Birgit Hein, Kanak-TV, Angela Melitopoulos, Ayşe Polat, Natascha Sadr Haghighian, *Social Impact*, Hito Steyerl, and Florian Wüst, among others, seek to break with the confining genre patterns of narrative cinema. This chapter focuses on their attempts to develop new forms to express the experience of migration. These artists have steadily shifted their' work from film to video to new art forms. This chapter also discusses how they incorporate lyrical poetic styles, explore expanded cinematic and installation work, undertake engagé interventionist projects, and provide new documents of vibrant cultural complexity.

CHAPTER 1

The Film Apparatus

A (Noncinematic) Example of the Apparatus of Communication

The towns of Aurith and Urad lie across from each other on the banks of the Oder/Odra river. They had once been a single town, Aurith, connected by a ferry. The western, lower side had been the site of the farmlands, while the eastern, higher side, had been the primary site of the town itself. A ferry had connected the sides, taking farmers and livestock back and forth between the narrow banks of the shallow river daily. The declaration of the river as the border between Poland and Germany sealed the town's division into two separate fates. The ferry was destroyed at the end of the World War II and not rebuilt. The next closest bridge was 42 km in one direction. Aurith developed as a German village with roughly 70 inhabitants, populated mainly by German refugees from the former German eastern territories. Urad developed as a Polish village, with roughly 450 inhabitants, populated mainly by Polish expellees from the former Polish territories in the East. Even after tensions diminished on the border, there was little reason to traverse the shallow waters to interact with the people on the other side. Language was a barrier and the inhabitants looked to Berlin or to Warsaw more than to the figures fishing on the opposite banks. These towns developed in what we could describe as two separate zones.

In 1989, at the point of the *Wende* citizens of the GDR began to cross the border illegally in makeshift boats in order to make their way to the consulate of the Federal Republic in Warsaw. These new refugees tested the permeability of the border; the boats and inner tubes they left drying in the morning sun on the Urad banks were signs that a transformation in the region was taking place. An area that had become quiescent in the Cold War, a bucolic backwater, began to turn, once again into a crossroads. In the 1990s the pattern changed and until Poland entered into the open internal region of the EU, this area was the site of nightly forays in the other direction. Passing through Urad/Aurith, smugglers brought migrants from Eastern Europe, Central Asia, the subcontinent, and the Far East into the EU. Especially on the western bank, the sirens and helicopters of the *Bundesgrenzschutz*, the border patrol, that pierced the night created a great sense of tension. Tightened security did not stop the smuggling; it only made it more desperate, dangerous, expensive, and profitable.

Those people who connected Aurith/Urad to Ukraine, India, or Vietnam kept moving through the town. The smugglers who brought them over returned to the other side. The global pressures and flows that passed through did not result in an immediate transformation of the villages; this activity of global smuggling was predicated on impossibilities of filiation and affiliation with the local. It was not actually until the move toward ascension into the EU that what we can identify as an interzone began to form here. The ascension brought an expanded map of the region, a new awareness of connections to the people on the other side. Here, culture and cultural production came to play a decisive role.

In 2004, Anschlaege.de began the project "Oder|Odra" in the towns of Aurith/Urad. Anschlaege.de is a Berlin-based collective begun by Axel Watzke, Christian Lagé, und Steffen Schuhmann. They organize their work around three principles of: communication, design, and "phorschung" [hreesearch]. Communication indicates an orientation toward interventions in the public sphere. The collective does not just contribute to but actually gives gestalt to the nature of public communication. This point connects into their idea of design, which is not simply a matter of the production of pleasant objects but the conceptualization of projects that bring various possible participants into interaction, for which there may be reason but no foundation. Design offers vantage points and new perspective, "design is part of the solution." *Phorschung* plays on the German *Forschung* (research), and in this playful spelling as *hreesearch*, it connects precisely play and research. For Anschlaege.de, then, research is site-specific, and develops out of a personal engagement with the locale, the participants, the ideas and conflicts at hand.

Of particular interest to this study, Anschlaege.de took note of the region and began a research project that did not assume that there were two distinct cultures that existed on the sides of the river. In the context of the Polish ascension to the EU, they turned to the old practice of the *Wandzeitung*, the hanging of a public newspaper on a wall, to develop an awareness of and connection to the other side. Anschlaege.de established a simple wooden structure for each side and pinned up on it a life-size photo portrait of one of the inhabitants of the other side on a weekly basis (Images 1a-c). The portraits were accompanied by a story of the person, biographical stories that described the person presented, revealed something of his/her interests and aspirations, hopes, and anxieties. The fact that these figures were presented to the "other" side, and that their stories were often about personal worries and dreams—stories that were not spoken out loud on the "other" side—meant that in some ways the readers from across the river became intimates with their counterparts across the way. Across the banks, they knew things about each other that were not even known in the immediate locale.

On May 1, 2004, the thirty entries to the "newspaper" were set up again and became the basis of a rebuilt ferry that spanned, at least for the day, both sides. The project drew two thousand visitors to the towns on that day and it led not to a bridge but to the actual permanent rebuilding of the ferry. So far, the ferry travels seldom, only annually. However, this ferry as communication represents the inventive quality of cultural production to bridge geographical obstacles and draw together participants into new forms of affiliation.

Images 1a: Oder/Odra Exhibit, May 1, 2004

Images 1b: Oder/Odra Exhibit, May 1, 2004

Images 1c: Oder/Odra Exhibit, May 1, 2004

The physical interzone established by the ferry was preceded by the ideational connection that Anschlaege.de initiated. It derived from an almost archaic form of media: the portrait and the public newspaper. Yet in this very direct material form of media, Anschlaege.de drew upon the medium to mediate. The structures were not passive conduits of some reality or information from one side to the other; rather, they instantiated a new system of communication that brought into contact potential communicative partners who are already present. Before the project there was no compelling need to draw these potential partners into communication. The project, however, developed a desire to connect through the material association. The portrait is important here, as is the living person on either side represented by the static image. The portrait, standing in for the other, raised interest in the inhabitants on the other side. However, also important here is the simple wooden scaffolding on which the image was tacked up. That structure created a surface of presentation and fostered the space of communal gathering.

The mechanism, structure, and artifice of communication here is a complex matter of connectivity, dependent on the design and the research of Anschlaege.de in this particular moment. The mechanism established here that draws these sides into connection functions like the bridges along the river. The medium of communication here is not separate or additional to social structures; rather, it is dependent on and constitutive of existent social and ideational possibilities. We can describe the medium of this project, like the bridges along the river, as an apparatus that draws together existent social structures into new and specific dynamics.

Debating the Cinematic Apparatus

I have identified the interzone as a physical and ideational space of communication. This designation of space, physical and ideational, could be understood as provisional, a placeholder for the understanding of apparatus that is now emerging in this study. The apparatus, as seen in the preceding example, is a technology but it is also a communication. It has the ability to connect, to realize community, to underscore the *communis* of communication. As seen in the preceding example, the apparatus of communication and that which is communicated are inextricable.

It bears noting that in Film Studies, this term *apparatus* has played a significant role. In the 1960s during the emergence of Film Studies as a discipline, the question of the cinematic apparatus was a hotly discussed and debated concept. The term apparatus quickly took on an international dimension: in French, *dispositif*; German, *Dispositiv* or *Apparat*; Dutch, *Filmapparaat*; Polish, *aparat* or *urządzenie*; and so on. And it offered a means to consider precisely the study of film as more than formal analysis of the projected image. Apparatus theory sought to arrive at a more comprehensive discussion of cinema as medium and mediation of social organization. The production of the image was understood not simply as an industrial tale: who wrote the script and what studio produced the image, but as a matter of signification, social relations, modes of production, methods of projection, space of reception, and subjective effects on spectators. What took place on the screen in the projected image and how that image came to be were understood as inextricable as the "base and superstructure" of cinema. Indeed the exploration of the cinematic apparatus extended the analysis of film to questions of what role film plays in the establishment and maintenance of social order. How does cinema support an existing social order and how does it support change in the social arrangements?

Currently, however, the discussions of apparatus in Anglo-American Film Studies has become quiescent. The term represents unfortunately a certain almost sectarian legacy of the discipline. In 1978, the Center for Twentieth Century Studies at the University of Wisconsin-Milwaukee hosted a conference on Apparatus Theory in Film Studies, bringing together a set of leading scholars from France, England, and the United States to address the question of the cinematic apparatus. An immediate controversy erupted as scholars around the journal *Jump Cut* criticized the lack of women and the narrow focus on a Lacanian line of inquiry. The debate around and pursuant to the conference grew to an international scope and generated two subsequent anthologies.[1] Even as the considerations of the apparatus entered into the canon of the young discipline, the debates they inspired led the discussion into certain impasses. Considerations of social configuration and transformation became focused on the term ideology and especially on an Althusserian understanding of ideology.[2] Then with the end of the Cold War, much of the impetus for this line of Marxian analysis dissipated. By the 1990s, the once lively debates on the apparatus became the object of derision by David Bordwell and Noël Carroll. Their rejection was based on almost a parody of the original goals of apparatus theory; it marked the starting point of their backlash against the general canon of film theory.[3] And subsequently, the term *apparatus* has taken on an almost anachronistic quality.

The loss of considerations of the cinematic apparatus from the center of Anglo-American film studies has left a lacuna, even forced a break. At this point, film studies have diverged such that discussions of production or industry and discussions of image or content rarely take place together. If we return to the early contributions of the 1970s before the focus narrowed, we see there that the initial impulse was to take the full extent of the apparatus into account: the projected image and its relationship to the viewer as well as the process that produces that image to be projected. Importantly and suggestively contributors to the debates like Stephen Heath argued against an industrial history that had taken technological changes, advancements in recording and projection devices, as the motivating factor for change in cinema (a reductive approach to historical development that has returned in much of the contemporary discussions of digital imaging).

Revising Apparatus Theory: The Social Configuration

The revision of apparatus theory, which this project undertakes, can take place easily by returning to the initial strengths of the project. In apparatus theory, working against technological determinism, for instance, became important, so the factors considered in the development of cinema expanded to include the relations of production that bring images forth, the mechanisms of distribution, and the modes of reception. This research inverted certain received expectations. For example, considerations of the apparatus revealed that the ability of the audience to read increasingly complex methods of visual narration was as much a cause for change in cinema as the invention of new technologies such as the camera crane. The idea of connection precedes the building of the bridge. The interest in the other side precedes the launching of the ferry.

Recall Jean-Louis Comolli's considerations of *Machines of the Visible*, written in 1971 in part as a summing up of the positions of the period, in part as an instigation to further the debate:[4]

> [T]he cinema . . . functions with and in the set of apparatuses of representation at work in a society. There are not only the representations produced by the representative apparatuses as such (painting, theatre, cinema, etc.); there are also, participating in the movement of the whole, the systems of the delegation of power (political representation), the ceaseless working-up of social imaginaries (historical, ideological representations) and a large part, even, of the modes of relational behaviour (balances of power, confrontations, manoeuvres of seduction, strategies of defense, marking of differences or affiliations). On the other hand, but at the same time, the hypothesis would be that a society is only such in that it is *driven by representation*. If the social machine manufactures representations, it also manufactures *itself* from representations—the latter at once as means, matter and condition of sociality.
>
> Thus the historical variation of cinematic techniques, their appearance-disappearance, their phases of convergence, their periods of dominance and decline

> seem to me to depend not on a rational-linear order of technological perfectibility nor an autonomous instance of scientific "progress," but much rather on the offsettings, adjustments, arrangements carried out by a social configuration in order to represent itself, that is, at once to grasp itself, identify itself and itself produce itself in its representation.[5]

In Comolli's analysis of presentation and representation, especially in the last line, "produce itself in its representation," there is a clear and purposeful connection to Marx's discussion of production and reproduction and the general notions of base and superstructure in Marxism. Yet Comolli refuses a reductive materialism based in shallow economics and instead deftly intertwines technology, techniques of representation, and social organization. Here Comolli raises the stake of representation, removing it from a marginalized position as superstructural phenomenon. Representation is "not only" a matter of signification. Rather, within the apparatus of production, representation as reproduction is not distinct from the material world, nor is it just a duplication of the material world; its images are the practice of the material world as such. Thus the joining of technology, technique, and representation in the apparatus is nothing less than the means and the mode by which a particular society or social configuration maintains and perpetuates its order.

To draw it away from the impasses of subjectivity and a focus on the *psyche*, the project of rethinking apparatus theory needs to turn to the *socius* and take up this question of social configuration.[6] Comolli's approach did establish a restrictive connection between cinematic apparatus and social configuration. In Comolli's description it appears that the apparatus is determined by a single social configuration. Such an approach aligned itself easily with Althusserian considerations of repressive and ideological state apparatuses. This was part of the general tendency of the period, to align state and capital as forms of power and control. Rarely were there investigations of various state forms and never was it understood that capitalism has various forms and that market economy is not immediately equivalent to capitalism. It was forgotten that there are ideological apparatuses that are not state-based and there are state apparatuses that are not ideological (or repressive). And there are apparatuses that are neither ideological nor state-based.

Immediately for the investigation of the interzone, we can withdraw from an approach that derives from an understanding of a single social configuration—*an* (ideological state) apparatus. The project of the interzone presumes multiple and competing social configurations, multiple and competing social imaginaries, multiple productions and reproductions that make possible a dynamic coupling and decoupling of individuals, images, spaces, zones. The cinematic apparatus is not an ideological state apparatus; to the contrary, even in moments of extreme totalitarian censorship, the cinematic apparatus proves constantly capable of eluding state control, consistently confounding to propagandistic tasks, and always able to produce polyvalent signs that bewilder ideological homogenization.

The project of the interzone, however, aligns with Comolli's description inasmuch as Comolli highlighted the role of cinema in the reproduction of the material world. Apparatus theory highlights the materially constitutive power of images; it accepts that *images effect social relations*. For instance, we have already considered that the idea of bridging precedes the spanning of two sides and that the awareness of a need or desire to connect compels the material association. The ferry in Aurith/Urad was rebuilt only after a sense of interest in communicating with the other side developed. But lest we descend into neo-idealism, cinematic apparatus theory adds more complexity to this understanding of the relationship of the ideational to the material. *The relationships in the cinematic apparatus are not simply relationships of human to image, but rather human to human, machine to image, machine to machine, and image to image, i.e., relations of individual subjects, technology, technique, and signification. Changes in signification entail changes in spectators and in material relations of production as much as changes in spectators or in technology affect the other factors.*

Historically, we have aligned the cinematic apparatus and the state apparatus. We have discussed national cinema and offered histories of German, French, Dutch, Polish, Turkish, Egyptian, Indian, American, Sri Lankan, Brazilian, and so on as if these were coherent systems. We need to ask: Is the cinematic apparatus largely there to represent the national community to itself, or does it represent something more and/or less than that community? What happens if we assume that the nation-state is neither the only nor even the dominant social configuration? Inasmuch as this study of the interzone focuses on the prenational imperial and the postnational project of European Union as other "social configurations," as globally unique "delegations of power" and historically distinctive "modes of relational behavior," what is of interest here in recalling these debates is this question of the relationship of film to various and changing social orders. How does the film apparatus produce and reproduce, for instance, the European social configuration? How does the new European social configuration develop through the representations of the film apparatus? We saw in the example earlier how the project developed out of Aurith/Urad, two autonomous zones, a communicating continuity; currently, what Anschlaege.de accomplished on a small scale for the five hundred inhabitants of Aurith/Urad, the audiovisual policy fostered by the European Union seeks to develop as a condition on a grand scale for the more than five million inhabitants of the EU.

EU Social Configuration: Harmonization, Subsidiarity, Synergy

If we look at the European Union we can note that audiovisual and especially cinematic production has played a significant role in the development of a new European social configuration. In the introduction here we discussed some models where by the films of the EU produce images of Europeanness. But we also noted behind those images a tendency to, for example, more coproductions, indicating the legal and funding relations in the apparatus of production. Not only have coproductions grown, but overall production has increased. In the EU we note the expansion from 1992–2004 of the audiovisual market at a steady pace: e.g., it rose from 61.5 in 2000 to ninety-nine billion euros in 2004.[7] Along with the overall growth in 'production we can also identify a steady growth in the European share of the film market from 2003–2009. More screens, more films, more films from European neighbor countries, and more European neighbors attending films made in Europe mark the period following European unification from 1992 onward. This development is neither a product simply of market forces nor does it derive solely from decisions taken autonomously and serendipitously in the twenty-eight member states of the EU. Rather, it results from a meeting of the directing hand of policy decisions at all levels of the Union with the producing hand of aesthetic and profit driven interests within the industry. Film and media in general play a key and successful role in a new social configuration. They are central to what we can describe as a process of Europeanization. European cinema, precisely through its production mechanisms, is delimiting a kind of market-oriented cultural space, the contours of which we have yet to apprehend clearly.

In addressing the specificity of the social configuration in Europe, I am not suggesting that the nation-state, small or large, has disappeared from the geopolitical map. Postnational celebrations of the death of the nation-state have continually been proven premature. National film in Europe, inasmuch as it is still an important apparatus of representation, is defined in its relationship to Europe: i.e., a national film is a European film, participating in the social configuration of the EU. Nevertheless the preconditions for the state have changed. In the process of Europeanization the unified states of Europe have voluntarily relinquished significant aspects of state-sovereignty, a process unique in global history. They operate now within a new system of associated sovereignty and legitimacy that calls for a more thoroughgoing theorization.[8] Indeed, the fact that the processes of decision-making and principles of organization characteristic of the EU differ largely from Jeffersonian democracy and Enlightenment state models has led many political and social scientists to characterize the EU as a weak, fragmentary, and disorganized union—in effect, to dismiss it.[9] Precisely this description, however, underscores the need to consider more precisely the specific mechanisms of production and reproduction of the European social configuration.

We need not debate the merits of the new mechanisms for arranging economics, politics, and culture; rather, we can take the terms of regulation and coordination in the process of Europeanization seriously and recognize them as inherent bearers of an organizing social configuration that urgently invite inquiry and theorization. We can approach as strong signifiers of real material and cultural processes the terms by which the EU itself describes its structures: e.g., harmonization, cooperation, decentralized competencies, subsidiarity, proportionality, synergy, solidarity, mobility, multispeed integration, opt-outs, enhanced cooperation, soft law, and so on. Such terms might appear at first to be better suited to discuss specific legal or economic arrangements, but as designations of modes of relation and communication they likewise inflect the cultural arrangements and creative production in Europe. Let us consider how just three of these terms of Europeanization: harmonization, synergy, and subsidiarity inflect the apparatus of film production in Europe.

Harmonization describes the process whereby laws and economic structures are brought into a form of translatable comparativity (Image 2). We can con-

Image 2: Harmonization

sider that member states are not required to accept a unified European tax code; however, they are required to foster economic union by making their tax codes transparent and comparable to other member states. This transparency does not require that the Italian or Spanish system adopt the German but it does make possible a condition in which goods and services can flow more easily from one system to the other. Serrano ham, parmesan cheese, and Rhine wines can thus move more easily as exports in the EU. Harmonization in this way also makes film coproductions and cross-border cooperation easier. A result of such harmonization has been the dramatic explosion of coproduction markets at international film festivals. In 2008, the MEDIA program registered over forty different such markets designed to bring together potential partners in various genres and forms, from feature film through documentary to animation. Harmonization has also marked the individual national support structures for film production. From a restrictive focus we could recognize how in 2005 the Polish parliament established the Polish Film Institute (PFI), doing away with the remnants of the Cinema Committee from the old Socialist system. This development was a major step forward in securing the Polish film industry. However, when it was established the PFI signed on to the guidelines of the European Council of Film Institutes and in its organizational and funding structures it followed the model of the British Film Institute (BFI), the French Centre National du Cinéma (CNC), and the German Filmförderungsanstalt (FFA). While each uniquely fosters work in a national parameter, each of these national institutes and film boards also pursues its tasks in a harmonized fashion: funding production, promoting distribution, and ensuring training and development. Each is a national institute but none has an exclusive or exclusionary national quality. The PFI, like the FFA, provides subsidies that should preserve the national quality film while at the same time opening up the market to positive coproductions. Indeed, fostering coproductions is a stated part of the primary goal of both institutions. In the language of the PFI, an orientation toward Europe even plays a primary role: Europe as market, as source of funding, but also as common cultural realm. As such, the model of harmonization derives from an even more fundamental European understanding of synergy.

Within Europeanization, *Synergy* designates a principle of reduction of redundancies, bundling of resources, improved effectiveness, and enhanced interoperatiblity (Image 3). The Council of the European Union issued in this regard a characteristic Resolution on January 21, 2002: To Enhance the Development of the Audiovisual Sector (2002/C 32/04). That resolution underscored "the key importance of European content and, as a consequence, the need to uphold and foster support measures, while bearing in mind the need to promote complementarity and synergy between national and Community measures as well as

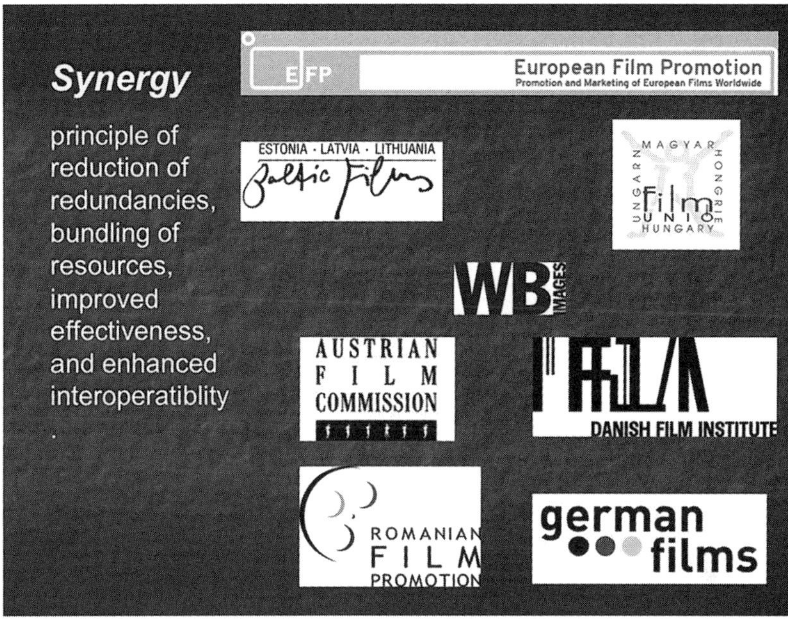

Image 3: Synergy

the need to safeguard cultural diversity." The Europa Cinemas Network is a good example of synergistic organization. The network brought together a series of cinemas as a common screening space for European film so that Europeans have a chance to see films from other member states. Or we can think of how the work of the Baltic Films Association, the German Film Export Union, the Magyar Film Union, the Polish Film Institute, and so on—each pursues a goal of promoting and marketing national film abroad. But each of these institutions is brought directly into contact with the other institutions through the Office of European Film Promotion (EFP), which includes all twenty-eight EU member countries plus three further applicant countries, including Turkey. The EFP helps members build up a presence at festival film markets in Cannes, Berlin, Sundance, and so on. It schedules the rotating film weeks that showcase national cinemas in major urban centers around the world, from Beijing to Toronto, Johannesburg to Buenos Aires. The bundled work undertaken by the EFP or the Europa Cinemas affords the diverse cinemas of Europe a necessary expanded market potential that limited national parameters could never accomplish. Important, however, for the social configuration of the EU, this activity is not a negation of the national level, but a radical transformation of it through the consequent application of the principle of subsidiarity.

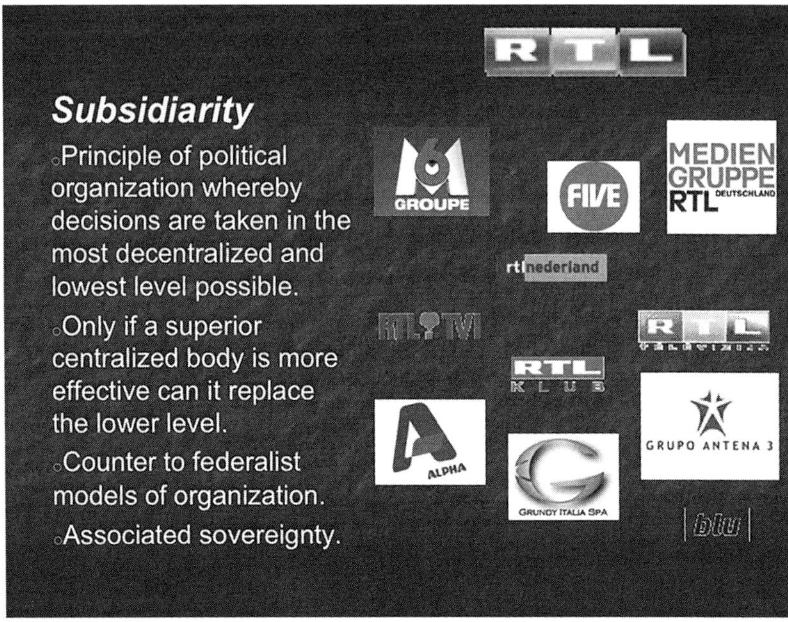

Image 4: Subsidiarity

In 1992 with the Treaty of Maastricht, *subsidiarity* became the central principle of organization in the newly established EU (Image 4). Subsidiarity is at first a principle of political organization whereby decisions are taken in the most decentralized and lowest level possible. Only if a superior centralized body is more effective can it replace the lower level. Subsidiarity developed as a counter to federalist models of organization like that of the United States of America. It is a principle of associated sovereignty that retains the nation-state as a fundamental level and addresses significant objections that had developed in the precursor organization of the European Community. For instance, in the 1980s, when the European Community implemented the Television without Frontiers directive, critics expressed fears that the transnational opening would result in a dominance of the image and especially an MTV-style contentlessness and that the informational quality of the media would be lost or simply reduced to a few national and local remnant broadcasters—in effect a condition parallel to the United States. What developed in the EU, as a reflection of subsidiarity was instead a reconfiguration and apparent diversification of national media industries with a dramatic expansion of total broadcast hours. Such diversity and expansion is a cultural and economic condition that parallels political subsidiarity. Exemplary for this state are the media conglomerates of RTL and Springer, but also the simple structural formats of shows like *Big Brother*, *Hell's Kitchen*, *Super Model*, or *Survivor* put out by production companies like Grenada. The company develops formats that are sold to national broadcasters and tweaked to be culturally specific. These formats then can be produced in a assembly-line structure, where the "Help I Am a Star, Get Me out of Here" jungle camp in Australia serves a cast and crew from Germany for three weeks or so, and once they "break camp," it turns over to the French crew, followed by the British, and so on. Such programming is easily capable of being integrated into a broadcast model like that of RTL, where each country has its own station with a certain autonomy but as a conglomerate they follow a similar format. RTL Hungary and RTL Germany may differ significantly in terms of time of offerings; however, they are subsidiaries of the same conglomerate with the same market orientation, intellectual *niveau*, and entertainment aspects, relying on the same formats. Such production appears national and yet has a Europeanized model uniting it. The decisions and content appear tailored to the local but on comparison evidence a homologous quality such that we can say that there might not be one European audience that watches the same show, but European audiences are watching the same type of show.

Curiosities arise in the subsidiarity model in which, considering for instance print media, the conservative Springer press, publisher of the boulevard newspaper *Bild*, can in 2003 begin production in Poland of *Fakt* according to the same marketing model as *Bild*. *Fakt* quickly rose to become the most popular newspaper in Poland—the same position *Bild* occupies in Germany. As of 2003, both newspapers have engaged in the construction of media controversies around Günter Grass, Erika Steinbach, the question of war reparations, and the 2008 Europa Cup, among others. The editorial staff denies reports that they jointly agree on what controversies to ignite. Clearly, however, the extreme nationalist rhetoric that the two internationally connected newspapers express serves them both well in their respective struggles to maintain their position in a competitive market. Even if they do not agree on their disagreements, the condition presents simultaneously an older "industrial form" of nationalism. And it shows how Europeanized subsidiarity can nevertheless draw such nationalist extremism into a homology. *The nation here becomes a kind of replicated zone of production and consumption. Given that it is homologous from state to state, zone to zone, the form of contact developed in the apparatus is not immediately apparent to the inhabitants of the zones and is not immediately readable from the image. The apparatus behind the image establishes a form of spatial contiguity but not ideational continuity.* Only a comparative supranational approach can identify these structures.

The National Social Configuration and the Apparatus of the Interzone

European filmmaking does not replace national film; rather, it resignifies what national film means, and it reconfigures what national film can do. Consider for a moment not the coproduction, but how a smaller-budget film with a very German and even local eastern German appearance participates in this new dynamic. We could think of how such films might not be *coproductions* but rather *codistributions*, a dynamic that occurs when a film enters almost immediately into a distribution circuit beyond its national market. For instance, Andreas Dresen's *Wolke 9* [*Cloud 9*] (2008)—a touching tale about a woman in the autumn of her life who, after thirty years of being faithfully married, enters into an affair and leaves her husband—was released in Germany but then screened in rapid succession in ten further countries beyond Germany. This possibility derives from the synergy and harmonization of the distribution mechanisms in Europe.

The question here of apparatus and interzone is not a question of the "being" of film, e.g., what *is* a national film, but rather a question of activity: What does a film do? How broadly does the dynamic activity of the new film apparatus reach? Or in EU-speak, how does a film bundle, harmonize, and synergize forces in the EU and beyond? Such a question is, again, not easy to answer if one concentrates only on the surface of the film, the image that is projected. Recall Hannes Stöhr's tragic-comedic episode film, *One Day in Europe* (2005), four tales of events that happen in four European locations in conjunction with the same soccer game. This film seems to reveal clearly that it is a European coproduction between Germany and Spain with its clever attention to that most important of European annual mass phenomena, the Champions League and its multiple locations, in, among other cities, Berlin and Santiago de Campostela. The space of the film may not be contiguous but it seeks to present a continuity of action across the expanse. On the other hand, films like *Irina Palm* (Gabarski, 2007), *Perfume: The Story of a Murderer* (Tykwer, 2006), *Zwartboek* (Verhoeven, 2006), and *Takva* (Kiziltan, 2006) follow a more common dynamic of production. They do not reveal the fact that they are all coproductions, allowing each of these films to be celebrated as a significant contribution to British, German, Dutch, and Turkish cinemas, respectively. In point of fact though, all are in some ways German films as well. Not just *Perfume* but rather all received significant if not primary funding from Germany and are listed as German films by the German Federal Film Board [*Filmförderungsanstalt*].

In 2006, the German federal government, to be in line with EU financing models, initiated a new *Produktionskostenerstattungsmodell* (Film Production Incentive Program) that supports producers who develop projects so that 25 percent of the film is *developed* in Germany, meaning it does not have to be a German location but can be German-based postproduction, and also fulfills a "character test."[10] Such a transformation was greeted warmly by the major German production firms. Characteristically, Stefan Arndt from X-Filme Creative Pool noted that this funding supported his company's own orientation with the foundation of X International. The point of such funding is not just to compete on the international market but also to draw international production to Germany, Brandenburg, and Berlin so that as a region it benefits from the production aspect and not just the sale and distribution of smaller-budget German productions out onto an international market.[11]

In the social configuration of the EU, the principle of subsidiarity creates, thus, a condition in which film appears as a national film even as it is produced with a European and even global market orientation. A transcultural film like Stöhr's is obvious, but the national-appearing film, masks this infrastructure of production and distribution. As a result, something curious and worth noting arises, i.e., a condition in which economic and social configuration become distinctive although not separate. *Perfume* or *Takva* appear to reproduce the nation while at the same time they are producing a European economic configuration. There is something of a rift here between European economic and national social configurations in which the cinematic apparatus functions as an interzone joining the two configurations.

In harmonization, synergy, and subsidiarity, the national configuration may continue to reproduce itself, but at the same time the economics of the national configuration come to depend on other nonnational systems production. If we focus only on what a film is, we will probably consider *Parfum* and *Takva* as German and Turkish films reflecting and reproducing a national economic and social context. But if we explore what these films do, we see that they actually produce a very different economic configuration, one not explicitly national, a more complex economic and social configuration. We discover a dispersion or heterogenization of the economic configurations that produce themselves and the social configurations that reproduce themselves in the cinematic apparatus. The national configuration remains, but gives way to other configurations, flexible social configurations, whatever appears able to draw together potential spectators into a film-viewing public.

A Critical Return to the Apparatus: Agamben and Power

Recently Giorgio Agamben has taken up the consideration of the apparatus though largely in ignorance of the discussions of cinema. Nevertheless Agamben's discussion highlights in part the reason why a revision of apparatus theory is in order but also what the strengths of the historic apparatus theory were. Agamben took up the term through his development of a specific and narrow Foucauldian perspective on the *dispositif*, describing the term as a configuration of power.[12] Agamben begins his discussion drawing his principles of apparatus from Foucault's general reflections on *dispositif*, given in an interview in 1977. The interview with Foucault, "The Confessions of the Flesh," can be understood as a somewhat minor contribution to the larger debate that reached a certain zenith the following year at the Center for Twentieth Century Studies.[13] Agamben's discussion ignores the larger context and the complex discussions of the period, failing to situate Foucault in a historical moment.

The turn to power is, of course, helpful in revision apparatus theory in that it opens up a broader understanding of the social configuration than that alignment of nation-state and capitalism, which had been understood as the singular bearer of negative power—i.e., control and censorship—in apparatus theory. Moreover, in not attending to the specificities of cinema, Agamben did bring a further expansive quality to the discussion, considering the apparatus as a matter of heterogeneous elements, "that includes virtually anything, linguistic and nonlinguistic."[14]

The expansion to elements beyond the cinematic is welcome. However, what in turn allows him to group these heterogeneous elements under the single term, *apparatus*, is what he identifies as a capacity that enforces a coherence on these elements. These elements he considers are not constitutive or structural elements but rather formations or networks with a restrictive regulative function. He calls "an apparatus literally anything that has in some way the capacity to capture, orient, determine, intercept, model, control, or secure the gestures, behaviors, opinions, or discourses of living beings."[15] Against the apparatus, then, Agamben sets "living beings" who in the apparatus become subjects.

Although the renewed attention to the term apparatus is timely, the idea here of an apparatus as anything that captures and exerts power is both more open than the previous focus on the cinematic apparatus but also a more highly restrictive notion that positions the discussion of apparatus solely under the question of power. For Agamben, apparatus is *only* a structure of power, control, and regulation. In setting the apparatus up and against "living beings" he states "I wish to propose to you nothing less than a general and massive partitioning of beings into two large groups or classes: on the one hand, living beings (or substances), and on the other, apparatuses in which living beings are incessantly captured."[16] The sentence is unclear in its formulation, a problem in which living beings are set up against living beings, suggesting that there is some state of being outside of apparatuses and that living beings in that state are distinct from those "captured" beings. In general, then, the apparatus is reduced to only a question of capture and the struggle of living beings.

The problem here is not just that this approach simply replaces capitalism and state as negative apparatuses of power with a consideration of power itself. The Foucauldian reading here sets power and apparatus as equivalent and negative forces on living beings. Subjectivity and desubjectification are treated as dialectical and negative phenomena. Agamben's understanding of apparatus takes away the positive and productive capacities that Foucault described in his discussions, and he ends with a turn to religion as a means to restore some humanity to living beings in the confrontation with the profane apparatus.

Agamben's turn to cultural pessimism and religious mysticism as ersatz for liberatory action derives from the focus on the entrapment of living beings and a failure to consider *the apparatus as a structure for the conflicts and contestations of a social configuration.* Agamben suggests an apparatus may restrict and regulate; it may "capture, orient, determine, intercept, model, control, or secure the gestures, behaviors, opinions, or discourses of living beings."[17] However, as a web of human activity it may just as well allow, or even more likely, liberate, ally, invent, open, envision, author, or strengthen the gestures, behaviors, opinions, or discourses of living beings. The apparatus need not be understood purely negatively. Certainly if we consider the apparatus not as heterogeneous elements bound by a totalizing power but instead as an aspect of social reproduction à la Comolli, we could arrive at a more general position in which rather than see the apparatus as inherently directed toward control and restriction, we can recognize *the apparatus as scaffold, foundation, network, or system that also allows or empowers.* Although Agamben's essay did bring renewed attention to the apparatus in the Italian and English-speaking realm, this approach has extreme limitations.

The Apparatus beyond Ideology

Less known in the English-speaking context is the work on apparatus theory that has emerged in Germany over the last decade.[18] In April 2001, a significant gathering took place in the newly inaugurated home of the Kino Arsenal on Berlin's Potsdammer Platz. Gregor Stemmrich organized a film and discussion series under the title *Eine andere Kunst—ein anderes Kino* [*A Different Art—A Different Cinema*] that took as its goal a revisiting of the apparatus debates.[19] Following on this gathering, Eva Tinsobin's 2007 *Das Kino* [*The Cinema as Apparatus*], suggests provocatively in its final section that the consideration of apparatus in the German-speaking literature has a much longer pedigree than in the French or English. She sees the work of Vilém Flusser, Siegfried Zielinski, Hartmut

Winkler, Friedrich Kittler, and Peter Weibel as continuing and expanding the discussion of apparatus after it had lost momentum in the English- and French-based investigations.[20] If we accept Tinsobin's characterization of their work as fundamentally a consideration of apparatus, they are considerations that are distant from the once central focus on ideology and spectators that led to the impasses of the 1980s. Furthermore, they develop a radically different approach than Agamben, considering the apparatus as something more than a negative mechanism of power. They shift attention in the discussions from the large questions of class, economics, gender, i.e., large scale social configuration, and focus more specifically on the relationship of technology to reception.

Drawing phenomenological and cognitive approaches to the discussion, Zielinski's and Kittler's work in particular has developed new models for considering industrial history.[21] It is also worth mentioning that with *Was geschah wirklich zwischen den Bilder* [*Film before Film*] (1986) and the five part *Media Magica* (1995–1996), visual artist and historian Werner Nekes has explored these questions in the medium of film itself. As new histories of the apparatus, these works engage the constitutive qualities of the cinematic as such: how we come to see what we are given to see. Furthermore, without hinting directly at the term *apparatus*, their work has influenced scholars in the English literature, such as Anne Friedberg, who have elaborated more fully the dynamic between technology, physical capacity of the human body, and imagination-driven invention.[22] For their part, Flusser and Winkler have explored more extensively the relationship between technique (or *tekhnē* in the Heideggerian sense) and the image. For instance, in recent work like *Diskursökonomie* [*Discourse Economy*], Winkler explored the exchange and interchange of economy and communication. Discourse economy explores the political economy of the media and how semiotic mechanisms travel as signs within the networks of a society.[23] Winkler pushes apparatus theory further discussing how media do not transparently mediate; rather, they constitute material possibilities of connecting and communicating.

This work, contrary to Agamben's, does not presume an inherent relationship between apparatus and restriction, control, or capture, i.e., negative power as such. On the other hand, it does also not continue to investigate explicitly the question of social configuration. The focus on technology is brought typically into connection with economics, Hollywood, and entertainment, but not with state or other forms of communal organization. The initial incentive to consider the apparatus was, of course, driven by an interest in how a social configuration in its reproduction is open to conflicts that shift modes of relational behavior, "balances of power, confrontations, manoeuvres of seduction, strategies of defense, marking of differences or affiliations."[24] As much as this new work extends and advances the consideration of the apparatus, it is, however, largely unconcerned with this once central aspect of apparatus theory. Technology, signification, and subjectivity become key to the analysis without the discussion of how these relate to social reproduction.

East, West, Central European Film

The revision of apparatus theory is interesting only insofar as it serves to describe real conditions and elucidate material practice. The consideration of terms must stand in a close relationship to practical experience. Theory develops out of attentiveness to material practice, processes of production, and cultural artifacts. We have with the transformations that followed upon the collapse of the East Block a clear period of rapid transformation in social configurations. The meaning of nations and the configuration of states shifted dramatically at that time. The relational behaviors of ethnic, class, political, gendered, sexual, and religious groups rearranged. New market conditions of exchange and use value developed. Old possibilities of representation closed down and new ones emerged. Old possibilities of communication were silenced as new ones arose. Old conversants slipped from center to margin or from periphery to the limelight and newly emergent ones eclipsed them. That period could not be described as a loss of apparatus but rather as a transition from one apparatus to another. Or rather this was a transformation in a plural form; thus, that period could be described as a move from ossified social configurations to a plethora of new ones.

Returning briefly to Agamben's position on power and the apparatus, it is not the case that this transition resulted in a condition of loss of power or freedom from power; however, it is clear that the delegation of power that followed the collapse of the authoritarian states opened up potentials for new subjective experience. Agamben's equation of power with negative determination of subjects, or desubjectification, can not obtain. It is clear that most people experienced the loss of authoritarian power as liberation into an apparatus in which they had more self-determination. Such an observation does not mean that the reconfiguration of power from authoritarian to liberal, from command to free market, resulted in an ideal condition, or that there are no grounds for critique of the current social configuration. It does mean that we have to develop a more nuanced understanding of power and pay attention to how the apparatus is a productive capacity conveying potentials of positive subjectification. But how do we understand the social configuration of the former East Block? What new communicative possibilities arose?

The standard discussions of film history continue to understand the former East Block as a unit, drawing on common film industrial infrastructure. In particular the experience of authoritarian state Socialism is treated as defining both its structures and themes. To be sure, cinema was produced in command economies as an ideological apparatus for the reproduction of the authoritarian state. And it makes sense that this basic structure of production and social reproduction should be understood as creating a system that distinguishes the Central and Eastern European film industry from the Western. It did imbue it with a history of planned production, censorship, artistic excellence, and second-world aesthetic quality. Yet the standard contemporary description sees the commonality of the past as providing a continuity of the region into the postrevolutionary era of the 1990s. The European Audiovisual Observatory, for instance, notes that the region shares as common experience from this period the fact that in a short frame of time, five to six years, the film industries of Poland, the Czech Republic, and Hungary undertook a complete reform of their financing systems, creating in effect a new private sector of production.[25] Freed from the former social configuration, the narrative of central Europe has the propensity to quickly become an economic one. The Central European film apparatus had to become part of a western economic order.

In her groundbreaking study, *Cinema of the Other Europe*, Dina Iordanova looked beyond the economic changes to explore in more detail the experiences of storytelling and image-making shared throughout the region. Looking in effect to the cultural artifacts produced in the post-Communist era, she offers a precise *localization* of the film apparatus. Iordanova describes an "East Central European" film region that continues to share a common past and likewise continues to develop in a common contemporary dynamic. Such an approach does go beyond the national and is attentive to the larger regional apparatus of production; it sets the national imaginary as part of the system of images of East Central European film based on a detailed economic and sociopolitical context.

However, critical questions arise immediately as to where one draws the limits of such a region. Imaginary and territory do not necessarily easily correspond in the European film apparatus. Daniela Berghahn, for instance, noted that such an approach that divides Europe into the East and West tends to neglect the central importance of East German cinema.[26] Even though it would be a historical conversant with the Polish, Czech, and Hungarian film industries, in this analysis, DEFA film falls off the map of Central Europe as belonging to Germany—and hence part of the West. (She notes further that in German and Western European film studies, East German film also tends to be neglected, most frequently relegated to a side question.) Moreover in this map, the further east complicates the region. Yugoslavian cinema stood in a different relationship to the West. Romanian film production experienced the opposite effect of liberalization, doubling production in the 1990s and winning prestigious awards. Mike Wayne seeks to take this expanded terrain into account but does so by inverting the discussion away from a Central Eastern European self-understanding to the understanding projected onto the East by the West.[27] Yet this approach too has its limits.

Too much emphasis on the economic and ideational coherence of the Central and East European film industries creates a condition of essential difference to the West that clouds the reality of the West and falsely subordinates the East. The West appears in such a comparison as a static entity, an existing social configuration and economic order to which the East has to accommodate itself. What if we shift the consideration to a broader reflection on the changes in the apparatus of *European* film production during this period. What happens if we recognize that all of Europe was placed into a new system of communication? What happens if we attend less to the *localization* and more to the *universalization* of the film apparatus during this period?

Aniko Imre and Aga Skrodzka have sought to situate Eastern European film in a larger context.[28] And certainly rather than treat Eastern Europe as a distinct autonomy, we can recognize that during the same period *all of Europe*, East and West, underwent a fundamental transformation of its audiovisual apparatus. The collapse of the East Block transpired along with the formation of the EU. The return to national autonomy took place in a new transnational context. German unification took place in 1990, marking the resolution of historic divisions. The formation of the European Union took initial shape in 1992, unleashing a process of ongoing transformation. The collapse of state Socialism belonged to the past while the process of European unification belongs to the future. Nationalization and regionalization need to be placed alongside the process of Europeanization. The logic of a new social organization became implemented across the space of West Central Eastern Europe; upon coming out from under the tutelage of the Soviet Union, the region from the Baltics down to the Adriatic turned toward the EU.

Here, the nature of communication in the new system is defined by the language of Europeanization. We can look again to the constitutive quality of the terms of harmonization, synergy, and subsidiarity. The harmonization of the national apparatus, as discussed previously, took place across Europe. To be sure the transformations in the West did not require the establishment of a private sector. The West did not go through economic "shock therapy." However, during the 1990s the significance of the private sector certainly changed in Western Europe as well. Synergization pushed a free-market liberalization of film industries; not just in Eastern Europe. The 1990s across Europe is characterized by a shift from state funding agencies and subsidy systems toward joint ventures and for-profit private production companies. In this period not only of post-Socialist transformation in the East but of European unification across the continent, the audiovisual sector underwent thoroughgoing transformations. Silvio Berlusconi could consolidate a private media empire begun with the breakup of the monopoly of Italy's state television RAI. The small private broadcaster Radio Télévision Luxembourg (RTL) could become one of the grand winners of this transformation growing to become Europe's largest television radio company with stations in the vast majority of European countries—including those beyond the EU, such as Russia. Film, in particular, underwent dramatic changes. Understood in the 1960s as a particularly valuable form of national cultural expression and a vehicle for high cultural critical expression, it becomes increasingly embedded in an expanded European culture industry with a largely mass entertainment orientation. It is not only in the Polish or Hungarian film industries that we can detect a turn to comedy and action genres. Distraction and amusement replace goals of information and education across the European media. These transformations harmonize all European national film industries and markets, albeit individually and uniquely, depending in particular on the level of state subsidy and control. Where they exist, public monopolies in the broadcast sectors, once understood as protecting a vulnerable electorate from populist propaganda are broken and forced into competition with an enlarged private sector. The more state control up to the 1990s, the more drastic the changes.

In Central Europe, the immediate result of the introduction of the free market on film production was the disruption of funding schemes, the breakup of existing studio structures, and the disintegration of distribution mechanisms. Centralized state funding gave way, but private funding did not immediately appear and when it did, it oriented itself toward profitability. Production dropped to record lows. In the years from 1989 to 1992, Polish Television produced up to half of the films made in Poland. Likewise across the border in Germany, 1992 was a record low point in cinema audience. In the wake of the *Wende* the DEFA studios in eastern Germany were closed down and privatized, former workers let go, production stalled. Moreover, Western German production of films sank significantly. Helmut Kohl's government pushed the united German economy into free-market conditions and for film, the state initiated a transition to private funding. These changes in Germany did not have the same drastic effects as in Poland. They were not the "shock therapy" to which the Poles were subjected. Nevertheless, the changes in Germany and Poland brought both countries into economic harmony and they created a similar restructuring of a European film apparatus, East, West, and Central. In the 1990s in both Poland and Germany, the films that offered a hope of attracting broad audiences benefited most from the investment of capital, and across the board the strategies of filmmaking shifted from an auteurist concentration on the director to the financial organizing work of the producer.[29]

This is a differential process proceeding according to the principles of subsidiarity. In countries like Germany or Denmark where the film industry was largely a state-subsidized auteurist project or in countries like France and Italy where quotas insulated the industries against competition, such control was transformed and often fundamentally broken apart. In general under these conditions the audiovisual markets moved from largely state-protected, state-organized, or state-controlled quasi-Socialist conditions to conditions of for-profit competition. In a for-profit orientation, mass audiences play a central role, and across the board in Europe, the 1990s are characterized by the rapid expansion of comedy and action genres in film and television designed to draw in such audiences. The first success of the new Polish film industry belonged to the action films of Władysław Pasikowski: *Kroll* (1991) and *Psy* [*Pigs*] (1992). Paralleling these developments across the border, the German film market began to expand in 1994 with the Comedy Wave that gained momentum from the success of Sönke Wortmann's *Der bewegte Mann* [*Maybe, Maybe Not*].[30] This pattern repeated itself across Europe—West, East, and Central.

If we understand these changes solely as national or even regional developments, we do not recognize how in effect the principles of European harmonization and subsidiarity influenced these developments so that in the new millennium West, Central, and Eastern systems have come in line. The German and Polish states, for instance, have come to occupy the same role in this apparatus, now serving as quasi-guarantors of film projects. They both provide funding that has a fundamental goal of profitability, and they both stabilize the foundation of the private sector.

Iordanova notes that the system of distribution that had exchanged films between East Block and developing world countries broke apart.[31] In their place an orientation toward the West and a dependence on major distributors and television arose. Already one year after the *Wende*, Germany replaced Russia as Poland's most important trading partner. At the same time, Russian film disappeared from Polish screens.[32] Maria Kornatowska noted that France and Germany became Poland's primary co-producing partners within the new strategies of film production.[33] Yet in Western Europe as well the European Union and its directives such as Television without Frontiers forced in place free-market structures that established similar demands on the industries. Existing enterprises with reserve capital and profit orientations moved in to fill in the spaces opened up in the free market across Europe, such as the now-defunct giant Vivendi Universal, HBO Polska, or Warner Brothers Deutschland.

Attending to market conditions, certainly in the new producer orientation of filmmaking, the majority of capital for investment and production came initially from the West. However, we must be careful about how we assess this financing. It did undermine quality production, and critical auteurist directors who had dominated the New Wave into the 1980s in the West and the East found it difficult to receive financing. Older established generations of filmmakers across Europe who could not accommodate themselves to entertainment and genre formats, suddenly faced great difficulties in accomplishing the projects. Andrzej Wajda *and* Werner Herzog had to struggle with financing. The private companies that developed during this period often represented Hollywood interests, but those interests cannot be localized to a location in California. This period also represents the period in which the processes of globalization transformed Hollywood such that the profit structures and audience orientations came to include and even focus on markets outside of the United States. A company such as Vivendi Universal was a French company producing global blockbusters in Hollywood studios, while companies like HBO Polska or Warner Brothers Deutschland were backed by American funds but recognized that their profit lay in fostering projects that appealed to local and regional markets. While we can identify companies from the West like HBO, Vivendi, or RTL as racing into Eastern Europe to fill the gap left behind by the break up of state monopolies, we should recognize that those companies also grew in the West and their rising profile changed the media landscape there. Out of this process there is no better example of subsidiarity than Axel Springer, once Germany's largest publisher of yellow-press newsprint. Springer Press expanded over the 1990s into the new millennium to become the major newsprint company for all of Central Europe (with significant holdings beyond the EU, e.g., in Turkey and Russia as well). In this expansion the once ultraconservative populist press has actually diversified its political profile and interests.

Europe acts as a market and a source of funding, but also as common cultural realm. Here we see how Europeanization affords smaller national cinemas a necessary expanded market potential that can no longer be accomplished in national parameters. This mode of production takes on a logic of its own, supplanting limited national markets. Jäckel describes, for instance:

> [T]he form of networking encouraged by the European and pan-European initiatives is unlikely to stop, whether a particular government opts out of a programme or not. As production and marketing costs rocket, film-makers seek new

> ways of turning a profit: new patterns of film-making as well as new clusters of partnerships are emerging, whether between countries with a similar approach to film-making such as Hungary, Poland, and France or between neighbouring countries such as Italy, Austria, Germany and Hungary, Poland and the Czech and Slovak Republics.[34]

We can survey from North to South and East to West in Europe and recognize that the market portion of coproductions has expanded dramatically. In the U.K. at the start of the 1990s the number of films made as coproductions was twenty per year; in 2003 it was over two hundred. In Germany in the course of the decade coproduction rates went from roughly 45 percent-54 percent of overall production. In some documentation, the Polish film institute estimates that with the entry of Poland into the Eurimages program, 70 percent of Polish films are produced as coproductions.

Acknowledging this condition, Iordanova concludes her study by revising the position of local coherence, noting how "the interaction moved beyond the European dimension to a truly global one. Worlds that were unlikely to touch (unless they collided) now interact and overlap. The world is on the move, bringing together Russians and Catalonians, Hungarians and Bolivians, Czechs and Afghans. Alliances and confrontations that were unlikely just a few years ago are now commonplace."[35]

Cinema, the audiovisual apparatus, extends out across Europe materializing new possibilities of contact, just as on a very small local scale the apparatus of newspapers and ferry materialized an interest in "the other side" into knowledge and real contact. As a result of the transformations of the national markets, we can say that there is no small cinema in Europe today but rather an audiovisual apparatus of border-crossings. There is no country that produces films in isolation. *European cinema has become a cinema of interzones, crisscrossing and traversing the continent and well beyond.*

CHAPTER 2

Interzone History

(Pre-)National Social Configuration and the Cinematic Apparatus

The previous chapter focuses on the cinematic apparatus. We considered the debates and the possibilities of revising apparatus theory and we explored how the cinematic apparatus participated in the large social reconfiguration that took place in the post–Cold War era: the East West Central European film apparatus. We discovered the possibility of considering the period of the 1990s as unleashing a process of Europeanization that developed European audiovisual production within a common apparatus. Harmonization, synergy, and subsidiarity were explored as characteristics defining the "state" apparatus structuring European economic, political, and cultural union. Throughout the discussion the complex connectivity of the transnational and the local, the regional and the European, and the bridging of European economic and national social configuration were understood as outcomes of various interzonal arrangements. In the last chapter the focus was on the shift from nation to union.

A number of scholars and critics of contemporary discussions of transnationalism have noted that cinematic complex connectivity is not a new phenomenon. Anne Jäckel and Wendy Everett have offered histories of European film production as European. These are important extensions of their foundational work on contemporary European transnational production.[1] Mark Betz has considered European art film's historical complexities.[2] Tim Bergfelder has conducted extensive studies of coproductions and industrial connections in popular film production from the 1930s to the 1960s.[3] Andrew Higson and Richard Maltby helped remind us of thc project of Film Europe that formed in the interbellum.[4] In all this work there is an attention to the industrial aspects that underlay the images projected onto the screen. These scholars among others, myself included, have struggled with the questions of how to identify what is new in the contemporary period, sometimes even suggesting that there is nothing new.

Important, though, is that in describing complex connectivity as a consistent aspect of the cinematic apparatus, we not efface epochal differences and make sure to distinguish qualitative differences from period to period. For example, the current condition of coproduction in Europe is facilitated by the presence of the EC's Television without Frontiers Directive (1989), the Council of Europe's European Convention on Cinematographic Co-Production (1992), and the EU's Audiovisual Services Directive (2007). These treaties transformed the conditions of bilateral national coproduction agreements that had dominated the postwar period.[5] In a simple phrase we can insist that before there was transnationalism there was internationalism. Mohammed Bamyeh made the point already at the turn of the Millennium that there may always have been a world system but it was not always defined by the conditions of contemporary globalization.[6]

This chapter addresses the historical phases in the cinematic apparatus. I want to explore historically this quality of complex connectivity that characterizes the apparatus and constitutes its potential to create interzonal relations. The work of the colleagues cited above has focused largely on the move from the national to the transnational. What happens if we move the time frame of analysis further back to the imperial era, the prenational instead of the postnational? Currently the imperial period has lost much of its specificity in cultural analysis; in some recent literary and film studies the imperial has been too quickly associated with colonialism. Or, in the rush to consider the term *transnationalism*, the terms *imperial* and *international* is passed over as, for instance, in the otherwise interesting study of Mark Tilse: *Transnationalism in the Prussian East*.[7] The recent work of Gregor Thum on the German East, Annemarie Sammartino's study of the "impossible border" or Omer Bartov and Eric Weitz's excellent collection *Shatterzone of Empire* offer by contrast very nuanced understandings of the polylingual, multiethnic, multireligious complexity of the imperial and international world.[8] It balances an understanding of long periods of concord with a focus on increasing national tension and regional conflict. The historical view of these scholars does not employ a term from the current moment to grind its lens on the past.

Following the model of such work, this chapter thus offers four historical considerations from the end of the imperial period. The goal is to set the distinctions of the cinematic and state apparatus into high relief. It turns to the imperial period, not as a naïve celebration of some lost multicultural utopia—imperial structures were certainly not utopian. It offers a consideration of that period because precisely the contemporary period of transnational arrangements revives certain forms of governance present in the imperial that had receded in the era of (inter)national arrangements. And furthermore it turns to the imperial because the period of rapid decline in classical empires corresponds roughly to the period of emergence of cinema. Cinema not only records this process but the shifts in sociopolitical and economic arrangements that necessarily structure the cinematic apparatus.

What role did cinema play in the grand shifts in systems from empire to nation? In *Theorising National Cinema*, Valentina Vitali and Paul Willemen argue that at the start of cinema, the "clusters of production" that we now understand as national cinema bore little national significance.[9] Similarly Richard Abel, Giorgio Bertellini, and Rob King have documented how national cinemas had to be constructed out of an otherwise permeable market.[10] Tom Gunning has noted that "cinema crossed borders easily in its first decades [following] global pathways opened up by worldwide capitalism, colonialism, and imperialism."[11] It is this mobility and market orientation that distinguishes the cinematic and state apparatus; this mobility can align them but even set them at odds to each other. Abel describes in great detail how U.S. producers and distributors whipped up nationalist sentiment to counter the dominance of (French) Pathé.[12] Charles Musser described the transformations of cinema in the United States in the first decades of the twentieth century as one "from cosmopolitan internationalism to jingoistic nationalism."[13] Much of this analysis has developed through attention to the United States, Hollywood and to the nations and cinemas of Western Europe. In Central Europe, however, that crisscrossing terrain of empires, the story of the cinematic apparatus follows a similar trajectory yet has its own important distinctions. To consider the interzone, I want to highlight those complexities here.

Under consideration in general in this study, as well as the work of other colleagues seeking to historicize the work of European cinema, is how these shifts in the apparatus of cinema stand in relationship to the apparatus of governance. What is the relationship of the cinematic to the state apparatus? Is it a relationship of total correspondence? Althusserian analysis understood cinema as a part of the ideological state apparatus and as such a more flexible mechanism than the repressive state apparatus. While Althusser devoted little attention to cinema directly in subsequent discussions of apparatus theory, the question was considered extensively and only "counter-cinema" was understood as offering an alternative. The question as to what constituted counter-cinema remained a tautological point of contention. However, the analysis of this chapter reveals that the cinematic apparatus resists total alignment with the state apparatus. It is in the fissure that the alternative possibilities of cinema are revealed.

The national apparatus asserts a certain coherency as localizing and particularlizing system on the cinematic apparatus, but the cinematic apparatus proves capable of operating according to parameters that exceed the national. The difference between the systems, that point of contention, is the point that generates repeatedly the interzone: the moment of an imaginative representational negotiation of difference.

History 1: German and/or Polish Film History

The history of film, especially in German language film histories, is often traced to the inventors Max and Emil Skladanowsky, brothers who worked actively on the development of new technology to produce moving images.[14] The Skladanowsky brothers developed the *Bioscop* as a technique for creating the illusion of "living images" and it famously premiered in 1895, two months before the Lumière Brothers premiered their *Cinématographe*. Eventually, though, the Bioscop technique proved more cumbersome than the Cinématographe, and the Skladanowskys folded their business. Whatever the outcome of their business, the famous Skladanowsky screening at Berlin's Wintergarten vaudeville theater does allow a claim that the origins of cinema are German. And in 1995 a centenary celebration in Berlin's Friedrichstadtpalast took place with a guest list of thousands, broadcast on television, to celebrate the birth of "German Film."

We could, however, consider this nationally inflected history differently. In its earliest stages the moving image arose out of an immediate connection in all aspects of the apparatus among inventors scattered across the globe engaged in experiments within the new industrial means of production. "Filmmakers" at that moment were more scientists and technicians rather than artists, industrial inventors developing new technologies with immediate control over their new techniques. The Skladanowskys were in communication with their counterparts across the globe in France, the United States, Britain, Japan, and so on, allowing us to recognize the immediate broad parameters of communication structuring the cinematic apparatus. To ascribe German origins to cinema at the height of German imperialism is to retroactively nationalize film history, limiting its complexity. Like industrialism itself, film was part of a process that stretched across the globe. Thus we could develop a film history that underscores a more universalist prenational quality of the apparatus at its point of emergence.

There is, however, a further different way to frame this history. We can localize the frame and focus on the very specific parameters of the story. Born in Berlin-Pankow during the period of the foundation of the Second German Reich, Max (1863) and Emile (1866) Skladanowsky were the sons of the glazier Carl Theodor and Luise Auguste Ernestine Skladanowsky. Carl and Luise had moved from Pomerania in the east of Prussia, lured by the economic promises of rapidly industrializing Berlin.[15] The Skladanowskys belonged to the community of Polish Prussians and Prussian Poles, coming from a region where ethnicity and language were quite complex, where dialects like Upper Silesian, Masurian, and Kashubian bridged Polish and German, a region that later would belong to Poland. Their last names marked them as Poles in the German Reich at a point in time when Poland as a kingdom had ceased to exist, partitioned between the German, Russian, and Austrian Empires. In his treatment of Max Skladanowsky, film historian Joachim Castan notes directly that "the name 'Skladanowsky' does not sound particularly German."[16] Castan traced out the roots of the family to Obersartowitz (Górny Sartowice). His father was born in 1830, the same year as the November Uprising in Czarist Poland. Carl Theodor and Luise Augustine grew up during a time in which the Germanification pressures in eastern Prussia were intensely deployed as a means to standardize the empire. These pressures unsettled many people in the region and drove them to the rapidly industrializing imperial center in Berlin. This localization of the history would attend to the very specific qualities of the environment of production in Berlin and the Prussian East of the German Reich.

Thus in the absence of a Polish state as such, we could ethnicize the Skladanowskys and just as likely underscore the origins of cinema as Polish. Not a matter of a *German* film history, the first event of cinema could belong to *Polonia* in diaspora, a sign of the significant industrial contributions the imperialized Poles made to the German Reich. As a caution to Castan's ethnicizing interests, like many residents of eastern Prussia, the Polish name does not convey easy ethnicity. It is unclear to what extent this family understood themselves as ethnic Poles, whether they were advocates of an independent Polish state, whether they had suffered through and resisted the hardships imposed by Germanification, or whether they understood themselves as belonging to the multiethnic and multilingual part of the Prussian kingdom that flowed easily between German and Polish. Nevertheless, later the National Socialists wanting to celebrate German ingenuity over the Lumières were certainly cautious about the Skladanowskys. Suspicious of their Slavic origins, they refused to highlight their work and through that lay claim to the centerpiece of their modern propaganda apparatus. In the various and competing possibilities of how to construe the Skladanowskys' contribution to cinema we recognize easily how *nationalization* quickly counters other possible paradigms based in *localization* (the Skladanowskys were just typical Berlin industrial inventors) or in *universalization* (the brothers belonged to a larger fraternity of global engineers of the moving image).

History 2: Polish and/or German Film History

The Polish national historiography develops its historical framework within the prenational era. This process of national cultural historiography offers a foil to the German (and French or U.S.) models of film history. While the German national film histories typically overlook the ethnicity of the Skladanowskys, Polish national film histories generally invert that approach. If German ethnic nationalism incorporates German imperial history, it does so through the exclusion of the German Poles. Where nation-state parameters proved determining for the approaches to the German Reich, almost paradoxically Polish ethnic nationalism by contrast excludes the German, Russian, and Austro-Hungarian Empires to which the Polish territories belonged. It relies on the fluid concept of *Polonia*, without the typical connection to state and country. By contrast to other national paradigms Polonia actually requires simultaneously forms of universalization and of localization. The development of early cinema is acknowledged as extraterritorial and the Polish diaspora, reaching across territories, means that Polish engagement and know-how is universally present in the developments. At the same time, even though they did not have political autonomy or unity and were split and under the control of the Prussian, Russian, and Austro-Hungarian Empires, territorial attention localizes to the space around Warsaw and Cracow. Poles are everywhere while the soul of Poland is not bound to a state but to a place, to Cracow or Warsaw, perhaps there in the Holy Cross Church next to Chopin's heart.

So how does a national history mark the where and when of Polish cinema? Marek Haltof's book, *Polish National Cinema*, a classic text of Polish film history in English, speaks of the Polish territories and their divided status but also speaks frequently of Poland proper as a sovereign cultural state: "At the beginning of the century in Poland."[17] Similarly, film scholar Sheila Skaff considers *Polonia*, the diasporic Poles, as a coherent and cohesive unit and distinguishes between a Polish national cinema and a cinema of the nation-state.[18]

To nationalize this prenational cinema, the discussion of Polish early cinema has to rely on a very narrow frame that draws a focus to the center of the Polish territories, especially Warsaw and Cracow. Consider that typically Piotr

Lebiedziński as well as Jan and Józef Popławski are identified as founding figures in Polish cinema histories. They worked in Warsaw, but they traveled, were trained elsewhere, and were in communication with the Skladanowskys in Berlin and the Lumières in Paris.[19] They belonged to the community of visual scientists of the period, likewise undertaking early scientific experiments with the new process alongside the other pioneers starting in 1893. Finding in them the foundation of Polish film underscores their ethnicity while limiting their international scope to a national contribution. It localizes them in a diasporic history.

Attempts to recount the developments of the imperial period from a national perspective generate models that efface much of the complex connectivity of the period. Recall in this story that there is another large group of inhabitants of the eastern territories. The Jewish community comprised about a quarter of the population in the region and was as well a lively center of film production. Haltof incorporates this production into his history observing that "a significant number of early films made in the Polish territories were productions in Yiddish."[20] Haltof's study proceeds from an understanding of Poland as a cultural place before it was a Republic, but the gesture to include Yiddish production into the study compels a radical rethinking of what that culture is. Haltof nods in this direction but does not develop it fully. Such a move requires a *regionalized* understanding of cultural production as polyvalent, multilingual, and de-ethnicized.

History 3: Posen/Poznan as Interzone

Typically, then, in attention to film history the seat of governance or the metropolitan centers are taken as indicative of a qualitative if not quantitative aspect of the cinematic apparatus. Berlin, Warsaw, Istanbul, Vienna, Moscow, Paris, London, Madrid, Lisbon, and Rome receive the most analysis, often with good reason. Yet in the imperial era it is important to consider that the periphery may have had a particular productive role in the cinematic and state apparatus. In her study of Russian cinema, *The Imperial Trace*, Nancy Condee discusses insightfully how center and periphery relations functioned within the Russian imaginary.[21] Moscow and St. Petersburg, the metropolitan centers, the seats of governance, and the core of artistic life had as foil the provinces with their plurality and heterogeneity. The province was where the heart of Russia was imagined. Time and again the retreat from the city to the province offered and continues to offer a push and pull of the Russian cultural imaginary. Similarly *Völkisch* paradigms of the II and III Reichs likewise located the heart of culture not in the bourgeois urban life of the urban centers but in the countryside and in the *Heimat*.

One could explore the narrative tropes of Empire, and yet what is of interest for this study is what happens if we focus more concretely on the apparatus? In the period of early cinema Posen played an important role as German-Polish interzone in the German Empire. It was located at the "frontier" of the Reich in a region of ethnic, linguistic, and religious pluralism. Posen had had a twin-city structure since 1253 with the establishment of a German settlement on the West Bank of the Warta river.[22] After 1793 and the second partition of Poland, the Polish residents of Posen enjoyed equal rights in the city, but increasingly Posen was a center of Germanification efforts.[23]

Posen was also a center of film distribution, screening, and production. From the earliest days of cinema Posen was one of the six film centers in the German Reich and Posen served as a central distribution point for wandering cinemas in the East. Important as its role was in the cultural life of the Reich, it has fallen off the map of German film histories as in general has the entire German East. The standard text, *A Second Life: German Cinema's First Decades,* filled with a plethora of insightful essays by leading film scholars orients its perspective to the West, considering film relations with France, Denmark, and the United States.[24] It treats these relationships as forms of international competition. None of the analyses, however, considers the complexity of imperial relations; none of them attends to the dynamics in the East. Posen, the sixth most important center of film in the Reich is not mentioned. The intellectual map of Germany that informs the study is in effect equivalent to the contemporary spatial parameters of the Federal Republic.

Attending here to Posen accomplishes some of the dynamic regionalization noted above. It requires a rethinking of the film apparatus away from presumptions of national homogeneity and into an imperial condition in which cinema is a vehicle of complex communication between and among ethnicities and languages in the imperial regions. Importantly, in Poland, Małgorzata Hendrykowska and Marek Hendrykowski undertook a project in the late 1980s in the People's Republic of Poland *Film w Poznaniu 1896–1945* [*Film in Posen*]. This project of extreme localism offered an alternative to dominant modes of national film historiography in general and Polish in particular.[25] Its attention to the particular and local countered centralizing aspects of national film history, achieving simultaneously an impressive and radical universalization. The study chronicles the history of film in one of the most complex regions of Prussian Poland, a multiethnic and multilingual territory, particularly subject to Germanification pressures and increasingly fraught with tension in the course of the nineteenth century.

Hendrykowska and Hendrykowki's study begins with discussions of imperial complexity avoiding an ethnic approach defined by *Polonia*. They note already on the first page that in 1903 Leon Mettler reserved a room in his restaurant to exhibit films. The book contains initially images of signs and newspaper items in Polish and German. It describes moreover the international scope of film of the period, identifying the presence of Edison, Lumière, Méliès, and Messter films in the screening venues of Posen. They trace out multiethnic work; e.g., how the second permanent movie theater, The Palace, opened in 1907 and was run by Franciszek Dymarski and Herman Mittelstädt.[26]

They actually begin their study even before 1895, taking an industrial view and making the point that Posen was an early center of photography and experimentation with the recorded image. They note that Ottomar Anschütz, one of the early pioneers of film, came from Posen from a family of photographers. He published his significant early work, *Augenblicksbilder* [*Instant Images*] in Posen in 1887, a book that displayed a new strategy of high-speed serial photography that could record various stages of motion and extended Eadweard Muybridge's practice into the protofilmic realm. He moved to Berlin in a move common at the time, given that the rapidly industrializing imperial center exercised lucrative attraction on much of the eastern territories. His connection to Posen recalled in the study underscores pointedly a German-Polish past that has been all but forgotten.

The study then chronicles the nationalization of the region in the second chapter entitled, "Film w Poznaniu w dobie kina niemego (1919–1929)" ["Film in Posen in the Silent Era"].[27] Of course the preceding era was also a silent era. What is truly distinctive here is that this is the beginning of a new era of Polish nationhood during which Poznan became the major city in the West of the new Polish Republic. Quickly, the study notes the development of journals such as *Kinematograf Polski* in 1919 and other signs of a specifically Polish film industry. Posen is one of the centers of that production, giving rise to films in various genres including nationalist dramas like *Odrodzona Polska* [*Poland Reborn*] (Wesolowski, 1924). In this phase the study itself takes a turn that might be described as inward; the attention to international complexity fades away and the study focuses on the production by Poles for Poles in the Polish Republic. This shift is understandable given the flurry of activity; however, it frames out the complexity of the market and the continued permeability of the national and international in the cinema of the period.

In the analysis of the interzone, then, eastern Prussia and Central Europe in general played an important role, positioned in the developing apparatus as a crossroads of experimentation and production going East and West. It is a space of complex connectivity and polyglot communicative potentials. The goal should not be to deny the impact of the national social configuration on defining other parameters of the film apparatus; rather, a discussion of the film apparatus allows us the ability to attend to other communicative potentials available. Yet it also requires that we recognize how—inasmuch as cinema quickly expanded in the imperial space of the new German Reich, the old Austro-Hungarian, the Russian and Ottoman as well—cinema also established its own potential for later nationalizations, e.g., Polanization, Czecho-slovakization, Magyarization, Turkification, and so on in the great wave of nation-building that followed World War I.

History 4: Ottoman/Turkish Film

Throughout the region, similar questions arise in how to contend with the imperial parameters of cinema in national film histories. Traveling further south we find that Turkish film historians have come to identify a recently discovered short view of Sultan Mehmet V from 1912 as the first Turkish film.[28] Yet as Savaş Arslan points out, the filmmakers Milton and Janak Manaki were Macedonian and they were recording the Sultan's visit to Salonika. The complexity here of the image is much deeper; rather than understand it as the first Turkish, we might describe it as one of the last Ottoman films. Filmed after the Young Turk Revolution of 1908 and the beginning of the constitutional era, during the Second Balkan War, a battle primarily over Macedonia, the military images here portray a moment in the transition from an imperial patriotism to Turkish nationalism.

Arslan and Canan Balan have recently addressed critically the paradigm by which early Turkish cinema is discussed. Arslan questions "the possibility of a Turkish film when there was no Turkish state."[29] He charts out the different complexities of the introduction of cinema but within a system of "belated modernity."[30] He sees cinema as part of on the one hand an outside to "western" modern technology and on the other hand a project of "Turkification-from-above" suggesting that elsewhere the apparatus of cinema was demonstrably different.[31] A comparative perspective reveals these dynamics, the adaptation of new technologies of representation and the intervention of authoritarian state tendencies, to be common aspects of modernization and one that is by no means belated. These dynamics are present in the German, Austrian, and Russian Empires in very similar structural ways and within the British, French, Spanish, and Portuguese Empires as well.

Arslan comes to the conclusion that Turkish cinema developed via a "self-colonizing cultural mentality."[32] What Arslan describes through the term *self-colonizing*, we can find repeated elsewhere. In the German Empire, Kaiser Wilhelm II drew on the new media for authoritarian purposes; the first historical newsreels and deployments of the apparatus of cinema for political propagandistic purposes can be traced back to the images of Wilhelm.[33] In the literature he even earned the nickname "Media Kaiser." But these images have two valences. In the imperial metropolitan center, the novelty of the moving image combined with the image of the Kaiser in the newsreels promoted patriotism; in the diffuse provincial locales, it promoted patriotic Germanness. In eastern Prussia this media served the colonizing policy of Germanification.

Balan approaches the typical distinctions of West and East, modern and traditional, critically. She notes that commonly "cinema-going was imbricated with Westernism."[34] She surveys various discussions in the Turkish literature that aligns cinema screening and spectatorship in the late nineteenth century with the introduction of a new "foreign," i.e., European technology. Balan challenges this approach, however, noting first that the very notion of foreign being applied here needs to be interrogated given that a city like Istanbul in 1885 was only 44 percent Muslim. It is not just a matter that the city was populated with ethnic Turks and Greeks, Arabs and Armenians, Protestants, Orthodox, and Jews. Rather, the conception of foreign in an (Ottoman) imperial context differed radically given that only the smallest minority of the subjects of the Empire identified as Ottoman. The forms of identification in imperial conditions are much more decentralized, overlapping, ambiguous, and mobile. Most subjects of the Ottoman Empire as with the Hapsburg, Russian, Spanish, French, or British Empires considered themselves "foreigners" in their empire, coming from its periphery and not center.

Further, numbers of scholars have sought to position the emergence of cinema against the visual culture of the Ottoman Empire, striving for a more complex understanding of the technological history of the film apparatus. Nijat Özön, central founding figure to Turkish film studies explored how the adaptation of the new technology of representation drew on the local precinematic period in the region, especially puppetry and shadow plays, i.e., the Karagöz.[35] Scholars such as Özön and Balan point to these precinematic forms as signs that an expansive audience already existed, as did a culture of entertainment defined by a form of moving image. The question is not so much why did the production of the moving image proceed so slowly in Turkey but rather how did the transition from one moving image form to another take place?

The first moving pictures were brought to Istanbul and introduced in the Ottoman Empire by noncitizens. However, this was also the case in the Russian and Hapsburg Empires, in Latin America and Asia, even Canada. *In the Ottoman Empire, as in other imperial spaces, the communicative potential of cinema was not defined by state borders and it exhibited an ability to move and spread quickly*. We should underscore that the introduction of moving pictures in the empire, took place as quickly as in all other European capitals; by 1896, the screening at the Yıldız

Palace took place only a year after Paris and Berlin. And, as with the rest of the world, cinema rapidly took off in Istanbul and throughout the empire albeit mainly through the distribution and not production of images.

Sigmund Weinberg already offered regular showings to the public in 1897 in two locations.[36] Weinberg is often taken as a sign of the foreign quality of early film exhibition. Balan notes that the early cinema in this environment had a quality of cosmopolitanism about it. She, Arslan, Burçak Evren, and others approach him as "a Polish Jew from Romania." However, in this typical description it is often overlooked that he had been born in Romania while it was still Ottoman at a point in time when the Polish state did not exist.[37] He moved to Istanbul from the new Romanian kingdom and went to work as then a foreigner in the capital of the former empire. He rose to become one of the central importers of new entertainment technologies, especially gramophones, and quickly took on the display of Pathé films in Istanbul. Weinberg is not an exception but rather a fairly commonplace figure of the period in Istanbul. He is not a symptom of westernization but rather a sign of a very practical imperial subject accommodating himself to new conditions. Weinberg may not be a Turk, but he *was* an Ottoman.

This imperial character of the cinema in the early period can be understood as contributing ultimately to reformist demands moving through the Ottoman Empire. It was a vehicle for new forms of publics. This role as public sphere thereby actually prepared the cinema to be, as Balan describes, "overtaken by patriotic concerns by the end of World War I."[38] The cinematic apparatus could become a vehicle of Young Turkish nationalism.[39] Arslan describes that the first Turkish feature films, melodramas and patriotic films, were commissioned by the army during World War I. Indeed the process began with the start of the war such that the first film understood as Turkish was *Ayastefanos' daki Rus Abidesinin Yıkılışı* [*The Destruction of the Russian Monument at Ayestefanos*] by Fuat Uzkınay. His 1914 documentary, now lost under some controversy, recorded the demolition of the Russian church and burial ground that had been built after the loss to the Tsarist forces in the Russian-Ottoman war of 1877–1878. The demolition followed quickly upon the declaration of war against Russia and was said to have occurred as a spontaneous sign of patriotism among the citizens. Uzkınay, who was an officer at the time, was supported with equipment by the Messter company.

Like Arslan's notion of self-colonization and his deployment of the paradigm of belated modernity, Balan ends her essay by alluding to these transformations as "discontinuities," specific to Turkey and especially "created by the irreversible tide of nationalization."[40] While I am not interested in denying a national and regional specificity to Turkish cinema, these positions of Turkish particularism deserve some skepticism. Comparisons between and among the histories presented here reveal that Turkish cinema arises like other cinemas emerging out of the imperial condition. This move is a movement of rapid transformation in the cinema as such, the move from a cinema of attractions to a cinema of national styles, from exotic actualities to feature fictions, from global views to domestic propaganda, from silent to sound. In effect what Balan, Arslan, Evren, and Özön describe as a Turkish condition is a transformation that actually roughly parallels the cinemas of the new states of Central Europe. The parallels are so striking that we could describe on this basis *a region running down from Poland to the Turkish Republic in which entertainment and the apparatus of culture are exposed to similar structures of nationalization, industrialization, and standardization.* The concern with female spectatorship may have its specific inflections in Turkey, but it is a concern shared in various forms with the rest of Europe, North America, Far East Asia, and the Middle East. The irreversible tide of nationalism is likewise a tide washing over Eastern, Western, and Southern Europe; North and South America; South and East Asia; and not just Italy, Germany, Spain, and Japan.

The Pre- and International Film Apparatus: Limits to Antagonistic Film Works

These four histories mark out a complex structural relationship in the state and cinematic apparatus. The end of World War I can mark a caesura in the history of film inasmuch as it also represents a broad transformation in the state apparatus. But it is important to note that there is not an easy alignment of cinematic and state apparatus at that moment. The breakup of the Hapsburg, Ottoman, and Prussian Empires began a wave of nation-building in Central and East Europe. Out of these new states a specific national culture could be asserted. The establishment of the new Polish republic meant the possibility of developing an industry with a local national orientation. Thus, for Poland a real emergence of Polish (and Yiddish) film could begin. The same could be said for many other new countries: Czechoslovakia, Hungary, Turkey, Austria, and Weimar Germany. We can describe a region running down from Poland to the Turkish Republic in which entertainment and the apparatus of culture, once part of imperial flows, are exposed to similar structures of nationalization, industrialization, and standardization. After 1918 we can talk about Polish, Turkish, Hungarian, Czech, Slovak, Austrian, and German cinemas in a form we could not discuss previously.

Nevertheless, we should be cautious to understand the role of the cinematic apparatus here from within a national paradigm. Although in many instances we can identify a celebratory assertion of a new largely ethnic-based national liberation, we should not assume that the population of the new republics were immediately good citizens. In Central Europe it was not the case that the cultural orientation of the citizens automatically followed the shift in the political apparatus. For instance, as Andrew Behrendt has shown in his research, the new media and culture industry addressed the people of the new Hungarian republic to reorient them toward Hungary. Most of the citizens still moved in the world in which they had grown up, a world largely defined by imperial parameters. They traveled on a train and road network designed to connect imperial centers. They vacationed in Austria just as Austrians continued to visit the spas in Hungary. They watched German films and celebrated the success of Géza von Blováry and Marika Rökk on the international screen. Behrendt describes how the state supported the new culture industry through film, travel, and entertainment regulation in general to capture the population and form it into a national consuming public. Famously in Turkey, Attatürk undertook a thoroughgoing transformation of the new republic's citizens, creating a culture industry, reforming orthography, changing vestimentary habits, reforming the arts, and so on. In Poland, similar processes unfolded, made complex by destabilizing territorial battles. Annemarie Sammartino has shown how on both sides of the border, the new Polish and German states fostered Polanization and Germanification among the populations often ethnically mixed and diverse.[41] In a process that could be described as the transforming of population into a people, the new republics had to fashion new Polish, German, Hungarian, Czech, Slovak, Austrian, and Turkish citizens.

During this period we recognize how the national configuration came to rely heavily on the cinematic apparatus to manufacture images in which an audience could experience itself as a national audience. We noted above the role played by the nationalist *The Destruction of the Russian Monument at Ayestefanos* for Turkish film. Already around the time of the Balkan Wars (1912, 1913), Grigore Brezeanu provided films with nationalist patriotic content for the Rumanian audiences. Similarly, the German war effort required the images of the *Vaterland* films to promote nationalistic fervor. Such tendencies developed throughout the region. After the end of World War I in the early years of the Polish new republic, nationalist works, *Bartek zwycięzca* [*Bartek the Conqueror*] (1923) by Edward Puchalski for example, offered national patriotic films portraying a history of Polish suffering during partition. These films served to bolster the identification with the nation-state, presumed a Polish audience with common sociopolitical interests, and offered films that fostered an antagonistic relationship to Germany and Russia. Jaroslav Jerry Siakel's film *Janosik* (1921) proved a great hit among the Slovak audience with its tale of an antimonarchist anti-Magyar robber and folk hero à la Robin Hood.

However, at this moment we should not assume an easy correlation between citizenship and allegiance. We noted Sigmund Weinberg in Istanbul earlier; a further interesting case is that of the Hungarian Arzén von Cserépy. In 1920 in the young Weimar Republic, von Cserépy began directing the four-part Fridericus Rex (1920–1923). The series celebrated the life of Friedrich the Great and was a complex film filled with patriotic and authoritarian sentiments. However, those sentiments do not easily align cinematic and state interests: a Hungarian former citizen of the Austrian Empire goes to the center of the German film industry to initiate a long series of "Prussian Films" that were designed to evoke German nationalist sentiments.

Films did foster a sense of commonality among the new national spectators; however, antagonistic film works in the new republics largely subsided by the midtwenties. Within their new borders the new national film industries confronted limitations on audience size that forced them to be oriented to markets beyond the national borders, frequently toward the old imperial centers in Austria and Germany. The Polish film industry, for instance, dropped the production of the anti-Prussian and anti-Russian films. By 1939 the Polish film industry produced thirty films per year. Some of this output sought to entertain a *Polish* audience with stories of the antics of *Polish* figures, reproducing an image of Poland and its people. However, much of it relied on the fluid market quality of silent film that continued to function. In spite of explicit nationalist parameters and localizing tendencies, the Polish and German film industries remained in close communication. In Germany during the 1920s, the film industry reached a rate of up to six hundred films per year. In the face of such numbers, the smaller Polish industry could not avoid hegemonic push and pull influences from the West. And certainly the borders to the German industry were permeable. The Polish actress Pola Negri, born in the Russian empire, did not remain bound to a Polish national film apparatus. After her successful premier in films in Warsaw in 1914, she became the first great film star of the Weimar Republic, defining the role of vamp. And her hiatus in front of the German camera was part of a longer route to Hollywood.

The Cinematic Apparatus and Monolingual National Communication

The national apparatus asserts a certain coherency as localizing and particularlizing system on the cinematic apparatus, but the cinematic apparatus proves capable of operating according to parameters that exceed the national. It is this mobility and market orientation that distinguishes the cinematic and state apparatus; this mobility can even set them at odds with each other. In this contradiction, the possibility of the interzone arises. Consider how within the preceding history we can detect flows and connections that opened up or kept intact communication and even counter public spheres between and among agonistic and even antagonistic populations.

The advent of sound placed a limitation on the ability of film to move. It created a fetter, attaching film first to a linguistic market. Bound to language in new ways, once-global suppliers of moving images MGM, Pathé, or UFA, İpek Film suddenly confront producing films oriented first to an English, French, German, or Turkish-speaking audience. Before the nineteenth century, the notion of social organization within empires contained de facto various conceptions of multiethnic polyglot states. By contrast the rising nation-state evidenced centralizing and homogenizing tendencies, supporting in general monoethnic monolingual conditions of governance. Yasemin Yıldız has convincingly argued that this drive toward monolingualism marked the German nation-state in particular.[42] But throughout the globe, territories, in which sometimes conflictual heterogeneity was once a norm, were redefined by notions of commonality and majoritarian mores. Linguistic communities, ethnicities, and peoples once a part of the coherence of a territory were positioned as minorities that limited the integrity of the state; they were even framed as posing a possible endangerment to its stability. In this work, the advent of sound cinema played an important role, fettering cinema to a linguistic community easily defined nationally.

The nation-state appears to develop with an almost teleological necessity, yet there is nothing necessary or inherently progressive to this form of sociopolitical organization. Likewise, just because sound cinema has been a dominant form of production for almost a century, we should not assume that the cinematic apparatus is limited to any particular spoken language—nor is it limited to sound itself. The success at the box office and awards ceremonies for the silent film *The Artist* (Hazanavicius, 2011) attests to the continuing possibility of other strategies to sound film. The cinematic apparatus is not inherently bound to the spoken word in any way.

MLVF and Interzonal Film

To be sure, sound technology changed thoroughly the apparatus of cinema, but filmmakers did not accept easily the limitation to a status of "small cinema" that arose out of the orientation toward particular linguistic communities. Studios developed various strategies of responding to this fetter on market circulation brought about by the new technology. Best known of the methods, of course, is the use of subtitles, a basic extension of the intertitle of silent film into the frame of the moving image. In this way visual language became subordinated to the spoken word. The introduction of sound film was the end in the apparatus of visual communication to an ease of *transport or transfer* and the introduction of a need to *translate*. Yet along with subtitles, however, we can recall a rather forgotten strategy from the period, the Multiple Language Version Films (MLVF). The MLVF is a sign of other communicative possibilities within the apparatus of cinema, indeed of the fundamental ability of cinema to elude determination by a state linguistic apparatus and generate interzonal relations.

Chris Wahl has done great service in extensively working up this history.[43] The heyday of the MLVF was in the years between 1929 and 1935 with some five hundred films being made for the European market alone. Concretely, the MLVF was a further film shot simultaneously with sometimes the same cast, as in the case of *The Blue Angel/Der blaue Engel* (von Sternberg 1929–1930) or Laurel and Hardy's *Pardon Us/Hinter Schloß und Riegel/De Bote en Bote/Sur les Verrous/Muraglie* (1930–1931). While Marlene Dietrich was famously polyglot, this strategy often resulted in heavily accented films, especially as in the case where actors like Stan Laurel and Oliver Hardy pronounced German, Spanish, French, and so forth only phonetically. Thus studios experimented with a different strategy of translation, filming with two or more casts on the same set. Paramount Studios set up a studio in French Joinville where variations on a basic script were filmed. Leonardo Quaresima reports that the Joinville studio was divided into six "ateliers" where French, German, Hungarian, Portuguese, and Spanish versions were filmed by day and Italian, Polish, Swedish, and Czech versions by night.[44] These films relied on a base U.S. version, but it can be considered a form of visual translation not to just change the language but actually seek to add cultural specificity into setting and filming strategies. Such films could be a matter of just changing actors or of a full exchange of cast and crew.

Jesse Lasky, president of Paramount studios famously announced at the outset of the Joinville project that "Film is no longer international; it is rather a purely national matter."[45] Lasky would have done better to suggest that film is a purely *national-appearing* matter. Important for an understanding of multilanguage version films is that they were not simply understood as oriented toward a single "other" national audience. It was not the case that the MLVs were primarily filmed in English as a means to enter the lucrative U.S. market. Rather, under the project of Film Europe, many of the multilanguage version films were understood as oriented toward a system of circulation among a polyglot European public.[46] Hence, Ivan Klimes and Pavel Zeman make the point that E. A. Dupont's film *Atlantic* (1929), a British film based on the story of the Titanic, was also filmed in a German version as *Atlantik*.[47] This film traveled not only in Germany and Austria but was marketed in Central Europe, especially in Czechoslovakia and Hungary, with the awareness that over 40 percent of the Czech and Slovak populations also understood German in these territories. And in truth, such multilanguage version films were particularly important not for the German market but for the smaller countries where cinematic production could not meet demand by any means. Exhibition in countries such as the Netherlands, Belgium, Hungary, Poland, Czechoslovakia and so on was inherently *international.*

Thus for the consideration of the multilanguage version film, a country like Czechoslovakia plays an extremely illustrative role. Language politics were complex in the new republic. Czechs and Slovaks produced films in their particular languages at the main studios in Prague.[48] The languages were not taught to the other communities in the new republic but were similar enough that Slovaks and Czechs could attend films in the other language without problem. Nevertheless, the output in both these languages was relatively small. Thus with the introduction of sound, the Prague cinemas were primary vehicles not only for films from Germany but also for Hollywood German language version films. Petr Szczepanik describes how the market was dominated by nonnational productions in Germany.[49] In 1930, thirty-six German language premiers took place and by 1932 this activity reached one hundred and twenty-one films. Czechoslovak audiences felt much more comfortable with German films than English and preferred language to subtitles. Szczepanik suggests that for Czechoslovak audiences, the production of a German language version actually initially offered Hollywood films a veneer of increased respectability. This trend continued, although the numbers declined in the next few years because of a boycott of Czechoslovakia by major Hollywood studios. By 1934, however, this example of the project of Film Europa began to break apart in the face of aggressive national linguistic politics. The Czechoslovak government prohibited "second party" multilanguage versions and required Hollywood to supply the market with English originals with subtitles. The MLVF project comes ostensibly to an end not because of the failure of the strategy to reach audiences but because of the stricter fettering of film to the national market in the 1930s and with the effects of World War II.

Interzone Interdependence: Polylingual Moving Images

The history here—of regional and imperial, national and international, silent and sound, MLVF versus subtitles—has charted out shifts in the apparatus of cinema and its relationship to the state apparatus. This history has also offered signs of other and expanded communicative possibilities in the cinematic apparatus, communicative possibilities that foster complex connectivity and generate interzonal relations. Those relations develop across divides here—ethnic, linguistic, political, cultural, and antagonistic rifts. The cinematic apparatus was compelled historically by market interests to reach the largest audience possible;

but it was also compelled by the propensity of audiences to discover the world through the cinematic lens. The ethnographic quality of (early) cinema made that which was distant proximate and that which was proximate unfamiliar enough to hold our interest.

Cinema spread rapidly within the imperial condition, but it emerged too late to stabilize imperial divides.[50] The potential of the cinematic apparatus struggled with the fetters of the postimperial nation-state. Its potential to draw conciliatory lines across old rifts is realized most fully in the contemporary condition; offering new images to imaginative communities is the work of the moving image in the age of transnational production.

Thus, leaping forward to the contemporary moment, we can consider that the MLVF need not be perceived as a dead end. There have been a number of attempts to use this strategy in various ways over the years, especially within European filmmaking from art cinema to popular and animation: e.g., *Nosferatu: Phantom der Nacht* (Herzog, 1979), *Prince Valiant* (Hickox, 1997), *The Lorax* (Renaud and Balda, 2012). Quaresima, moreover, sees the contemporary DVD with its ability to choose forms of subtitled, commentated, dubbed, or even other versions as the direct inheritor of the MLVF practice.[51] Furthermore, we can hold up a recent project associated with the "Declaration of *Inter*dependence" as a sign of ongoing experimentation. In this declaration, Interdependence as a collective mutual responsibility counters the liberal individualism enshrined in the U.S. Declaration of Independence. The project from 2011, organized by a group, Letitripple.org, seeks to foster the possibilities of the internet to form social networks that cut across typical and traditional boundaries of state and economics, gender and age, religion and education. While I am enchanted with the Declaration of Interdependence as a statement, I want to focus on one of the outcomes of the project in that it generated a crowd-sourced moving image—that is, a collective film.[52]

The filmmaker, Tiffany Shlain, in this film would be better described as editor or moving-image compiler. She drew together individual films of people alone or in groups reading the Declaration of Interdependence in sixty-five languages. Transforming these readings into clips, she set them within a collage of text from the Declaration in other languages. Those graphics are in multiple non-Latin scripts and often those text graphics illuminate like a karaoke text, soliciting the spectator to speak along, even if the text is illegible to the individual reader. At the same time the collage strategy recalls historic legacies of collage from early twentieth-century visual culture. In its new deployment of new moving-image technologies it maintains a connection to the MLV film of the past. However multiple languages appear in the film as opposed to presenting multiple versions of a film in different languages. This piece has a different strategy that entails a repetition of the text setting up a sort of coda and refrain structure at times, with the main statement in English and then multiplied in various languages and texts. Set to swelling music by Moby, the meaning of the Declaration is also given further emphasis by a gesture that the readers repeatedly make of interlocking thumbs and forefingers.

We can highlight this work as illustrative for the question of visual communication and in general for the discussion of the interzone as a sign of polylingualism. This is not a silent film but the moving images here strategically deploy new technologies, communicative connections, and editing possibilities to operate outside market systems and state apparatus. This film actively seeks to violate through a new deployment of the moving image the ossified apparatus of governance and economy. As a moving-image project, it generated a very different relationship of image to text, producing importantly a dynamic admixture of spoken and written and visual languages. As a free web-based openly distributed film, it is not part of a liberal market model of profitability. It exhibits a visual language that has the ability to cross and even rupture borders in ways not driven by logics of profitability or domination. This project represents a truly transnational project that relies on the new and unique possibilities of global communication. Historical in its allusions, nevertheless it is a product of its moment and highlights the difference between imperial, national, international, and transnational potentials.

CHAPTER 3

Contiguous

The German-Polish Interzone

We attend to the interzones that conciliate because we cannot assume that neighbors have contact with each other or that people living side by side will communicate with each other. Interzones are more than and less than points of contact; they are the spaces where that which is sundered, rent, and divided, adjusts, concedes, compounds, and ameliorates; the interzone is that space in which a negotiation of difference transpires. This negotiation allows contact between and among those who would otherwise not find themselves on common ground. In Posen in the early part of the twentieth century, precisely during that period of rupture and division, in the "shatterzone" as Bartov and Weitz have called it, the Palace cinema of Franciszek Dymarski and Herman Mittelstädt offered an important meeting space in the context of the new technology of cinema and its entertainments.

On the geopolitical level it is indeed possible that state borders can demarcate a barrier across which there is silence. It is a matter of understatement to note that World War II had devastating effects on German Polish relations. The Palace and all such spaces were gone. It is a further matter of understatement to note that the war had a devastating effect on both the German and the Polish film industry. The common cinematic apparatus was sundered and silence dominated for decades. If the previous chapter focused on the period of the postimperial, this chapter then returns us to the period of the transition from the national to the transnational. It explores the quality of the cinematic apparatus to reach across borders and to conciliate the divided.

Interruption in Communication: The Image of the West in Poland

In terms of nation-building in the postwar period, one of the "positive" results might be considered that it resulted in a clear distinction of film industries. The cinematic and state apparatus on both sides of the border aligned well if not fully. Under the planned economy in the People's Republic, the annual Polish film production was around thirty feature films per year, roughly the same number of films produced by the DEFA studios in East Germany. The West German film industry, although it experienced significant market swings, was larger than both the East German and Polish film industries by two to four times. Nevertheless, in these new (inter)national conditions, it lost the role it played in the past as the center of film production for Central and Eastern Europe. The relations among the three film industries were tenuous at best, with a general turning away of all three from the immediate neighbors.

In these conditions we can note a turn to national oriented spectatorship. In the 1950s and into the 1960s, in West Germany film could contend relatively successfully with strong competition in the theaters from Hollywood productions. The productions of the DEFA film studios in the GDR confronted a repressive Stalinist cultural dictate and frequent censorship so that the blossoming of GDR film took place later than the neighboring countries. In the People's Republic of Poland, the orientation toward national productions was strongest and longest lasting. Stanisław Kuszewski reports, for instance, that although Polish films comprised only 11–12 percent of the market, they drew 34 percent of the audience, indicating an audience with a strong orientation toward the productions of the national cinema. This number is made more significant by the fact that the films had to compete with an equivalent number of films from the Soviet Union and from Hollywood, as well as significant numbers of films from France (twenty-one in 1973), Italy, and Great Britain.[1]

Thematically in Germany, both East and West, the neighbor to the East did not appear on the screen. In Poland however, the German was a constant figure. The new conditions removed the market limits to antagonistic filmwork discussed in the previous chapter, and thus the German figure came to serve as a negative national foil. Just as the III Reich and antifascism served an important ideological function in the cinema of the GDR, the III Reich and the German as Nazi occupier was a repeated motif of Polish cinema. Furthermore, though, the Poles reached further back into the Prussian past. In building on a memory of division and occupation through representations of the Germans, in part Polish film also alluded, albeit obliquely, to that which could not be displayed or discussed. The image of the German was an image of trauma and anxiety that referenced both the Nazi and Prussian past but also the Warsaw Pact present and the Russians as occupiers. In the period 1946–1975 every sixth film was set in World War II, and Kuszewski notes that numerous other films contained sequences set during that period.[2]

As noted there are a few exceptions to the disruption in communication. *Na Krawedzi* [*On the Edge*] (Podgorski, 1972) tells an action espionage cross-border tale under the influence of the Cold War. A decade later, during the period of martial law in Poland a few directors worked outside the country under conditions of greater artistic freedom and during that time Krzysztof Zanussi filmed *Imperativ* (1982) in Germany.[3] A wordy art film with an international cast, the film exhibits a certain neutrality toward Germany.

Perhaps the most significant exception was Andrzej Wajda's adaptation of *Ziemia Obiecana* [*The Promised Land*] (1975). Władysław Reymont's classic of Polish literatures is set in turn-of-the-century Łódź and tells the tale of three friends—a Pole, a Jew, and a German—who set out to make their fortune in the booming textile economy. In an interesting twist, the film works against a national-ethnic paradigm present in the novel; given that Reymont had positioned the Polish character as a déclassé member of the nobility. In Communist Poland, it was not possible to imbue the nobility, even if Polish, with exclusively positive attributes at the time. The film thus transformed the original novel, making the Polish character a more problematic and negative figure. The changes resulted also in a more positive portrayal of the other two friends than in the novel, with the German actually becoming an advocate of artisanal craftsmanship and workers' rights. These films remained exceptions in the representation of Germany and its citizens.

THE IMAGINARY EAST IN THE GERMANIES

In Germany the experience of flight at the end of the war and the subsequent expulsion from the East, was a source of directly experienced trauma for more than nine million people. While without the war there would have been no such fate, only a few understood the loss of home and the disruption of culture as a justified exchange for the ethical moral bankruptcy of the Germans during the Third Reich. For the majority of these refugees and expellees the term *German East* [*deutscher Osten*] shifted from being a term of lived experience to one of historiography and the politics of remembrance. The expulsion *and* the further flight from the GDR into the West meant that in Germany, *the East* became the term for a lost homeland, indeed a stand-in term for the German concept of *Heimat* as such. Historian Gregor Thum pointedly describes the transformation of the German East as "a romanticized, 'German East,' a screen onto which West

Germans projected their longings for stability and tradition.[4] Real existing Poland (or Czechoslovakia) played no role in these considerations.

For instance, in *Green Is the Heath* [*Grün ist die Heide*] (Deppe, 1951), the first significant German *Heimatfilm* and one that revolutionized the cinema culture of postwar West Germany, the expellees appeared not just on the margins but played a central role in the story. Alasdair King details how they provided an image of folkish custom and community that reconfigured similar imagery instrumentalized during the Third Reich.[5] Fundamentally important to the film's success, however, is the scene of harmony that arises in the end as the local community and the community of expellees gather together in celebration at the village festival, dressed in traditional costume. The conflicts that motivated the film resolved, the male and female leads finally having found each other, the villagers old and new can sway to traditional music together as a whole and resolved German community. It is not the Poles who appear here; rather, the East is represented by ethnic Germans in the territory of the Federal Republic. Eastern Europe is absent otherwise in representation and hence for the German imaginary a blank screen represented neither by direct memories nor by any contemporary reality.

We will return later to take up this question of projection; however, at this point we can consider the different conditions with similar outcomes in the GDR. Directly on Poland's Western border, for the GDR, in spite of state Socialist fraternity, Poland was a site of a number of unstated taboos. The state censor and official policy forbade that expulsion be addressed openly in the East and in general the GDR took distance from the entire history of Prussia, the German East, and therefore the history of Poland in general. Thus in the history of the DEFA studios, we can note Kurt Maetzig's *Der schweigende Stern* [*First Spaceship on Venus*] (1960) as a significant coproduction with Polish studios. And we can note that to accomplish this imagining of solidarity they had to a distant future and another planet entirely.

Most importantly at the DEFA, and offering a real exception, was Egon Günther's *die Schlüssel* [*The Keys*] (1972). As a major exception this engagement with Poland and Polish-German contemporary relations offers a momentary flash of the potential of cinema. It shows how even at that time cinema can actually establish a communicative connection across rigid and absolute barriers in the cultural imaginary. The main characters, the couple Ric and Klaus, heading to Poland for a vacation, meet a couple from Krakow. The Polish couple is on the way to Paris. Out of a sense of hospitality they give the German couple the keys to their apartment. It is a gesture of real human solidarity and not political sloganeering.

Günther's film takes place at a moment of liberalization in GDR film history in which the quest for individual happiness was thematized more actively. Having arrived in Poland Ric and Klaus experience a crisis in their relationship, realizing that they have different goals in life. But their self-realizations are set against a backdrop of semidocumentary scenes that show the more progressive Poland that existed during the period. We see liberal art and music scenes and political discussions, but we also meet concentration camp survivors and engage in confrontations over the past. In the end, tragedy befalls the couple as Ric, having realized a new commitment to Klaus, is hit by a streetcar as she is returning to the apartment. The Poles, only acquaintances up to that point, evidence real concern and indeed solidarity. They prove to be very supportive of Klaus as he tries to cope. The film, with its exploration of contemporary Poland as avant-garde of the East, also revealed much of the legacy of the war and the problematic of German-Polish relations. The representation of these real dynamics and cultural transformations had been silenced and forced under the surface out of fear that the liberal Polish model of Socialism might influence expectations in the GDR. The film experienced a number of criticisms right from the start, including from the Polish side. The vision of a progressive Poland in the film made the GDR leadership uncomfortable. Then with the rise of Solidarnosc at the start of the 1980s, the film disappeared completely out of the repertoire of GDR film screenings. In general, the political upheavals in Poland led the GDR to close the borders and return to a state of silence vis-à-vis the neighboring country.

In the most general of terms we can identify *two distinct patterns in national historiography* at work here. *In Germany*, history is something to be overcome and the past is something from which one generally has taken distance. The response to the negative and horrific past is to find orientation in the present. The act of taking distance from German history in turn offers a kind of basis for national identification: "we" Germans are the ones who have overcome that past. *In Poland*, by contrast, history is something to be celebrated and recalled actively. The past is the source of the collective "we" in the present. Ultimately, however, as divergent as they may be, both approaches prepared German and Polish historiography well to make a transition into the post- and transnational parameters of Europe and the European Union.

REESTABLISHING CONNECTIONS

On a material level borders can fall very quickly. Already one year after the *Wende* Germany replaced Russia as Poland's most important trading partner. At the same time Russian film disappeared from Polish screens.[6] On a cultural level borders have the potential to structure imaginative communities much longer. Although Poland's economic future became bound up with its relationship to Germany, and as Maria Kornatowska noted, France and Germany became Poland's primary coproducing partners, nevertheless Germany as it is did not appear in the Polish cinemas.[7] The primary depictions of Germans continued to be drawn from the experience of the Third Reich. On the German side of the Oder, at first a general silence continued to be maintained. Even as a film apparatus developed that fostered interzonal cooperation on a material level, that foundation did not translate into images.

As a foil to the relationship with Germany we can consider Krzysztof Kieslowski's Polish-French coproduction, the trilogy *Troi Coleurs: Bleu, Blanc, Rouge* (1993–1994). Those films marked the first great successes of the Eurimages project, belonging to the first round of funding. Eurimages, a grand project of the Council of Europe, sought to further European unity through film, especially between East and West. Kieslowski's films fulfilled that goal admirably. The trilogy represented a dynamic cultural French-Polish interzone that comes into existence in the films through transnational border-crossings. The characters, French and Polish and French-Poles, move about in European space; one character, Karol Karol, literally travels inside a suitcase from Paris to Warsaw. Although Germany lies right in the middle of that crossing, the country does not appear at all. It is a lacuna in the middle of this crossing; filmically, Germany is the border to be passed over.

But, as caveat, with a few notable exceptions in the documentary genre, we can say the same for German film. Poland was a space to be passed over. In *Die kaukausische Nacht* [*The Caucasian Night*] (Maugg, 1998) Poland is a lacuna on the way to Russia. *One Day in Europe* bypasses neighboring countries for a more complex imagining of European connections. Two divergent attitudes can inform our assessment of this silence. We could note that it took almost a decade before work similar to Kieslowski was undertaken between Germany and Poland. Or we could state more positively that the history of German Polish relations was marked by a history of occupation, cultural tension, silence, and anxiety-laden projection, and yet in spite of that history it took less than a decade before similar kind of work would arise between German and Polish partners. This normalization of relations proceeded at the same rate then as had those on Germany's western border in the immediate postwar era.

THE RETURN OF COMMUNICATION: POLAND IN EUROPE

Recall the discussion in Chapter One of the general transformations in Eastern and Western Europe after the collapse of existing Socialism. Just as in the other former East Block countries, in the 1990s Polish film production experienced a dramatic decline. Accounts vary, some recording under five films in the first years of the 1990s while others record larger numbers by including made-for-television films and HBO Polska productions. The European Audiovisual Observatory began recording production and release statistics in 1996 and at that point, they noted seventeen films with four coproductions. Since the silent era, Poland had produced over thirty films a year. In 1985, the People's Republic noted thirty-nine feature films released (Table 3.1).

By the mid-1990s a number of critics had come to describe a new, European orientation in Polish filmmaking. Since 1994 there have been thirty-one Eurimages sponsored coproductions with Polish production companies, starting with Kieslowski's *Three Colours* trilogy. The new millennium marked a general increase in production and a greater expansion resulted after Polish ascension to the EU. Tracing these developments, we can note that, importantly, 30 percent of contemporary film production in Poland has taken place as coproduction. Roughly 30 percent of Polish films are produced in a way that is inflected with a European outside.[8]

Marek Haltof identified the Polish orientation toward Europe that developed in the 1990s through the slogan "catching up with Europe."[9] He underscored that the task for Polish filmmakers and artists in general was to produce a "post-totalitarian art, which, while addressing some universal issues, will reflect national uniqueness."[10] Where other critics rejected the nonnational quality of the first post-Communist films, action genre films like *Kroll* (Pasikowski, 1991) or

Table 1. Annual Film Production in Poland

Year	Number of Films	Number of Coproductions
1975	36	
1985	39	
1996	17	(4)
1997	21	(3)
2000	27	(5)
2002	24	(6)
2003	25	(4)
2005	25	(7)
2006	38	(10)
2007	31	(7)
2008	38	(13)
2009	41	(11)
2010	42	(6)
2011	32	(11)

Psy (Pasikowski, 1992), Haltof saw in the work of Wladyslaw Pasikowski not a betrayal of the ethical artistic legacy of Polish New Wave cinema but rather a savvy engagement with Hollywood visual codes that bespoke a high-level awareness of conventions.[11] Alexandra Sosnowski, echoing Haltof, described Polish film from the 1990s as supporting a middle-course production that negotiated genre and national interest: "While creating works with wide cross-cultural appeal is not easy, the potential rewards make this challenging route worth taking."[12]

Janina Falkowska considers the orientation toward Europe as providing a "dreamscape" for Polish national fantasy, suggesting in effect that the Polish imagined community develops in a relationship to a space beyond the Polish border.[13] Where Benedict Anderson suggested that the historic national community developed in a relationship to the metropolitan center of the capital, Falkowska describes a development in which a current national community has a more complex and bifurcated awareness of capital, of border, and of the space beyond the border. She does not suggest that somehow Brussels replaces Warsaw but that Europe and Europeanness play a central role in national identifications: "idealistic Europe [acts] as a futuristic phantasm."[14] For Falkowska, Europe was, in the period before ascension to the EU and even after, not a concrete place but a future possibility that entails notions of belonging and becoming. Europe is a place into which Poles are moving, they are not yet there but will arrive soon. Thus in national discourse, Europe comes to serve as a measure for the better part of the imagined community. It is a matter of pleasurable fantasy or critical reflection.

What she describes as a "cinema of capitalistic fantasy," then, is a cinema set in the milieu of the new neoliberal winners of the market transformations, usually in Warsaw, with a nevertheless pan-European atmosphere. She sites *Tylko mnie kochaj* [*Just Love Me*] (Zatorski, 2006) as a good example, noting further, however, that the dramatically expanded role of television in Polish film production has made this genre of film an easily accessible and popular fare for Polish audiences. These films, generally romantic comedies, display a light and soap-operaesque world of the *nouveau riche*, where romantic intrigues occupy the foreground and the realities of capitalist accumulation are offscreen.

There is a second set of films being produced in Poland. These films are largely the films done in coproduction, films that screen outside of Poland and appeal to an international art house audience. Falkowska discusses these as "the cinema of the abject," the extension in post-Communist Poland of the Cinema of Moral Concern that dominated film production for decades. I would describe these films as the *new critical Polish cinema*. They eschew escapism and instead pursue a didactic critical function. These films are accelerating in their production. *Sztuczki* [*Tricks*] (Jakimowski, 2007), *Wszystko będzie dobrze* [*All Will Be Well*] (Wiszniewski, 2007), *Boisko dla Bezdomnych* [*The Offsiders*] (Adamik, 2008), *Handlarz Cudów* [*The Miracle Seller*] (Pawica, 2009), being good examples, detail instead a society marked by economic decline and sociopolitical difficulties, alcoholism, violence, isolation, despair. The films tell stories not of the upper class of Warsaw or Sopot, but rather small regional towns or desolate environments like the train station in Warsaw. The films are generally in line with European auteurist strategies; however, in her observation Falkowska identifies typically a happy end, and that end has a European dynamic to it e.g., a return of the businessman father and restoration of family (*Tricks*), rehabilitation by entry into a (European) homeless soccer championship, or a redemptive journey (across Europe) to Lourdes (*The Miracle Seller*). This happy end gives the films a lighter and redemptive quality that helps it appeal to larger audiences, although their primary appeal is to the educated classes. Europe may not be the direct object of consideration in the films but affords the characters an expanded field of reference and a likewise new terrain of mobility.

We can add to Falkowska's category though a further distinction of films without a happy end. In these films the act of abjection forms a significant aspect of the films narrative. A series of darker pessimistic films came out in 2009: for instance, *Wojna polsko-ruska* [*Snow White and Russian Red*] (Żuławski, 2009), *Moja Krew* [*My Flesh My Blood*] (Wrona, 2009) or *Swinki* [*Piggies*] (Glinski, 2009). The portrayal of the underclass, of violence, and dead end hopelessness develops through antiheroes who call forth little sympathy and instead generate a sense of repulsion. These are not characters who display hope in the end, succeeding "in spite of" their milieu; rather, they descend further, accommodating themselves to their conditions. Interestingly again, Europe—an expanded Europe of globalized contacts—plays a structuring role. *My Flesh My Blood* portrays the relationship of a Polish boxer with an illegal Vietnamese immigrant, difficult to image without the context of globalization. *Piggies* is a name that describes the teenage boys who prostitute themselves along the German border. The narrative is only possible because of that cross-border sex trade.

This *cinema of the border* region as represented by *Swinki*, reveals a tenuous emergence of an interzone. This is the cinema of coproductions, especially German-Polish in which the films do engage with the interests of the two partners in a coproduction. There is little crossing in *Swinki*, but when it does occur it is dangerous; for Polish subjectivity, as with Tomek the main character of *Swinki*, to have contact with Germany, to cross the border is to subject one's body and psyche to pain and trauma. Nevertheless, it is a film struggling to imagine a new relationship, albeit threatening and potentially destructive. The cinema of the border regions is the cinema in which a vision develops that considers the rupturing of a national inside and outside explicitly. This cinema is likewise motivated by a sense of Europe. From a perspective originating outside of Poland, across the border, and actually crossing the border, a group of people is brought into proximity by the fact of Europe.

Unlike in Falkowska's cinema of fantasy, Europe is not a future fantastic projection; rather, it is a relatively accomplished fact that has resulted in new set of neighbors, with whom one may engage. The cinema of the border may be socially critical and didactic but it is distinct from the cinema of the abject. What I would underscore here is that in this dynamic, the films of the border develop a vision of Poland and Polishness that does not easily address a Polish spectator. It is an image that does not easily interpolate a Polish fantasy, although it is also the case, as Falkowska notes, that the cinema of the abject does not easily interpolate the audience for the cinema of fantasy. A new critical Polish cinema does not have an easy time addressing a mainstream audience. Across Europe as in Poland, positive rather than negative images, entertainment rather than socially critical messages bring in the largest national audiences. It is difficult to produce a profitable and aesthetically critical film in Europe.

DOCUMENTING THE INTERZONE

In the considerations of the interzone, documentary film has captured the rapid transformations in German-Polish relations and the emergence of new solidarities and configurations along the border and beyond. It is in documentary that we can discover the first and the more consistent, more engaged reaching out across the border region. This is not an easy engagement and for that very reason it is an interzonal relationship. Here, communication is tenuous, a process of conciliation. The ease of communication that defines the alignment of cinema and state apparatus does not take place here.

In East Germany, silence dominated but in West Germany, starting in the 1960s, a number of television documentaries began to emerge. This shift took place in conjunction with the new *Ostpolitik*, the New Eastern Policy of the federal government that sought normalization of relations with the neighbors on the other side of the Iron Curtain. The recognition of the new German-Polish border by the Federal Republic and the reconciliatory act of Willy Brandt's *Kniefall* in Warsaw in 1970 foreclosed the possibility of return, and Manfred Kittel and Maren Röger detail extensive television travelogues of journeys to the former German East from that period on. Kittel describes this genre of travelogues from the early days of German television broadcast history as explicitly addressing the German expellees, offering them a medial compensatory function as the political climate began to make clear that there would be no return "home."[15] I have addressed this work directed at and for expellees in detail elsewhere.[16] In this moment I am interested in considering those documentarists who reached out at the collapse of the East Block, their cameras in hand, to travel across a once closed border and explore an expanse of Europe suddenly open.

Headed East: New Historical Films

In the wake of the collapse of the East Block most people traveled west, but a few filmmakers set out in the opposite direction. The works of Andreas Voigt, Helke Misselwitz, and Volker Koepp stand out as the first to engage with the people and lives on the border. These filmmakers, each trained within the DEFA studios of the GDR as documentarists explored the borderlands on both sides of the Oder and Neisse rivers. They then continued this exploration of the present, moving further east, not as tourists but indeed as documentarists with an interest in capturing and conveying something of the lives of real people in their contemporary conditions. These films were not made as coproductions and represent an often intense investigation of the present, sometimes motivated by personal history, but fundamentally indicating a commitment to an eastward orientation inculcated in the GDR. It is not Socialist fraternity in the manner of the old official sloganeering that motivates them; rather, as films they have a new historical humanistic interest and an affiliation based on a commonality of experience. Their films seek to document a multifaceted and vibrant world; their work counters nostalgic projections. For that and out of their training, they display a complex visual aesthetic strategy that considers the artistry of the image directly. In general in these films, we can say that their orientation toward the present allows the viewers the possibility of catching a glimpse of the interzone, but their orientation toward a German audience restrains their engagement with the complex connectivity of the region.

ANDREAS VOIGT, TRAVELER FILMS

"There are those who travel and those who stay home." ["Es gibt die Reisenden und die, die zu Hause bleiben."]

Of all German filmmakers Andreas Voigt has perhaps the most intense and most serendipitous relationship to Poland. In 1971, as a seventeen-year-old student in the GDR he was given the opportunity to study in a foreign country. At the time that he took the entry exam, he was hoping like all the other candidates that he would be sent to Russia. Instead he received the offer to go to Poland to study physics. During the year he spent in Krakow, he learned Polish and realized that physics was not his métier. He also traveled and attended a number of film festivals, including the famous Konfrontacje in Warsaw, where he was able to see a broad selection of foreign films for the first time in his life. A similar dynamic of serendipity developed at the point that Andreas applied for a job at the DEFA studios. Having been prevented from pursuing a Polish dissertation topic, he was looking for a new direction. He had worked as an assistant during vacations for the documentary group at the DEFA and sought at that point to begin working there full time as a director's assistant and script editor. He got the appointment precisely because there was a delegation from Poland at the DEFA studios at the time and they needed someone who could read and speak Polish. The period was 1978, just before the declaration of martial law.

Contact with Poland was easy at the time. In the 1970s the border was relatively open. Voigt notes however that in his experience there was an anxiety in the GDR vis-à-vis Poland that as a pluralistic land it could have a negative influence on the citizens of the GDR. As discussed earlier this atmosphere of relative freedom was captured in Egon Günther's *Die Schlüssel* (1973). Voigt had the most advanced linguistic and technical knowledge in the film sector of the GDR and would have been the person to develop joint projects in Poland, but by the time he began actually studying to be a director and documentarist, the border was closed and *Die Schlüssel* was taken from the screen. It was not until after the *Wende* that Voigt, then a newly trained director of the last generation of the DEFA studios and a documentarist auteur, was able to realize a film project about Poland that could draw on his talents.

Grenzland [*Borderland*] was filmed in the fall of 1991 into the summer of 1992 as a series of trips along both sides of the Oder and Neisse rivers, that is, along both sides of the German-Polish border. The film is a mixture of documentary, travelogue, and interview. It has no voice-over narrator offering the audience insights and facts about the environment. It is more of a solitary exploration, Andreas Voigt on a journey to the East, capturing the transformation of life that has taken place since the collapse of the Socialist states that once bordered each other there.

Voigt's trip to the East and this border for that moment was a direction off the beaten path. What it reveals, however, especially if one reviews it today, is that Voigt indeed went to the future. The tourism to the West was simply a matter of gathering present experiences, catching up with the opportunities that the other Germany had always had. The trip to the East was an ethnography that charted out all the problems that would become formative of the future: loss of industry, unemployment, shrinking cities, far right violence, sex trade, the insufficiently examined history of expulsion and suffering on both sides of the border, and the implications that this insufficient coming to terms with the past has on national sentiment and international relations.

This film, as well as Voigt's films in general, can be described as a *traveler film*. As opposed to what Tobias Ebbrecht has described as the *Spurensuche* films of the expellees, here the journey is not a search for the lost home or overcoming a personal trauma.[17] In a traveler film of this kind the documentarist takes up a critical relationship to his own work; the very act of traveling is directly thematized. In this regard, Voigt noted in an interview that "There are those who travel and those who stay home [Es gibt die Reisenden und die, die zu Hause bleiben]." Voigt as documentary filmmaker is one of those who travels, who goes away from home out into the world. He develops an anthropological openness that is open to the inhabitants of that great wide world.

Grenzland begins with a shot of a ruin of a bridge. We are given no explanation although the image returns a number of times in the course of the film and we come to understand that it formerly spanned the river. At the moment, there is no explicit marker of location. The film offers no initial information about its intent. This scene is followed by a sequence on the Polish side of the border. A far shot pans through a forest across a statue of the Virgin Mary. The statue and its surroundings are in a state of neglect yet there is a quality of a Romantic ruin that permeates the environment. An interview follows with a man in a uniform who relates the story of how the statue was decapitated by the Russian army and only later was the head placed back. The interviewee expresses a certain hostility to the Russians, saying that the Germans would never have behaved this way. When pushed to consider the history of atrocities committed during the German occupation, the man shrugs his shoulders and says, "that's how things were back then."

With this remark bespeaking either a shocking amount of historical forgetting or a shocking amount of generosity, the film cuts to the river. And as the camera moves between the shores, the title appears, *Grenzland, eine Reise* [*Borderland, a Journey*]. The principle of the film that follows is one of back and forth, a weaving of stories from both sides of the river. The next sequences, for instance, introduce a German couple celebrating their fifty-fifth wedding anniversary. They are originally from the other side of the border and share with the camera the history of their marriage.

The opening scene with the uniformed Pole is short but worth considering a bit more at length because it indicates a number of dynamics of an interzone. First and, perhaps as foundation to the film, most importantly is the voice that poses the questions to the man. This is Voigt's voice speaking in Polish. And here

Voigt's ability to engage linguistically with people on both sides of the border reveals itself right from the start. Certainly it is not necessary to speak Polish to go the eastern side of the border. Travelers can prepare themselves with travel guides of various kinds. A trip across the border can be organized in a closed environment of a bus in which as a passenger one travels in a collective and is mediated by translators. Other filmmakers who have traveled to the East like Volker Koepp, Hans-Christian Schmid, or Rosa von Praunheim, lacking linguistic skills, have solved the dilemma of how to develop a documentary about people and the past by relying on translators who accompany their journey. They act as intermediaries for the filmmakers. Or filmmakers like Andreas Dresen, Henner Winckler, or Christoph Hochhäusler have developed fictional narratives that film the landscape and people but establish a convention in the story that results in distance from the population, e.g., Dresen's *Halbetreppe* [*Grill Point*] (2002). Or a film might include characters who serve as a sort of native informant for the other side. The Silesian musician Bartek Blaszczyk played the role of Marek in Winckler's *Klassenfahrt* [*School Trip*] (2002) with the conceit that as an employee in a tourist attraction he naturally spoke some German.

The difference, however, is that as a documentarist, a dynamic develops in which the camera can record the moment of interpersonal contact. Periodically, Voigt's films represent this moment of "first contact," in which Voigt calls out from behind the camera a question in Polish to passersby. They may respond with indifference and keep walking, or they may stop and engage the question with an answer; they do not, however, express surprise at being addressed by someone speaking Polish. In conversations there may be moments when a linguistic barrier arises and Voigt has to repeat the question, but the conversation continues at that point. Of course this is not a necessary aspect of documentary filmmaking. However, it is a possibility and that it occurs here derives from Voigt's strategy of filming and editing. He gives us to see the development of contact with people. Voigt's films frequently have long takes in which people come into view and are addressed and engaged without a cut. There are moments in which people on the street stare into the static camera that has been observing them, and they ask each other what it is that that person is filming. Voigt describes documentary filmmaking as "wandering through the world telling stories about others and always about oneself." Precisely this potential is enacted here with the voice from behind the camera speaking out to the person in front.

At those moments, the camera may record a surprise that there is a camera recording. This surprise results, of course, from the fact that Voigt is indeed wandering and not preparing contact with people through a preceding research.

He was not here before. He is here now. Thus. there may be surprise that a camera has appeared in a small town or a defunct factory on the banks of the Oder, but the general lack of surprise at being addressed in Polish indicates certainly that the documentarist has entered into a moment of the quotidian. The camera may disturb the flow of life as camera but not as a foreign camera per se.

That last point requires a bit of a correction and that correction points to the third dynamic of the interzone. In interpersonal communication, even with strangers, a dynamic develops in which history and historical legacies give way to an openness in the present. Repeatedly, Voigt meets on the other side people who exhibit the same sentiment as the uniformed man at the start. There is the old couple that owns the photography shop, the counterpart to the German couple celebrating their fifty-fifth anniversary. The Polish couple met during the Third Reich as forced laborers in Germany. They describe their meeting without *ressentiment*. Voigt finds a man who tends to the ruin of a villa that once belonged to King August of Saxony. The camera takes in the ruins at first before the figure emerges to relate a bit of the history. They track through the rooms in decay as the man tells that the house was once a residence for unwed mothers and then a convent. He tells about the Russian occupation and blames them for much of the devastation. He also relates his own personal biography as a Polish expellee from Kiev. When questioned about his historical knowledge and his appreciation for the German past, the man turns from historian and guide to philosopher and organic intellectual. He speaks generally about humans and in tones that are pointedly indifferent to nationality: "Germans and Poles are humans and everyone should be a human [*Mensch*] to each other but not all of them are." In these interactions Voigt records moments of this principle, moments in which a German meets Poles on simple human terms, or simply as human.

At the same time, there is the sequence with the group of Polish workers who had been employed since the 1970s in the textile factory at Guben in the GDR. In the face of competition and privatization, the factory is already, one year after unification, set to close and they are laid off. These women denounce the situation and describe their years of laboring for the factory as wasted. The present here trumps the profits of the past. Nevertheless, their frustration over their pending unemployment is not expressed in nationalist terms. Economics and not German economists are to blame. The interzone may be conflictual but it is dialogic and focused on the present. It derives from interaction and engagement with the other.

Such is generally not the case, however, when Voigt interacts with people on the German side of the border. On the German side, in the absence of interaction with Poles, the interzone as dialogic space remains absent. Voigt visits the first local branch of the Bund der Vertreibene, [Federation of Expellees]

(BdV).[18] We meet the local organizer of the BdV, a machinist who quickly lost his job and has now opened his own fast-food stand. The scene cuts from the outdoor setting in front of the stand to an office where the head of the organization reviews a history of injustices perpetrated by Poles and the rest of the world on Germans dating back to World War I. A bit later, Voigt finds a couple camping on the banks of the river. They have binoculars and spend their time staring across to the other side at their old home. When expelled, they went to West Germany. As soon as the *Wende* occurred, they came to the border to take up this position. Standing in the grass in a far shot they describe to each other what they see and how bad the state of their old home is and how desolate and decayed their once thriving and prosperous village looks. The couple is able to take advantage of the open German-German border but does not make the next move to take advantage of the open German-Polish border. Voigt does not ask why the couple prefers to camp on the West Bank and peer through binoculars rather than park their RV on the East Bank.

We are given a sense though as to why. Voigt interviews the German couple at length in a medium shot, seated in front of the RV. When asked about the experience of the end of the war and expulsion, the woman simply states that it was indescribably horrific "and if anyone says they can tell you what it was like, they were not there." With this statement she closes down conversation and retreats from any dialogue into a hermetic silence based on this experience of suffering. The past appears in this moment and on this side of the Oder to overwhelm the present. To camp on the other side of the border would require the couple to interact with the location in the present and disrupt this condition.

If Voigt struggles to contend with this position, his interaction with a neo-Nazi pushes him to his limits. Voigt's film documents how quickly such groups emerged to fill in the vacuum left behind by the collapse of the Socialist state apparatus. He meets a local leader in a pub who appears clean cut and relatively articulate. He certainly is not shy about answering Voigt's questions, discussing his readiness to engage in violent force or what it means to be a "proud German." The responses though are confused and when asked about what it means to be a German they devolve into clichés listing attributes like industriousness and hard work and not having sex with foreigners.

One could accuse Voigt of offering a more appealing representation of the Polish side. The painful interactions with the neo-Nazi are followed by interviews on the Polish side. Two men standing roadside, discuss with Voigt the German occupation and the atrocities of the Germans back then. They remember it first hand and question what could have possessed such a civilized country to behave so barbarically. But once again, in the interaction with Voigt, they set the past aside and focus on the present expressing a desire for a normalization of relations between Germans and Poles. After all, they note, "Germany and Poland are trapped together in Europe.

Voigt's work displays an attentiveness to this area as a region with inherent commonalities, often as yet unrealized. In its investigation of the present, it is also about a struggle to find an orientation into the future.

Here the work of the Traveler Film is clear. In an interview Voigt noted:

> We all live in thousands of different worlds. There is the world of the waitress at the counter of Anita Wronski [café where the interview took place] in whose life we are only a small part because the rest of the time she is a student or who knows what or a housewife. There is the world of the taxidriver and the politician and the police officer and the letter carrier, and so on. But these are a thousand separate worlds. And because society is organized in a complex division of labor, there is no possibility or necessity from world x to enter into world 127. Everything that mediates between these worlds [Alles was an Weltvermittlung stattfindet], everything that allows for communication between these worlds is in the end a result of media. Our knowledge of the world is first and foremost a mediated knowledge and not an experiential one. We confuse the two because we think that the mediated is reality. This confusion has fatal consequences. Although everyone knows that the two are not the same, the mediated has this effect. The image in particular has this medium specific ability to appear as truth or reality. Yet the beautiful and fascinating aspect of documentary film is actually that I, Andreas Voigt, have a real possibility to move from the world of the shepherd in the Caucasus to that of the radical right or left youth in Leipzig, or from the world of the old grandfather and expellee who is sitting on the banks of the Oder river fishing, reflecting on the fact that he comes from the other side and his house is over there and he can see it, but he has no desire to go back over there anymore, off into a completely different one. This is what I enjoy about the work.

Voigt sees his work as a form of interactive communication that is part of his life but as film can also be imparted to the viewer.

The Traveler Films are future-oriented films, witnessing transformations that affect the inhabitants of a region, developing sympathies and orienting the viewers toward a shared humanity. They open the viewer to the possibility of the interzone, yet, as will be discussed further, they are infused with a sense of traveling from a home to which one belongs that limits that possibility.

HELKE MISSELWITZ, INTERNATIONALIZING IMAGES

In 2000, the acclaimed documentarist Helke Misselwitz likewise turned her attention to the other side of the Oder. Misselwitz, like Voigt and Koepp, had been trained in the GDR. She is of the same generation as Koepp, meaning she worked for over a decade in the DEFA studios at Babelsberg. Her film *Winter Adé [After Winter Comes Spring]* (1988) offered one of the most poignant and insightful visions of the end of the Republic. It focused on the lives of women throughout the country and gave them a space in which they could express their dreams and frustrations with a seldom-found openness and clarity. It belongs to the masterpieces of GDR cinema. After the *Wende*, Misselwitz has continued to make documentaries but under increasingly difficult conditions, ultimately working with contracts from television.

Fremde Oder [Strange Oder] (2001) was done as a project for MDR, the Middle German Television, the primary station oriented toward eastern Germany. It is an audience that grew up on GDR television and DEFA films. It is an audience that understands some of the sensibilities of a filmmaker like Misselwitz and one that knows how to appreciate the style of documentary film developed by filmmakers like Misselwitz and Koepp.

Throughout, the possibilities of the visual are foregrounded as part of the work of the film. There are interludes that could be understood as simple melodic scenery in the rhythm of the editing but then the interviews work as part of that rhythm. The film moves between Frankfurt and Szczecin on both sides of the river. The camera indicates an interest in the land and riverscapes that we do not find in Voigt's work but do in Koepp's. It is, however, not a traveler film. It is an international film. The open space of Poland and the East are filled with memory fragments of various individuals reporting on their experience of the collapse of Communism and the hopes that had risen during that period and that generally proved naive in the face of capitalist reality.

Misselwitz's film includes a number of figures familiar from Voigt's work: Ukrainian sex workers, neo-Nazis, expellees. She finds Germans, Poles, and Russians reflecting on a place that is both lost and regained. The film is, like the works of her DEFA colleagues, often described as poetic or lyrical documentary. Yet where Voigt could be understood as investigating the present with an orientation to the future, the relationship between the images and the voices frequently results in a sense of melancholia, a kind of mourning not for a lost past but a lost period of promise and optimism. The internationalism of the film, its focus on the Communist past and the dashed hopes of the transition period and its move between the two countries again, like Voigt, alludes to interzonal possibilities but yet retains the national as a form of comparison. Complex regional connectivity is not an explicit part of the film, although the film reveals it as subtly implicit in the very work of the film as such.

VOLKER KOEPP, HEIMATIZATION FILMS

Koepp's films *Fremde Ufer* [*Strange Shore*] (1995), *Herr Zwilling und Frau Zuckermann* [*M. Zwilling and Mme Zuckermann*] (1999), *Flussfahrt in Ostpreußen* [*River Journey in East Prussia*] (1999), *Kurische Nehrung* (2001), *Uckermark* (2002), *Dieses Jahr in Czernowitz* [*This Year in Czernowitz*] (2004), *Pommerland* (2005), *Schattenland—Reise nach Masuren* [*Shadowland: A Journey to Mazuria*] (2005), *Söhne* [*Sons*] (2007), *Memelland* (2008), and *Berlin-Stettin* (2009) represent the most extensive and protracted engagement with the past and present of the former German East. This growing list of films marks the most intense interaction with that region devastated by Nazi occupation, culturally eviscerated by expulsion, terrorized by Communist dictatorships, and then tossed abruptly into free-market chaos. Koepp has earned numerous prizes for this work, including in 2005 the Georg Dehio Kulturpres of the Deutsches Kultur-forum östliches Europa.

Koepp has been referred to frequently as a *filmpoet*, a film poet, and this is no surprise; in his academic thesis, "Strukturen im Spielfilm—Poetischer Film" ["Structures in Feature Film: Poetic Film"] (1969), Koepp explored the lyrical possibilities of filmic representation. Koepp, understanding the potential of the moving image, produces beautiful atmospheric films. Skies and landscapes, light and shadows, past ruins and present habitations are central images in Koepp's films. However, whereas in melancholic relations to the German East, contemporary images of ruins offer a negative foil to the once flourishing German culture, Koepp offers an almost neo-Romanticist appreciation of the ruin. The German East is beautiful in its present. The *Frankfurter Allgemeine Zeitung* described Koepp in 2005 as a documentarist who within the medium of film is able to produce "objective documentations nevertheless with lyrical poetical elements and an idiosyncratic aesthetic."[19]

From 1974–1984, within the section of documentary film at the DEFA studios, Koepp achieved a certain fame because he was able to undertake the long-term [*Langzeit*] documentation at Wittstock. The project ran over a decade with the express purpose of documenting "conflicts and problems in the GDR." Yet already in the GDR, Koepp had considered the lost German East. The short film *Gustav J.* (1973) focused on the title figure's life; born in Lithuania, Koepp confronted the horrors of the war and its aftermath with a particular intensity. Koepp then filmed the short film *Grüße aus Sarmatien* [*Greetings from Sarmatia*] (1975) as a way of honoring the poet Johannes Bobrowski whose work took up motifs from the Memel.

There is a strong aspect of the traveler film here. Koepp takes as a motif for his work a quote from the author Wilibald Alexis, "the traveler who knows everything already, is no longer able to see anything on his travels." As with Voigt, the point of Koepp's films for him is to travel and to see new things. And for the question of the interzone, this travel as contact and discovery is central. Moreover, in considering the legacy of the post-*Wende* films, Martina Knoben describes Koepp's work as having established a "Europe of Regions."[20] His travels have taken him into parts of the East that recall old territorial names, places that to a great extent no longer exist on official maps but, as the camera's journeys reveal, seem to have a lasting ideational presence. It is not just the case that the Mazuria, or the Kührische Nehrung once held a specific meaning for the German population that lived there, but rather that those regions continue to have specific meanings that have been transmitted even to the new residents. To be sure there is a difference between then and now, but that is always the case. It is only in melancholic longing that that difference is effaced or rejected.

Koepp's projects review those regions, lost to the Germans and hidden behind the Iron Curtain, lost for decades to the West in general. His films evidence a complicated and complex relationship to the subject. There is a fundamental interest and openness to contemporary conditions. Koepp never overlooks or fails to interact with the populations that settled in the region after 1945. He does search out, however, the minorities with an ethnic connection to Germany. And the postwar figures that appear in his films are often selected because they have a connection to the German past, e.g., they currently live in a former home of a German family or work in a setting that was once a German industry or tend to some aspect of the past with particular care.

In conjunction with this last point, cemeteries, memorials, statues, and markers of the historic presence of Germans in the region appear with frequency in his work: the ruins of the German East beautifully transfigured. But perhaps more characteristic and remarkable are the landscape and nature shots of Koepp's films. Pan shots along sweeping coasts or over stretches of fields that often appear like pristine nature. Brilliant sunsets, moons hanging in the horizon, a beautiful close up of flora and fauna punctuate the interactions with people, often even becoming the primary images. Reviewers give Koepp's films the appellation *poetic documentaries* and see in the work a new form. Tobias Ebbrecht notes that this work does not look for traces of the past; rather, here the past appears as a trace in the present.[21]

There is, however, a certain undeniable aspect of nostalgia in his films. They are not random travelogues or documentaries about mushroom species along the river Bug. The films investigate a legacy in a region, inspecting to see whether the memory of the German presence still exists. It is possible that the images can be appropriated for revanchist and far-right purposes. A group calling themselves "Edelweissist," playing on notions of the Heimat flower Edelweiss—its meaning of noble white and the ending *ist* as a form of racist identification did just that. They extracted the landscape and ruin images from Koepp's film and used them as backdrop for a music video to accompany the song "*Memel bleibt Deutsch*" ["*The Memel Remains German*"] by the neo-Nazi hard-core band Kommando Freisler.[22]

To be sure, such revanchist goals are not the aim of Koepp's nostalgia. Instead, we find there a fascinating and unprejudiced representation of the complexity of the region and its history. Ralf Schenk suggested that the central dynamic to Koepp's films is the questioning of the meaning of "*Heimat* and uprooting [*Entwurzelung*]."[23] Koepp does not seek to define the terms of belonging and displacement; rather, he shows us the way that people negotiate them. Indeed this aspect lends the ability to identify the work as a *heimatization* film, a homelandification film. The Europe of regions is also a Europe of homelands, albeit not the understanding of homeland that dominated from the nineteenth century onward. Heimatization is rather about the active negotiation of the homeland.

The camera practices a sort of active awareness: knowing what the terms of exploration are but not seeking to produce them, rather to inspect how people themselves produce and/or negotiate them. Thus belonging and displacement are not reified as a matter of good and evil. They are not understood as objective experiences where some lucky people enjoy a fullness of belonging and many wretched individuals are forced into a cold world. Rather, belonging and displacement appear as a consistent and constant dynamic of human experience. Even for those who stay, the experiences of filiation and affiliation prove dynamic. Home is never static.

To accomplish this position of active awareness, Koepp's documentary camera generally takes up a distance to its subjects out of a kind of respect. The distance is almost like a visual posing of the question, "do you mind if I film you?" Clearly he has permission to film, but not always are his subjects comfortable in front of the camera. Pans and tracking shots often begin on a shot of nature and then move to bring a person or group into the frame, but the camera often continues until they are back out of the frame, left again to their activities. And this is also a frequent strategy of Koepp's films. The protagonists are filmed engaged in an activity, often cooking or eating, planting or laboring. We are given to see the actions with little or no explanation. The camera stays on them long enough that we understand what is happening without necessarily needing language. Thus his protagonists are in actions in their settings and those settings are situated against the backdrop of nature. Nothing in the films ever suggests some one or a group better belongs here or there than an other.

Perhaps most representative of this work is the film *Söhne* [*Sons*] (2006) which tells a tale from the *Kriegskindergeneration*, the generation of children during the war. The film focuses on the Paetzold family of five brothers, who were from Celbau/Celbowo, a village North of Gdansk near the Baltic. At the end of the war their mother Elizabeth fled the advance of the Russians, taking with her two of her sons, the elder Klaus and Wolf. She left Friedrich and Rainer with her parents on their estate. In 1947 she returned to find her boys but could only locate Rainer. Only in 1955 did they hear from Friedrich who had received the name Stanislaw from his Polish foster family. At the end of the decade. she is told that she has the "wrong" Rainer. The four brothers, separated by chance and circumstance, grow to five. In spite of the revelation of confusion, the film underscores that the two West German biological brothers never treated their Rainer any differently. Late in the 1970s the "real" Rainer did emigrate to Germany, while Stanislaw/Friedrich remained in the People's Republic. But the film shows that this Rainer, the German with the Polish accent, does not seek to replace his double, the Polish Rainer who speaks only German.

The brothers are over sixty at the time of the film and it opens and closes with their visit to the estate of their family. They wander around the overgrown and neglected estate. The forest is lush with trees; nevertheless, large chestnut trees stand out, not just because of their size but because they are not native to the property. They are a sign of the landscaping of the family's ancestors. One tree in particular attracts their attention because of its size. They set out to measure the trunk. The film unfolds from this point to the tale of the family and the complexity of its story. When it returns to the image at the end, we have learned not only of the crisscrossing paths of the brothers and the way their family grew without biological intervention. We are given to see how the five of them reach with outstretched arms just barely around the tree. And we hear the brothers remark that if they were not five they would never have been able to succeed. As five, however, the image suggests that they are able to encompass this tree and their past as it developed in Poland and across the border.

The documentary practice here is in line with Claude Lanzman's *Shoah*. Although there are a few moments of family photos, in general the past is not shown; rather, the brothers are taken to locations in which they remember and relate those memories. And what is important is that they tell their family story without a trace of ressentiment. In such a sequence the Polish Rainer is asked directly about his sense of belonging: Is he German or Polish? In his answer, like the image of the tree, he provides another powerful motif for the film: "I feel as if I've had two lives, the Polish and the German life. Neither was wrong [*falsch*]."

Of further importance here is the fact that the brothers know their history and know their rights. They are not naive or ignorant. That is to say, when asked whether they would consider trying to get back their family's historic estate, they note that this portion of the Pomeranian coast belonged already to the Republic of Poland as part of the Baltic corridor. They note thus that their land was not expropriated under the decree of 1946 and that their claim to it is more distant. This exchange is less evocative, set in a conversation with no nature shots or other visually beautiful sequences to transfigure it. Still, it is perhaps more important for the fundamental principle it exhibits vis-á-vis the past as the potential for a normalization of German-Polish relations. Beyond the legal considerations expressed, the brothers exhibit no desire for a "return" to an estate they can barely remember. Such a "return" could result only in a rupture with the lives they have lived since childhood. Rather, they insist that it's more important that they tend to their relations with each other, get to know Stansilaw/Friedrich better as the most distant of the family.

Knoben notes that the film tells its tale with a certain easy reserve and even lightheartedness. The film is not about the tragedy of the *Kriegskinder*, the generation born during the war; it is a story "without bitterness and without melancholia for life's missed opportunities."[24] Schenk observes, however, that the film's focus on the mother marginalizes discussions of the father as soldier in the Wehrmacht.[25] A more extensive focus on the father might have brought forward conflicts among the brothers vis-á-vis their own understandings of German and Polish history. As such, the film avoids controversy.

On the Horizon of the Interzone

In the work of Voigt, Misselwitz, and Koepp we find a form of documentary that engages with the border, with intercultural contact and with legacies of the past. Voigt and Koepp evidence a positive complex connectivity to the present and open up the possibility of a new relationship in the future. Nevertheless, with these two filmmakers we discover a relatively nationally delimited documentary form. With Misselwitz the interest is oriented more toward a common Communist past that does begin to transcend borders in its internationalism. With Voigt and Koepp, the trips undertaken are trips into a German past and while they engage with a contemporary condition, the information their films are not conducted in a universalizing position. Misselwitz's and Koepp's poetic documentaries are often stunningly beautiful and the picture postcard quality can afford a universal accessibility. Especially in the case of Koepp, the choice of subjects and the questions posed have a German audience in mind. These are images of the lost territories. They are postcards that will not circulate easily in the Polish or Eastern European landscapes they recorded.

In Koepp's *Mazuria* film, a moment of engagement with a local resident who is organizing a protest action against the transportation authority's deforestation activities along the historic allées of the region has the potential of giving information to the local population. However, the sequence comes to an end and is replaced by an interview with a local German. She had participated in the meeting of locals, speaking in Polish; but now she appears speaking German and the interview reveals that she has been a correspondent in Poland for over thirty years who has decided in her retirement to settle in Poland. There is nothing, of course, that prevents anyone from watching the sequence, but the questioning of the sequence focuses on why she is there and the logic suggests that it is unusual and of interest to know why a German is here in this area. Certainly, the overall question is why anyone has settled and remained in this rather beautiful but difficult landscape. However, the questioning, framing, and engagement in this sequence underscore a German perspective, a film made for Germans "back home." In a subsequent sequence with a young Polish architect and his friends, when he informs us that he is from Lyon originally, the questions do not explore this information. A Frenchman in Mazuria does not bear the same weight as a German. In the *Kursiche Nehrung*, Renate—one of the few remnants of the ethnic German community—becomes a central figure. The film shows us that the area (like Mazuria) is an active and functioning tourist area. The issue here is not to search as broadly as possible for people whose life stories and lifeworlds indicate a complex connectivity. Rather, it is to find the German in a world of less than six degrees of separation. In the end, we see Renate in the company of German tourists, embraced by a distant cousin of hers from the West. There is a certain gentle national romanticism that haunts Koepp's films, as in Karl May's stories where the conceit was that no matter where the hero of the story roamed, German speakers showed up in the terrain.

A repeated motif of Koepp's films, and one that appears in Voigt's as well, is the legacy of German presence. This does not surprise, but there is a tendency here to highlight the cultural accomplishments of the Germans that reminds us a bit of Gustav Freytag. A repeated motif is the German brick.[26] Bricks are frequently found or appear in various ways in reappropriated use. These are the very real material quality of the typical bricks of the German communities. The bricks mark not only a certain historic quality of architecture that was wiped away by postwar deprivation and the shortages of real existing Socialism, but we see, as a frequent motif in the films, the bricks also being taken from ruins to be used for other buildings. German engineering and German culture survive, even in the decay. Even as *Trümmer*, German industriousness left behind materials that continue to have value after decades and decades. In this work, the horizon of the interzone comes into view but it is not yet traversed; rather, the films remain bound in national paradigms with documentarists on international journeys. A new and different approach had to arise to move out onto that new terrain.

Envisioning the Interzone

STANISŁAW MUCHA, COMPLEX CONNECTIVITY FILMS, LOCATING THE NEW CENTER

Stanisław Mucha was born in Poland in 1970, and belongs to a younger generation of filmmakers than Koepp and Voigt. He came of age at the end of the Socialist era and the beginning of the free-market reforms. He began studying at a theater academy precisely at the start of the free-market "shock therapy" of the 1990s. He worked as an actor before leaving to go to Germany in the mid-1990s where he studied at the film school in Potsdam. Mucha subsequently settled in Germany, but his attention has been directed primarily across the border. He is mainly a documentary filmmaker, although he also directed one feature film, *Hope* [*Nadzieja*] (2007). *Hope* was the third in the unfinished trilogy *Heaven*, *Hell*, and *Purgatory* written by Krzysztof Kieslowski. (*Heaven* was directed by Tom Tykwer as an international arthouse production in 2002.)

In his first films, already in film school, Mucha gained notoriety for developing a strategy of traversing Central Europe that is at once comedic but also insightful. With *Absolut Warhola* (2001) Mucha went to the Carpathian region where Poland, Slovakia, and the Ukraine meet in order to investigate the origins of Andy Warhol. The filmmaker moves randomly around in the region, documenting the daily lives and sometimes absurd-appearing circumstances that draw into connection the great pop artist of the twentieth century with a rural farming community living under the shadow of Chernobyl. In *Gypsy* [*Zigeuner*] (2007), his most earnest film to date, he travels through Roma villages in the Slovakian countryside. In *The Truth about Dracula* (2010) Mucha travels further into the Carpathians in the direction of Transylvania to trace out the origins of the myth and also the reality of the ethnic German minority that once inhabited the region.

Mucha's film *Die Mitte* [*The Center*] appeared in 2004. Erica Carter has insightfully discussed this film as exemplary of postnational trends in German filmmaking and as a sign of a new focus on Central Europe.[27] As Carter notes, the film is filled with "incoherency, fragmentation, and border-crossings," all characteristics that lead me to understand the film as an attempt to depict European interzones.[28] For *Die Mitte*, Mucha took as motivation this question: Where is the center of Europe? The film shows that there is not an easy bureaucratic answer; rather to pose the question was for him "an assault on institutional Europe."[29] He traveled through various towns and villages that claim to be at the center of Europe, starting in Mücke in Germany and going east through parts of Poland, Slovakia, Austria, Lithuania, and the Ukraine. Repeatedly, he finds massive markers outfitted with official certifications of the sites, as well as people who resolutely and yet naively advocate that their out-of-the-way village is the center of Europe. The documentary takes on a similar absurd quality to that found in *Warhola*, but here the film has a more direct political aspect, a testing of the meaning of Europe after the Eastern Expansion in 2002.

In many ways, we are introduced to the problem of imagining a new space of Europe right from the start and in Germany. The Germans along the Rhine, in Hessen, and in Bavaria insist on the centrality of their villages. But in the interviews the partners express a certain confusion when asked: If this is the center of Europe, where does it end? In at least one instance, an interviewee refuses to even speculate on where those borders might be. The centrality of the site and of the self seems certain in their answers, but the limits to the terrain of Europe as it stretches to the East seem unimaginable. The film thus argues that the center of Europe is not a matter of topography but of belief or identity based on a self/other relationship with an imaginary other. The common sense of Europe in this film seems to be that "we" are different from those to the East of us. The people he meets never set themselves apart from the West, always the further east. Interestingly, though—and that is the drive of the film—it reveals this construction as just that and gently refuses to accept it by continuing on. In the journey that Mucha undertakes, the East continues ever to open and unfold.

To describe this as an interzone film we can consider how it actively seeks to instill a certain disorientation in the spectator. The episodes of the film are marked repeatedly by geographic titles following Mücke; we are given indications like "180 km to the North" or "1000 km Southwest, Rakhiv-Ukraine." These descriptions, however, do not establish an easy cognitive map; rather, they become increasingly dizzying and disorienting as the journey continues, crisscrossing the region. And the editing begins to add to the complexity. Already the opening sequence before the title showed locations from the East, but by halfway through the linear journey from west to east it breaks up and the scenes jump back and forth. At this point the film becomes less about the locations and more about the people. The film gives way to matching bits of longer interviews with similar thematic elements, such as religious identity, anti-Semitism, or questions of history and culture.

Mucha communicates with the locals directly in German, Polish, and English. He draws on translators periodically, including for Russian. But it is this ability to engage the locals directly that creates the primary dynamic of the documentary. As discussed earlier, this principle of direct communication marked also Voigt's films; his knowledge of Polish allowed him entrée in ways foreclosed to others. Although knowing a language is not a precondition for an interzone, communicative competence is, and that is what we find here. Thus the film is not the serious investigation of the markers and their histories, but a dialogic engagement with the people who live around them. Mucha seeks out a diversity of types: a Slovakian monk, a Ukrainian miracle healer, a Chasidic Jew, a Roma entrepreneur, and so on. In conversation these people move from a superficial type into a more complex figure with depth of character.

To be sure, these are in many ways characters. In German Cölbe, he meets a man who believes that his garden, filled with garden gnomes, is the center of Europe, and he certifies it through a marker with an EU flag in the hand of one of his gnomes. But for the most part, the investigation is about the individual's sense of centrality. That sense in this region differs from the others further east in that here the conditions of determination are older, more mythic, or official, for example, resulting from a pronouncement of Napoleon as he passed through Austria.

Markers of centrality bear specific ideological qualities, such as the signs of the Cold War. In Lithuania, figures of Marx, Engels, Lenin, and Stalin surround the marker. The marker clearly placed the center of Europe behind the Iron Curtain with propagandistic intents but now serves more as a moment of comical nostalgia, compelled in part by the fact that there is not just one Marx or Lenin but multiples of the heroes of Soviet ideology, including repeats of Stalin in various poses. The garden gnomes are outsized by Soviet monumentalism. Such a center is given a foil in the Lithuanian Hill of Crosses, a site with over fifty thousand crosses—the Soviet ideology gives way to religious legend. People travel to the hill to erect their own cross, in order to gain a blessing and luck as legends promise. Or we find a hint at the new consumer culture and throwaway mentality of the free market in the Labyrinth of Televisions. The labyrinth in the Lithuanian Europa Park holds over three thousand defunct antique cathode television sets from all over Europe. The TVs housed in wooden scaffolding create a labyrinth through a forest. Nature versus capital, art project or organized landfill; inspecting sites such as this one, the camera pans and tracks around but the documentary does not provide specific information or explanations. The spectator surmises about the background but in general is left in befuddlement. The comedic quality of the journey arises through such unexpected and unexplained images.

In Poland, Lithuania, and Slovakia, however, the markers of centrality are often related to the expansion of the EU. Suchowola, Kutno, and Piatek, Poland all have markers from the period of ascension to designate them as the center of Europe. After ascension, however, these locations are filled less with "Europhoria" and more Euroskepticism. Now disappointed by the hype of ascension, the center seems distant and a Piatek local quizzically assures Mucha that he "can shit in his pants but will not find the exact center of Europe." Such shifting sentiments vis-à-vis the "center" make clear that this is a matter of imagining community and not determining geography.

Beyond the borders of the EU though, the quality of the film changes again and in Rakhiv Mucha lingers in particular with the elderly Raja in her newspaper stand. Here the knots of the East are woven most tightly. Raja was born in Austria, went to school in Czechoslovakia, started her family in Hungary, worked as a seamstress in the Soviet Union, and is ending her life in the Ukraine, never having left Rakhiv. This is the region that Mucha himself comes from originally, the area in which borders and states have shifted radically throughout the twentieth century. It is on the one hand forgotten and out of the way and on the other hand a cultural center for the film. The camera follows one of Raja's customers home, Ernest Neumann, the last Chasidim in Rakhiv. Neumann survived the Holocaust by fleeing into the Soviet Union where he was arrested as a German spy. Upon his release in 1947 from the gulag, he returned to a town whose Jewish community had been decimated. Neumann speaks nine languages including Yiddish and German. After the meeting with Neumann the film begins a return journey, as if to suggest that Neumann and Raja both or the entire town or Rakhiv were limit and goal of the journey. It was not the markers set up by competing authorities that marked the center of Europe, but these people whose lives and identities bear marks of a tragic and comedic entanglement. The multiplicity of their regions and the complexity of their lives is set against the clarity and simplicity of the people, the ease with which they speak to Mucha, and the openness they reveal to the camera.

If the region stands out as indeed a possible center to Europe, it is precisely because here the East seems to settle in on itself and the question of distancing from the ever further east noted earlier dissipates. Here lies the center of Europe, because the orientalism of Europe disappears. Whether such a dynamic belongs to the region and its population or to Mucha's camera and editing work can remain an open question. Clearly the film is constructing an argument. In an interview, Mucha stated explicitly that for him the center is "in the Ukraine, the West Carpathians. Perhaps you know Joseph Roth. That's Europe for me. Where very many identities mix and very many languages. Where one does not really have an overview. When you ask someone about their identity there, you get the response, 'I'm from here.'"[30] The Europe he presents is not the bureaucratically regulated, democratically governed, free-market Europe organized Europe of Brussels. The center of Europe in the Carpathians is a Europe that extends back to Metternicht and the Congress of Vienna, "a Europe of the nobility, not a democratic Europe."[31] It is a Europe of affect and gestures that articulate a response to the overwhelming problems the population faces in its efforts to survive.

The film sets forward a way of living in a set of relationships that, within the parameters of the nation-state, appeared historically as paradoxes. Here, it is possible to experience complex connectivity *and* rootedness, localization *and* universalization. All the figures, even the most humorous characters among them, are aware of a larger terrain into which they are connected and their own sense of centrality, officially sanctioned as it is here, allows for that connection. Inasmuch as Mucha is critical of the EU, the ability afforded by his film to see repeatedly the same position taken up by numerous peoples from numerous places transforms the sense of connectedness here from a specific experience at one site in Europe to a more general human experience, an experience of all *Europeans*.

HANS-CHRISTIAN SCHMID, INTERZONAL ECONOMIC FILM

It is no surprise that Hans-Christian Schmid's engagement with German-Polish relations would continue. His film *Die wundersame Welt der Waschkraft* [*The Wonderful World of Laundry*] (2009) was a continuation of the work with cameraman and friend Bogumił Godfrejów. It is a film motivated by the kinds of questions of globalization already found in his film *Lichter* [*Distand Lights*].[32] We could consider the investigation of the documentary as a form of material anthropology—an exploration of material culture, work, and consumption patterns. Schmid and Godfrejów went to the German-Polish border to consider a particular work relationship: the world of laundry.

Germany is Poland's most important trade partner, a relationship that arose immediately at the point of the *Wende*. The primary economic relations with Russia characteristic of the East Block dissolved and were redirected fully to the neighbor to the West. Whatever kinds of tensions on an ideational level may exist between Germans and Poles, material relations became immediately intertwined. Goods, services, workers, and even their work traverse the Oder and Neisse rivers on a daily basis. Instead of the thriving economic centers of Warsaw, we find here the region most heavily devastated by the collapse of the old system and for whom interregional work means a real fundamental transformation in material conditions.

The film begins with a concentration on the company Fliegel-Textilservice [Fliegel Textile Services], which washes the linens of the elite hotels in Berlin, 5 and 4½ star hotels only. To do so they transport the wash from Berlin across the border to the town of Gryfino. There, Fliegel opened an industrial laundry capitalizing on the free steam produced by the new neighboring power plant. In that laundry, steam from the Polish power plant, which itself powers much of the region, the linens are washed around the clock, seven days a week, 365 days per year. Without interruption this material cycles between Berlin and Gryfino.

The film displays a complex relationship by focusing on an object or an action that is generally a background action: doing the wash. One typically gives little thought to the towels that land on the bathroom floor in an elite hotel. However, the gaze of the camera does not remain solely focused on the laundry; rather, it develops an ever-expanding perspective that focuses on the people who work in this cycle. In this way, the film supercedes the (Marxist) quality of reification. It does not fetishize the laundry but reveals the humans and the human relations that are constructed in labor.

Fredric Jameson in his work on cognitive mapping maintained that the phenomenon of globalization reached a level of such complexity and abstraction that humans can no longer map out the network of connections in which they live. Material relations operate on such a level of abstraction that the condition of reification becomes dominant. I am not interested in asserting that the most important or central function of novels and films, art in general, is the production of such a mapping in the recipient. However contrary to Jameson, clearly there are works of art that attempt this task and with increasing frequency and increasing success. The work of art in the age of globalization can facilitate the understanding that humans can go beyond their reified conditions and achieve new insights into their social and spatial localization. *Die wundersame Welt* offers its spectators precisely this kind of *perspectival localization*.

One does not have to be a worker on the Polish-German border to gain insights here. The apparatus of cinema is itself a part of the processes of globalization and, as apparatus, the moving image and the act of montage produced within it establish relations in a film that are not available to any individual eye. The apparatus of cinema affords the spectator an expanded consciousness; it makes the spectators capable of traversing their interzones with an awareness of their economic and cultural conditions and relations.

In *Waschkraft* Schmid and his longtime cameraman Bogumil Godfrejów charted out the flows of goods and services across the border. In Gryfino, however, the film comes to focus on two women, Monika and Beata, workers in the laundry. Here, the film's focus distinguishes it from the previous generation of German-Polish documentaries, relying on Polish protagonists and, like Mucha's film, opening up to a perspective not directed solely at a German audience.

Structurally, the format is such that the film is easily translatable into various languages—a format typically used by the French-German joint television station ARTE. In such work, voice-over commentary is minimal and can easily be replaced with a different language. For the premier at the Berlin Film Festival, the filmmakers developed a communicative apparatus for the film, providing subtitling for interviews with the protagonists in English.

In addition to the language, the filmmakers recognize the problematic of the film as a European problematic. They state in the press package that the two protagonist families "try to find their way in the complicated labor conditions of a united Europe." And likewise, within the interviews of the film they note that the CEO of Fliegel, in response to the attack that he is taking jobs from the Germans and giving them to the cheaper Polish laborers, stated, "I'm not doing laundry in Poland, rather in Europe."

The move in the film from the laundry and the labor of washing onto the families continues to expand the terrain of the documentary's investigation. We follow Monika and Beata to their homes and their private sphere. The film explores how labor, family structure, goals, and dreams in this borderland are transformed through these new possibilities of movement of people, goods, and services. It withholds a direct or negative judgment on these conditions, aiming more so for the material cultural portrayal of the processes. In the end though, it does note a transformation in the conditions; a title card describes that the Polish truck drivers have begun to earn more than their German counterparts. That observation alludes to a fundamental transformation of the material conditions on the horizon of the film. The Polish economy began to expand more rapidly than the German. The conditions that marked the border region for the initial decades after the *Wende* began to invert such that the Poles experienced a rapid increase in their standard of living, while the German economy caught up in the Great Recession stagnated.

THE NEW EUROPEAN, SUBJECT OF THE INTERZONE

In these films, the insistence on a new European subject is made clear, although in Mucha's film the new European is also a much older, imperial and prenational subject. Mucha and Schmid in particular have a universalizing potential in their work. The filmmakers engage with the locals in a way that makes them as interesting to local as to transnational audiences. Koepp, in particular, and Voigt, to a lesser extent, pose questions of the locals that communicate largely back to a public on the other side of the Oder. Mucha and Schmid develop approaches that tend more to address publics on both sides of the Oder.

All the filmmakers travel to meet people, to explore what their tragedies have been, how they live now, what their hopes for the future are. In doing so, they have to negotiate a polyglot region, bringing either their own linguistic skills into play, relying on translators, or seeking other means of expression. The point of the films is communication, not as a dialogue or a negotiation of past injustices; rather, the films are vehicles through which the locals speak to a European audience. The films constitute an interzone as *Öffentlichkeit*, a creation of a European public sphere.

CHAPTER 4

Interzone Dis/continuous

The Borders of Europe

The Border as Ideational Space

Borders are first ideational before they are spatial geographical. The liberation of the camera, the ability of the moving image to move in space, is crucial here. Cinema, the cinematic apparatus, provides an edifice whereby the imagination of spatial and geopolitical relationships come together. As an aspect of the cinematic apparatus, we can consider how visual aesthetic strategies, technological innovations, and social policy result in images with particular angles and perspectives. Choices of depth of field, establishing shot, and a distant or proximate frame position spectators vis-à-vis the image but also within an entire imaginative world of affective possibilities. The camera can reveal who is with and against "us." It can also give a sense of heterogeneous diffusion that undermines an easy distinction of us versus them. It can establish distance through a simple pan so that what is very immediate moves outside the frame and outside the visual field. It can establish closeness, zooming across galaxies to make a connection between two figures staring out two windows light years apart. The cinematic apparatus can support a world divided by cartographic borders and it can produce a world organized according to countervailing rationales.

The work of the cinematic apparatus can affirm spatial-political regimes of power or critical cinematic images can countervail dictates of reigning authority. The black lines running down official maps in order to divide nation-states could never fully contain or describe the lived experience of any of the people inhabiting territories they divided. People may live on borders, but that experience is not to be confused with the drawing of borders between people. The latter requires the envisioning of a divided world. The division caused by borders may be influential but it is never complete. And even, or especially when, the passage across borders is most restricted, the border space itself becomes all the more influential, a place of fantastic imaginative potential and affectively experienced disruption.

Borders are always permeable, never hermetic. Indeed, the opening discussion of bridges in the introduction highlights that borders are as much about connections as disconnections, placements as displacements. The very spatial orientation of borders as contiguous, a line running down a map through the middle of a river, is itself a visual construct, a historical convention. Critical radical geographers have developed elaborate systems of signification to represent the complexity of human interaction over expanses of space. The cinematic image has likewise and more spectacularly developed an extensive and detailed visual language to represent spatial relations. Parallel editing and jump cuts are standards of montage that enable the representation of boundaries *and* connections over expanses of space. A film like *One Day in Europe* (Stöhr, 2005) can resort to this rich visual language to offer various representations of the connections and disconnections across the vast continent of Europe. The cinematic apparatus can open and close borders and bridges even better than guards at checkpoints.

As we saw in the last chapter, visual regimens may come to define the political imaginary on either side of a border, but they are never commensurate with the lived experience of the border regions. In exploring the interzone to this point we have considered various aspects of the cinematic apparatus: production, distribution, projection, governance parameters of state apparatus, economic organization, reception, and so forth. This chapter begins with a focus on technology and imaginative space. As was explored in the insightful film *Videogramme einer Revolution* [*Videograms of a Revolution*] (Farocki and Ujica, 1992) the mobile handheld video camera played an important role in the opening of Eastern Europe. We could extend the analysis of that film to recognize how in general as the borders of Eastern Europe were falling and changing, the digital revolution further liberated the camera in its ability to record time and move in space. The liberated camera joined in the exploration of liberated space.

Liberating the Camera, Opening Space

From the point of its invention, the film camera has been central to the apparatus of cinema. By giving motion to the still image the camera immediately opened up new possibilities of representing the passage of time. The dynamic exploration of space, however, required further technological developments and aesthetic experimentation, especially the liberation of the film camera from the static tripod. To be sure, expanded spatial movements have a long history. The "phantom rides" of early cinema offered the first traveling shots by typically mounting a camera on the front of a train. In the 1920s, cinematographer Karl Freund developed fundamental techniques of the *entfesselte Kamera*, the mobile camera. Films like F. W. Murnau's *Der letzte Mann* [*The Last Man*] (1924) or Abel Gance's *Napoléon* (1927) transformed cinematic aesthetics and gave the frame new dynamism by liberating the camera's tripod. Dolly and crane shots quickly became standard techniques of classic cinematic language. In the course of the century of cinema, the mobility of the apparatus has developed through alternating advances in the size of the camera and the development of new support mechanisms. Light handheld cameras with 8 mm film were introduced already in 1923, and then the technological advancements of Super 8 made "small film" a central part of cinematic experimentation in the 1960s. For "large film" in 1976, the introduction of the counterbalancing support system of the steadicam stabilized the jerky handheld frame and expanded the possibilities of visual language even further.

The spatial liberation of the camera is not simply a matter of technological indulgence; rather, the liberated lens expands cinema's semiotic field. It captured new axes of movement so that rather than the standard eye-level shot of classical cinema, the mobile camera accelerated the disengagement of the frame from a human perspective.[1] The video monitor and robotic arm developed in the 1980s marked a new support mechanism. Wim Wenders used that technology to great effect in *Der Himmel über Berlin* [*Wings of Desire*] (1987) not just to develop an "angelic perspective" but also to infuse the vision of the divided city of Berlin with quite literally new perspectives. The introduction of digital technology in the 1990s again lightened the camera, liberating the gaze into new technologized angles, proximities, and perspectives. The cinema became more cinematic and new horizons opened up to the human eye. Exactly how the new techniques have been developed aesthetically or how they have expanded the language of visual expression varies; yet the exploration of space is a primary aspect of the mobile camera.

The EU Border as Mobile Border

The EU border is not just any border. In general the EU border is a fairly unique border in the history of the world. It is a mobile border not yet determined. Hence, films in the EU, films about borders—the changing, lifting, shifting of borders—play a central role in defining the space of the EU. Unlike expansive imperial or colonial borders, the EU border depends on a quasi-voluntaristic application rather than a hegemonic imposition. It requires a new imagining of belonging. This border has a possibility to be a state border, albeit one in which central state control becomes limited, even obviated. A chief benefit of membership in the transnational partnership of the EU derives of course from the removal of internal borders; indeed the Union promises in its treaties to "offer its citizens an area of freedom, security and justice without internal frontiers, and a single market where competition is free and undistorted."[2] In conjunction with the dismantling of the border as state security apparatus, we find the possibility of a border based on economic considerations. State control is diminished to facilitate in turn the transfer of goods, services, finances, and people. Such free-market economic boundaries prove typically incorporative, open to ever further inclusion. Countries that take voluntary initiative can apply for membership and if they evidence sufficient ability to undertake the market restructuring required by "Europe," e.g., free-market economics, they can theoretically belong to the club.

Finally, the EU border is a cultural border where Europe can be understood as denoting a set of common cultural and historical values. As we have seen already, work on crossing the cultural border characterizes vast portions of EU policy and supports a massive support system for cinema and other cultural productions. However, the cultural border is both the most fluid and the most restrictive aspect here. Consider that even though countries like Russia, Turkey, Macedonia, or Algeria play a central role in the broad history of Europe, the cultural border is invoked here to restrict and exclude them. And the cultural border is capricious. Geographically, Nicosia is east of Istanbul and South of Tehran, closer to Cairo than Athens, closer to Baghdad than Rome, and capital to the divided island of Cyprus; yet Cyprus is understood as part of a European culture and has been understood as belonging to the EU. That can change. Fundamentally, the possibility of political, economic, and cultural union under the term *Europe* relies on a new form of flexibility vis-à-vis borders. Hence, the EU's border is mobile; its exterior can never be fixed or permanent. The border can always expand, allowing the ascension of new states to membership. The periphery always has the ability to pass the border and arrive inside. Through the EU, a new "inside" and "outside" developed to a new Europe: a new space of material and imaginative possibilities.

"Inside" Europe: The Polish-German Border

"Inside" Europe, both German unification and European unification put Germany at the eastern front of a new European configuration. In these shifts, all too often Germany's politicians set it up against those states on its borders. Recall that in 1990 the conservatives under Helmut Kohl's guidance protracted the discussion of the new border treaties with Poland. This created no little antipathy and great anxiety that a united Germany would once again make land claims to the East. Moreover, unlike the long extensive engagement with France that characterized the Bonn Republic's western border, the initial relationship to the East of the united Germany was largely one of ignorance and lack of concern for Polish sensibilities. Recall that Roman Herzog in 1994 after having been invited as the first German head of state to attend the fiftieth anniversary of the Warsaw Uprising, gave an interview in which he confused the Warsaw Uprising with the Warsaw Ghetto Uprising. Many Polish politicians questioned how the Germans could develop any form of political policy vis-à-vis Poland if they lacked an awareness of the most significant moments in German-Polish history. Ideationally, in 1992 the European Union became synonymous with Western Europe, and Germany became a border guard state of Europe on the eastern frontier. To the East of the Oder were foreigners and to the West were the allies that required protection from them. These qualities, a lack of engagement with the other side of the border, a mystification of the East, and sense of border threat infused not just the state but also the cinematic apparatus and set the preconditions for the films of 2002/2003.

The previous chapter discussed first the postwar closing of the border between East and West, between Germany and Poland, and then the tentative reopening. As part of that opening it was possible to chart out a new interzonal relationship represented in documentary film. I want to turn here to feature film and fiction as a different form of representation, one that develops more directly in the imaginative realm and one that also typically draws the interest more directly of larger audiences. Feature film as a popular form of representation became a sudden and punctual vehicle for the representation of the Polish-German border. After, in effect, decades of silence, suddenly in 20022003 four films by German directors appeared, portraying the German-Polish border regions: *Klassenfahrt* [*School Trip*] (Winckler, 2002), *Halbe Treppe* [*Grill Point*] (Dresen, 2002), *Milchwald* [*In This Moment*] (Hochhäusler, 2003), *Lichter* [*Distant Lights*] (Schmid, 2003).[3] These years 2002–2003 encompass a significant period not just because it comes at the start of the new millennium, not just because it was a moment in which the borders of the EU and the borders of Germany were set to change dramatically and fundamentally, but because in a region marked by a traumatic history of border-shifting a qualitative transformation of the border as such took place.

That 2002 and 2003 resulted in a burst in filmic representation is important. Important for us here and signified by the cinematic output of 2002–2003, this

European border is a space that compels new imaginings of community. In that process, although the two-dimensional political map had been a useful tool in imagining the national community, the mobile camera proved a significant tool in the cognitive remapping of the border space. The sudden burst of border films that emerged around the point of Polish ascension to the EU draws our attention to a moment when few established connections existed. It is also a moment during which the ideational transformation of the border, the possibility of recognizing the space as an interzone rather than a disjunction or even diremption, becomes actualized. These films represent in some ways a kind of first contact after decades of separation, a reestablishment of film industrial connections after a forced disjunction.

Interestingly, of the films *Klassenfahrt*, *Halbe Treppe*, *Milchwald*, and *Lichter*, only one of them, *Milchwald*, is a German-Polish coproduction. The others take up contact without the "encouragement" of an established apparatus. In fact, as will be discussed in Hans-Christian Schmid's work on *Lichter*, the film as project proves important in establishing lasting connections and structures that subsequently work to facilitate further cooperative work. It is thus a moment in which, largely in the absence of other aspects of the cinematic apparatus, the imaginative relationship of the filmmakers to the border and its other side are central to the motivation of the film. It is a moment in which these four films, appearing suddenly and punctually allow us to explore the relationship of the work of culture and the work of politics.

How do these films imagine the border? The political aesthetics of these films is especially important given the work of film in establishing interzonal relations. The four films follow two divergent strategies. *Klassenfahrt* and *Milchwald* in particular belong to the Berlin School, an aesthetic direction in filmmaking that relies on a static, distant, understated camera. By comparison to the cool and distanced images of the Berlin School films, *Halbetreppe* and *Lichter* seem almost dizzyingly chaotic, relying importantly on the handheld camera. These differing visual strategies are not simply a matter of style or form, but rather they portray likewise two differing forms of borders, two differing worlds, the former a world in which borders develop a new ominous significance. *Klassenfahrt* and *Milchwald* presented clashing worlds. The latter two, *Halbe Treppe* and *Lichter*, presented by contrast a world in which contact, not always easy, is a reality, not always positive.

BORDERLANDS OF THE BERLIN SCHOOL

Note that when considering the first two films, there is already an aesthetic commonality in the way the filmmakers approach the production of images and of space. Christoph Hochhäusler, director of *Milchwald* [*In This Moment*] and Henner Winckler, director of *Klassenfahrt* [*School Trip*], belong centrally to the Berlin School, an aesthetic direction that has received a great deal of critical attention since the first decade of the new millennium.[4] Marco Abel characterizes the Berlin School as a counter-cinema, based in an "esthetics of reduction," "dominated by long takes, long shots, clinically precise framing, a certain deliberateness of pacing, sparse usage of nondiegetic music, poetic use of diegetic sound, and, frequently, the reliance on unknown or even nonprofessional actors who appear to be chosen for who they 'are' rather than for whom they could be."[5] For the discussion here, it is important that, as Abel points out, "these cinematic aspects stress the characters' spatio-temporal existence—the fact that, unlike the films belonging to what Eric Rentschler influentially described as the "cinema of consensus" cycle, these films unmistakably take place in a specific time and place: in the here and now of reunified Germany."[6] Picking up on Abel, Kristin Kopp echoes that this strategy of a "slow, contemplative aesthetic" makes their work particularly "well equipped to move into a new space so underexplored by German film."[7]

Certainly the images of the Berlin School filmmakers in general are filled with space. The far shot gives the viewer a broad frame in which the characters and action are only a portion of the setting. The action of the film appears as only a portion of the overall visual information and the image moves into a photographic, even painterly, condition. The long take underscores this quality, lending the eye a surfeit of time in which it can explore the plentitude of this image as if perusing a still image. Indeed, typically in the work of Winckler and Hochhäusler, the action of a scene takes up a smaller portion of the frame such that there is a significant amount of image eccentric to the action in each frame. Given the attention to space and composition, it is thus not surprising on some level that the geopolitical space of the borderland should have called out the visual and narrative strategies of Hochhäusler and Winckler.

Although the Berlin School is celebrated as a breakthrough in counter-cinema, a movement demonstrating "the emergence of a new film language in German cinema," of course this minimalism as visual strategy is not a new technique.[8] The asceticism of the camera here hearkens back to neorealist strategies and early work of the European New Waves of the 1960s. A motivation to realism reappears in the work of the Berlin School filmmakers. Abel describes this realism as "a-representational realism," a form of documenting that allows the spectator to experience reality as "more intensely *sensible*."[9] Abel and other critics see this aesthetic strategy as a form of distinction that sets the films apart from the general works, which are celebrated in the critical literature but rely on popular genre strategies. Any positive assessment of this strategy of filmmaking needs to be set against its limitations. Especially in the two films under discussion here, we note that the a-representational realism, the visual quality of the static image, proves to be an easy vehicle for mytho-poetic fascinations with the Polish landscape. In the films, Poland becomes a vehicle of a mytho-poetic fantasy that proves destructive to German subjectivity.

Nationalism, i.e., national identification, comes to place significant limitations on the work of the Berlin School. Unlike the Dogme 95 Manifesto, which was at first a Danish initiative but was open to the point that anyone could join in the strategy, the Berlin School, the criteria of which indeed recall Dogme 95 principles, is a phenomenon of a *German* filmmaking.

Berlin School filmmakers win acclaim from critics as a revitalization of German film. As Abel notes French cineastes have actually promulgated the designation *Nouvelle Vague Allemande*, emphasizing the German appearance of the films.[10] Abel himself underscores the significance of the school as a German movement: "the Berlin School films can be regarded as a cinema that is engaged in the difficult task of improving Germany's reality in the age of post-Wall globalization by providing better images for it."[11]

In these two films, the orientation toward Germany results in an odd regressive tendency in the face of more complex considerations of subjectivity and identity. Questions of Germanness come to play a key role in *Klassenfäht* and *Milchwald*. It is not just that they are travel films, but they constitute travel in a particular way, as the travel of Germans into a foreign space. Kopp noted that the move outside of Germany is into a nonspace. However, that filmic nonspace is indeed a real place, Poland, as opposed to a place of fantasy, Middle Earth or Narnia; not all nonspaces are equal. In spite of her appreciation for the School, Kopp herself notes critically of Hochhäusler in particular but Winckler as well, that the presence of Polish space in the Berlin School films is a matter of projection and not knowledge. Poland is "a nonspace that becomes the projection screen for a childlike fantasyscape of adventure and enchantment."[12] Interesting above all, this act of projection is not an inherent part of the Berlin School relationship to non-German space; it proves to have this particular quality only vis-à-vis Poland. We could compare these films to the work of Berlin School colleagues Angela Schanelec or Maren Ade, whose films take Germany's western and southern neighbors for their setting without turning France or Italy into a point of infantile projection. Yet it may make no sense to pose the negative question: Why is this type of nonspace not present in Berlin School films set in other non-German locations? Nevertheless, we can ask, what does Poland do to the imagination of film understood as German?

NONSPACE *MILCHWALD*

Focusing on Christof Hochhäusler and his film *Milchwald*, we can note that this was his major debut film and garnered him a certain critical notoriety. This attention was solidified first with the success at Cannes of his film *Falsche Bekenner* [*I Am Guilty*] (2005). His work with *Revolver* and then his inclusion in the omnibus film *Deutschland 09—13 Filme zur Lage der Nation* [*Germany 09: 13 Short Films about the State of the Nation*] (2009) affirmed his position among a German filmmaking elite.

Milchwald is one of the few German-Polish coproductions of the post-*Wende* period. It was supported by the Film- und Fernsehfonds Bayern, Mitteldeutsche Medienforderung, and with the support of the Polish film production company Filmcontract Ltd. In spite of Polish participation in the transnational European apparatus of film production, in this coproduction Poland appears as an extreme threat.

In this film Poland is literally aligned with the darkest forests of the Grimm's fairy tales. *Milchwald*, as with *Klassenfahrt*, entails a trip into Poland. Rather than a school group, *Milchwald* follows a German family in their tragic forays across the border into this strange space. From the start, we see Silvia challenged by her role as stepmother to Lea and Konstantin. Lea in particular challenges her authority to the point where the challenge proves too much for Silvia, and on a shopping run into Poland she stops the car and forces the children out of the car. Silvia drives down the road and pauses for a cigarette before returning, but the children, believing themselves abandoned have set off into the woods, echoing Hansel and Gretel's journey. In this regard, restating her point about *Milchwald* specifically, Kopp notes that "Poland is a nonplace onto which child-like fantasies of the "Wild West" as well as visions of fairy-tale enchantment are projected."[13]

Silvia returns home and does not tell her husband Josef what has happened; instead, she supports the idea that they are "missing," abducted by a stranger. Not revealing to him what has happened fully positions her into the role of the evil stepmother. The children wander through the woods until they meet Kuba, a traveling cleaning-supplies salesman, who has set up camp in the forest for the evening. Kuba at first brings the children to the next largest town, but then realizes that he can extort money from their father. Thus he comes to take on the role of the witch, holding the children captive. In the end, Silvia is dead, having met the fate of all evil stepmothers, and the children have poisoned the witch Kuba with his own cleaning supplies. As a result, Josef has lost the trail, and the children are once again abandoned in the dark forests of Poland. The fairy tale extends out into an ever-expanding horizon, ever further from home.

The cool distanced shots resemble, then, the work of the other members of the Berlin School, but here as in Winckler's film, Poland is truly a nonspace of increasing loss and alienation. However, with the allusions to Hansel and Gretel as basis for the narrative, and the idea of the threatening romantic forest, Hochhäusler clearly takes up a position linked to the postwar stereotype of Poland as backward fantasyland. This film does not even offer the kinds of insights vis-à-vis the location found in other "travel films" of the Berlin School, including *Klassenfahrt*. Instead, the locations are marked by Catholic rituals in the background, or desolate decaying buildings, "polnische Wirtschaft," all manner of clichés without critical reflection.[14]

If it is a question of remote wooded location for a fairytalesque setting, the narrative could certainly have taken place in Germany's Black Forest, or in the depopulated expanses of Mecklenburg's marshes. Or it could have been situated in any number of other borderlands; however, Poland proves important here precisely because the clichés deployed in this film vis-à-vis Poland typically come up only in relation to other Western European countries in comedies. One can compare here the vision of Italy in the German-Italian comedy hit *Maria, ihm schmekt's nicht* [*Maria, He Doesn't Like It*] (Vollmar, 2009) where Italy and the Italians are portrayed as comical disruptions to German orderliness. In that film, however, the orderliness of the German is as much the object of derision as is the clichéd satire of Italian chaos. In *Milchwald* and *Klassenfahrt*, the opposition between German order and Polish dissipation has no intentional comedic qualities.

Kopp and Abel seek to find in Hochhäusler's work a significant critical contribution to German film. Kopp discovers in the film a critique of the Germans as cold materialists, struggling to pursue the dreams of wealth offered by the new (neoliberal) economy. Kopp understands Kuba as something of an innocent, seduced by the prosperity the German reward money would bring him. Thus, in their analyses responsibility for the tragedy of the film lies with the Germans. Undoubtedly the Germans are to "blame," given that Sylvia and the children offer no grounds for our sympathy and Josef is like the oddly distant and weak fathers of the fairy tales, ineffective in his authority over his children.

However, whatever forms of motivation may derive from infectious German materialism, we need to recall that the film positions Kuba as "witch." In this position, he is by no means an object of sympathy and in the end, like all the evil witches, we see this corrupted Pole as not even a match for two German children. Kopp sees the film "as an extended metaphor of German identity in the postunification period."[15] And certainly it is the case that the film investigates visually the austere home of Sylvia and Josef as a place of always impending crisis. Germany is not presented in a good light. But this film functions as national allegory; it becomes Germany and the characters become Germans, precisely because the narrative travels into a fantasy of Poland.

This is the core of a *homogenizing* tendency in the film. It relies on a model of essential contact, travel across borders as travel into the realm of the Other, the radically alterior with whom there is no communication. It is a Poland largely eviscerated of people—this same quality appears in *Klassenfahrt* as well. The woods are empty, and even in the urban spaces, the Poles fade into the background, except for one significant scene in which they participate in opaque Catholic ritual processions. The Germans travel here as in a land of ghosts: no one notices the children. And as much as they are struggling to get home, the film presents Poland as lacking civilization; there is simply no chance for them simply to walk up to a policeman, minister, or adult and make clear that they need help.

Kopp notes that the opening and closing scenes rhyme each other. The children are walking along an empty road. For her, the fact that the first takes place in Germany and the second in Poland establishes a conceptual unity, suggestion that the space is continual and the countries are "connected by a shared set of challenges and anxieties."[16] The possibility of understanding Kuba as seduced by German wealth hardly speaks to a form of cultural continuity. It speaks rather to a massive income differential resulting from the retention of the border. Inasmuch as the film's minimal aesthetics keep the motivations of Sylvia, Josef, or the children from a certain clarity, we know what Kuba wants. He is a crassly materialistic Pole in an impoverished landscape. The opening and final scenes are not a matter of continuity but of discontinuity. In Germany, the children were headed in a known direction and picked up by Sylvia, who arrived late. In Poland, they are without orientation, lost on a horizon only of threat.

And it is certainly not a matter of any space whatever. We can compare the treatment of Poland to that of France in Angela Schanelec's films *Marseille* (2004) and *Orly* (2010) or of Italy/Sardinia in Maren Ade's *Alle Anderen* [*Everyone Else*] (2009). Shanelec and Ade, also considered members of the Berlin School, treat their settings as a place of investigation, both spatially and personally. Marseille offers the photographer Sophie a chance to get out of her life in Berlin and see things anew. Returning to her life in Berlin, Sophie feels displaced from the petty quotidian existence that was once so normal. A connection, however, is drawn between what was once a foreign and now familiar place and the space that was once familiar and now foreign. Sophie comes to live in a French-German interzone, both in Berlin and Marseille. *Orly* intensifies this quality. Filmed on location in the midst of the hustle of the Orly airport, it is one extensive exploration of the transnational space par excellence. In Maren Ade's film, Sardinia is a vacation site for Gitti and Chris, whose relationship is pushed into crisis by contact with other German tourists. The film explores Sardinia as a tourist destination, a realm occupied by Germans. It is a space that vacillates quickly between familiar and unfamiliar; Chris's parents "own a vacation home there, and Chris the architect is considering work on the island. Yet here the problem arises from their contact with other German tourist couples. In that contact Gitti and Chris develop a different dynamic and their quarreling becomes intense, even threatening. But in contradistinction to Poland, Sardinia is not the cause of their problems; rather, their own character flaws are exaggerated in the condition of travel and displacement. The film portrays this alienation and self-awareness in images and with minimal dialogue. In these films, the locations are not spaces of projection but rather of observation. Here, the spectator is equipped to be critical of the characters' interactions with their surroundings. In the case of Winckler's and Hochhäusler's Poland films, challenging aesthetics prove capable of representing uninventive visual spatial regimes.

In general, *Milchwald* exhibits a homogenizing strategy of community, making distinct and separate the German and Polish worlds—a tendency present in *Klassenfahrt* as well. These films lack engagement with a "real" Poland and promote instead a mystification of Polish space. This homogenizing strategy acts as a conserving mechanism of representation, representing the border communities as distinct. It promotes the existing logic of the border, showing the borderland to be a space of danger, and contact between the peoples from either side poses a threat to the individual and even to the communities at large. Here, a wholeness of subjectivity derives from the stability of ethnic community. Contact, exchange, or communication is largely foreclosed. When it happens it is a matter more of miscommunication and uneven exchange. The central characters lose more than they gain from contact.

In these films, the apparatus of the film, choice of framing and subtitling, forecloses communication and understanding. The spectator is placed rather in a position of alienation from the surrounding. Poland is incoherent. The images do not convey information; they devolve into stereotypes from active and dormant discourses: Poles as thieves but also Poles as blond seductresses or as "wild Indians." The border itself does not play a significant role; rather, Poland as a country in transformation constitutes a landscape of confusion and potential tragedy. It is the social Other located across the border. Poland represents a place of cultural opacity; its Catholicism, its language, its people prove to be strangers in ways that France or the Italians are not. To be a stranger in Poland is to be alienated, to experience a sense of confusion and being lost in cultural space.

Travel destabilizes the characters' and the viewer's orientation. But oddly, in the emptying out of Polish space that takes place both in *Klassenfahrt* and *Milchwald*, the Poles are made strangers to their own land. Historically, trips to Italy have benefited the German traveler, while excursions into Poland only bring loss. These films do not offer the German audiences a transnational relocation, a sense of new cross-border continual space or generalized unity. For the Polish audiences, they offer rather a confirmation of the type of stereotypes of Poles that populate a German imaginary.

In regard to these films, I would question the visual asceticism of the Berlin School in its eschewing of the camera's mobility. Rather than praise it as a critical visual innovation, this move actually can be understood as a turning back of the development of the camera. Certainly it sets up a set of restrictions that foreclose certain representational possibilities. The question is: Does this limitation actually make them "well equipped" to explore space? Does a refusal of the possibilities attendant on the mobile camera actually lead to a better depiction of the borderlands? Or is the high estimation of this technique in critical discussions an overestimation based on the way the Berlin School filmmakers distinguish themselves from popular genre film?

DYNAMIC SPACE AND THE HANDHELD CAMERA

Unlike Winckler and Hochhäusler, there is not a specific aesthetic orientation that unites the directors Andreas Dresen and Hans-Christian Schmid. Although similar in age, they grew up on opposite sides of the Wall, Dresen in the East and Schmid in the West. What does unite their work, however, is a matter of technology. Both relied on handheld cameras—a technological fact that should not be attributed to simple serendipity. Hochhäusler and Winckler worked with the super 16 mm camera, a lighter camera used particularly for low-budget and film-school productions. Dresen and Schmid turned to new technology. In the 1990s, rapid advances in high-definition video cameras took place that made the technology widely available to a general market. It was not until 2000, however, with the release of the Sony HDW-F900 that established filmmakers felt that a quality in recording technology had been reached that rivaled traditional film. In 2001, the first major projects in digital recording began to appear in theaters. The use by Dresen and Schmid of the then new visual technology to explore the space of the borders is a dynamic effect of the ongoing liberation of the camera from the static tripod. These films are nothing less than an avant-garde use of technology for creative representational purposes, expanding the language of cinema.

In 2002, not only did the high-definition camera improve in recording quality but it developed enough storage capacity that the cameras could film long takes of a record length. The historic achievement of Tilman Büttner operating the steadicam for *Russkij kovcheg* [*Russian Ark*] (Sokurov, 2002) must come immediately to mind. Büttner's use of the super-light digital camera allowed him to make the single ultralong take at the heart of the film. The single take was not simply a gimmick but an attempt to explore simultaneously the space of the Hermitage and the sweep of Russian history. Dresen and Schmid's work films may not have received the same level of discussion as *Russian Ark* but cameraman Michael Hammon's unique work on *Halbe Treppe* and Bogumil Godfrejów's display of skill with the camera on *Lichter* likewise prove historic in their use of the handheld camera. Their imaginings of border community follow Orson Welles's advancement of crane shot technology to allow his investigation of the border in *Touch of Evil* (1958). Like Welles's classic, the handheld camera in these two films offers the spectator new techniques for establishing a cognitive map of the border space.

Less a matter of concern for postproduction editing and filtering, the handheld camera in its new forms has opened up aesthetic horizons in the constitution of films as such. Dresen and Schmid praised the ability the handheld camera gave them to liberate themselves from complicated exposures and precision lighting: precisely the kind of filming work that necessitates blocking out the actions of the actors. The mobility of the handheld camera, its ability to follow action means that the actors have increased freedom to act, to fill the social space of their characters. Fundamentally with these two films we have the handheld camera deployed to inspect a doubled space of subjective and geopolitical interaction. Both films sought to describe and represent the borders between people and countries through new visual language pushing at the use of the handheld camera.

LOCATION FILM *LICHTER*: THE BORDER AS ABJECTING APPARATUS

Hans-Christian Schmid came of age in Altötting, a small town in the heart of Catholic Bavaria known as a pilgrimage site. As a new student in film school he chose to concentrate on documentary film. Schmid has always evidenced an interest in the relationship of culture, economics, and space, and his first film, *Die Mechanik des Wunders* [*The Mechanics of the Miracle*] (1992), was an experimental documentary film that took up precisely the organization of the annual pilgrimage in his hometown. It displayed the crass relationship between piety and prosperity at the heart of the pilgrimage business. As we discussed in the previous chapter, Schmid has maintained his relationship to documentary filmmaking, even as he has had major successes with feature films. Critic Daniel Kothenschulte has suggested that this training in documentary films instilled in Schmid a commitment to social criticism and social engagement that was missing from German film in the early 1990s.[17] In this way Schmid's and Dresen's aesthetic and socially critical interests move toward each other and away from that of Winckler and Hochhäusler.

For *Lichter*, Schmid drew his inspiration from a newspaper report of a group of illegal Pakistani migrants who had traveled through the Ukraine all the way to the German Polish border only to be abandoned there by their transporter who assured them that they were outside London. This story finds its way into the film in the opening where a group of migrant Ukrainians are let out in the woods of Polish *Słubice* and told by their corrupt transporter that they are right outside Berlin. The lights ahead through the forest, they are told, are the lights of Berlin. Ultimately robbed and abandoned, it takes a while before the migrants regain their orientation and realize the hopelessness of the situation into which they have fallen. Here is the core of Schmid's film: the contrast between the grand dream, the hope and belief in success and prosperity in the consumerist capitals of Europe and the reality of the shattered existence, the inhuman barrier of the border, and the endless economic reassignment of 90 percent of the world's population to the ranks of the impoverished.

Lichter has been repeatedly described as an episode film because it relates seven loosely intertwined tales. However, it is not an episode film in the classic sense of *One Day in Europe*. We could possibly describe it as a *location film* precisely because what unites these tales is that they all take place in the same space over the same period of time. Frankfurt/Słubice becomes the central organizing principle to Schmid's film and its narrative.

The film begins as the film's title appears in white, *Lichter* lights against a black backdrop. The action of the film opens with the camera in this same darkness until someone rolls a tarp back revealing a dim light. We begin to realize that the perspective is from inside a transport truck looking out. In silhouette, people unload from the back and a smuggler gives them instructions in Ukrainian, assuring them they are across the border in Germany near Berlin and that with sunset they only have to head for the nearest lights of a house at which they will be told how to proceed further.

Then begins fast-paced cuts between this and the subsequent narrative lines. Marko and Katharina work smuggling cigarettes across the border for Marko's father Maik, a father/Fagan type whose house is a dubious junkyard and underground hideout somewhere outside of Frankfurt. Andreas, Marko's younger brother, also lives here in this dysfunctional family. He has fallen in love with

Katharina and is jealous of Marko's relationship with her. Intercut with this narrative is an introduction to Ingo, the owner of a local mattress store. He is economically on his last leg, and total ruin motivates his burst of energetic salesmanship. He hires Simone to assist him in maintaining his business and fires his Polish cleaning woman Milena when she asks him for her pay. Milena returns home to the other side of the border. Milena is married to Antoni, and their daughter Marysia is about to have her first communion. Marysia begs Antoni to buy her a brand new, very expensive communion dress and he agrees, not knowing that his wife has just been let go from her work.

Among the Ukrainians, a central character Kolja emerges who argues that they should try to cross the river on their own. The couple Anna and Dimitri, however, separate out of the concern for the baby they are carrying. Anna and Dimitri will spend the night and the next day desperately looking for help until they meet the taxi driver Antoni. Antoni eventually steals their money to buy his daughter's communion dress. The German border guards catch all the Ukrainians except one who dies of exposure. During his interrogation, Kolja meets Sonja who works as a translator for the border guards. Rather than simply translate for the guard, Sonja lets her sympathy take over. Sonja drives Kolja herself across the border, hidden in her trunk. A final narrative line opens up with Beate, who works as a translator, and a former boyfriend, Philip. He is a German who is working as an assistant architect in the firm that has designed a factory for Słubice.

Ingo eventually loses everything and breaks down in front of Simone. Andreas, jealous of Marko and Katharina, betrays Marko to the border guards. Sonja, succeeding in smuggling Kolja across the border, arrives at the Potsdamerplatz, where Kolja gets out of the car, stealing Sonja's boyfriend's camera as he does so. Philip, while chauffeuring his boss to a celebration of the business venture, has to witness how the factory owner cuts the plans for his facade and how Beate's duties as translator spill over into work as hostess/prostitute. Antoni, having used the stolen money to purchase his daughter's communion dress arrives at the church after the ceremony has started, only to discover that his wife in the meantime has made a dress for Marysia. He collapses in the back of the church. The depth of field forces the communion celebration out of focus until it is nothing more than a white field against which Antoni, hunched over in exhaustion, forms a black field in the corner of the frame. These fields of color return us to the opening visual motifs. The lights for all the characters remain distant. The film ends and the credits role against a black backdrop.

Compared to the other border films, there was a daringness to Schmid's project deriving from his willingness not just to cross the border but to cross cultures. Schmid conducted intense research and scouting for the shooting on the eastern side of the Oder, but also drew on special support from a few people familiar with the territory. *Lichter*, as project, thus marks the opening up of cross-border production relations, which has made it easier for the realization of future projects. In searching for his actors, he turned to Claudia Geisler to play the translator Sonja because Geisler, known then as a rising German film star, had grown up bilingually and could believably undertake the part. For the characters from Eastern Europe, however, Schmid had to find actors beyond the scope of the typical German casting agency. With Zbigniew Zamachowski as Antoni and Aleksandra Justa as his wife Milena, Schmid found two significant Polish actors who themselves are married with a child. He went all the way to Russia in order to find trained actors to play Dimitri and Anna. English was the primary language during filming, yet Schmid wanted the characters specifically to speak Polish and Russian; those dialogues would be subtitled to give the film precisely a feel of accuracy.

Most importantly, for this film and his future work Schmid selected Bogumil Godfrejów as his cameraman. Godfrejów was only twenty-five and *Lichter* was only his second feature film, but already as a student in the renowned *Łódź* film school, Godfrejów had distinguished himself. In 2001, he had received an Oscar nomination for his camera work in the student short-film category. With Godfrejów's handheld camera and improvisational flexibility in the script, Schmid strove to achieve a naturalism in acting and a third-person-observing status for the camera. Godfrejów worked with Schmid to develop a visual relationship that connected both sides of Frankfurt/Słubice. Additionally, and central to this discussion, the handheld camera also afforded a realist precision in social-spatial exploration.

This is not the a-representational realism of Hochhäusler and Winckler. This is a cinema of abjection in Falkowska's sense but one that describes the Polish *and* German sides of the border.[18] In moving about the border, we see that Frankfurt is falling apart. Maik's house is a junkyard shambles completely disrupted by Andreas's betrayal. Ingo sleeps in a sleeping bag on the floor of the mattress store. His and Simone's social mobility becomes increasingly limited. More than Frankfurt, Berlin—the Gateway to the West—represents the first and best hope, the brightest light in Europe. This is a place toward which the Ukrainians strive, a place beyond Frankfurt. At the same time, the Polish side, Słubice, actually appears positive by comparison. While Słubice thrives, Frankfurt's economy stagnates and its population declines. Schmid noted that "the Poles live facing the border while the Germans have turned their backs on it."[19] Słubice is the city where familial and intimate relational aspects of the stories play out. It is the primary social setting for the families of Ann and Dimitri, and

Antoni and Malena, as well as Beate and Philip. Their stories transpire against the backdrop of a border town with its smuggling, black-market business, and illegal migrants. As such, it is a relatively positive vision of the city and Poland in general, in that the film does not offer a "heartwarming" positive vision of Germany either. The film offers a more complex vision of the Polish side than any other border film to date.

Schmid presents the border as an abjecting apparatus, an ongoing struggle to maintain a solidity of borders against a dissipation of migration. It is a German border designed to keep the Other out and the German social organism pure. The film depicts how abjection sorts the desirable from the undesirable, how the abjecting mechanism distinguishes between refuse and infuse. We see early on the abandoned Kolja and Dimitri walk in the woods while they wait for the sun to set. The camera tracks with them and then turns to take up their perspective. They are at the edge of a highway where two hitchhikers stand traveling toward the border. In a far shot, through the hanging tree branches we observe how, within moments, a black Mercedes stops and picks them up. We hear the two observers remark with some bitterness how easy "they" have it. The affluent hitchhikers will travel easily into Germany while Kolja and Dimitri remain stymied on the other side. The scene underscores how the border is a selective membrane allowing desired commodities and people to pass in while abjecting the rest. The film does not privilege German subjectivity; rather, it shows how German subjectivity is privileged by being on one side of the border.

In the film, the German authorities act as the agents of abjection, regulating the permeability of this border. When the Ukrainians are caught, the film includes a processing sequence at the detention center. In quick succession we see mug shots being taken, bags being inspected, a rubber glove being put on while a naked man stands spread against the wall, and so on until the sequence moves into the interrogation of Kolja. In a long cramped white room, Kolja, his interrogator, and Sonja sit. Here, the handheld camera provides particularly useful framing techniques to represent the social boundaries and connections of this space. The camera first assumes as much possible distance to give us an establishing shot, but then it begins in medium frames to switch perspectives from Kolja toward Sonja and the interrogator. Acting as translator, Sonja achieves her own frame only when she ends her complicity with the guard by giving Kolja advice in her translations. When she advises Kolja to ask for asylum, the guard suddenly switches into English and Kolja answers in English. Sonja remains in the diegetic space as an observer to the workings of the border guards but is kept then out of the rapid back and forth of the frame, no longer a part of the abjecting apparatus. A back and forth between the guard and Kolja transpires with the guard becoming increasingly aggressive at the possibility that he has been outmaneuvered by his own laws, until another uniformed figure enters the frame from a door in the background with a piece of evidence: a receipt from a restaurant on the Polish side. The guard stands triumphant in the frame over Kolja; with this bit of evidence, they now have the legal empowerment to deport him back to the other side.

To be sure, the abjecting force of the German authorities proves also directed at Germans. In such scenes, we witness the establishment of borders internal to German society. When Ingo is stopped by the police in a random traffic check, they discover he is driving without a license and his decline accelerates. Katharina is apprehended at Maik's by two social workers. She is brought to a juvenile detention center where we see her eventually caged in. Some critics described this setting as unrealistic, too brutal, even though Schmid did rely on an authentic detention center in the area in which to film. The objection of critics directed at how Germans treat Germans is worth noting. The challenge to the realism of the detention center setting derives from a lack of acceptance of the conditions of the abject. I found no critics who doubted the veracity of the settings on the Polish side.

The narrative does allow for one successful crossing. In a far shot, we see Sonja arrive in her car at the border. The long lines of cars stretching out in front and behind her, she creeps forward with Kolja in her trunk. At the guard booth she hands over her passport. The camera maintains a position from the front passenger seat next to her, so the focus is on her and her attempt to keep herself under control. The guard takes her passport through the window. He looms above and outside the frame as a force, and his voice comes back in asking her what she has in back. A momentary confusion ensues until Sonja realizes he is only talking about the camera equipment in the backseat. The escalation of tension during this entire scene, the mounting sense of threat posed by the border authority, suddenly ends rapidly into almost comedy as the guard still outside the frame instructs her that it would be better to keep her valuables in the trunk. Of course, at the moment the trunk is filled with a human fate. Sonja's privileged position as a German passport holder allows her to move with ease through the barrier much like the hitchhikers from the earlier scene.

This sequence takes place about two-thirds of the way through the film on the second night—the entire film taking place in the space of about two days. It contains key aspects of the film's exploration of the space of the border territory. The subsequent scene of this sequence begins with Maik making a delivery of cigarettes to Vietnamese dealers at a wayside. Sonja's car arrives into the scene and takes up a position where we can now see the action of Maik and the dealers in the background. While the two groups do not interact as she releases Kolja from her trunk, the camera occupies an axis that visually constructs these narrative strands as occupying the same social space. This visual crossing of narrative paths, facilitated by the flexibility of the liberated camera's wandering gaze, infuses the film with the sense that indeed every figure that comes into the frame is a potential character, a person with a separate story that could be told.

Upon their arrival in Berlin, Kolja recognizes the Potsdammer Platz from pictures his brother sent home. He asks to be let out, stealing the camera as he leaves. This act of exploitation of Sonja removes any redemptive innocence from Sonja's action. The border as abjecting mechanism attenuates and ultimately impairs the basics of humanity: trust, faith, hope, love, sympathy. Kolja steals the camera to take pictures of his triumph. He early on had said to Anna and Dimitri that his dream is to send back photos of the square to show his brother and family that he had succeeded. The mobile camera encircles Kolja as he shoots pictures of the lights of square, the lit skyscrapers and building cranes. The encircling shot taken from a low point looking up puts Kolja into a frame against the backdrop of these lights, and it would appear that he has succeeded in gaining access to the distant lights. But the constant motion of the camera begins to lose its status of jubilant triumph and turn over to precarious entrapment. Having arrived at the site of his dream, the distant lights remain just that—distant, out of reach—and the encircling camera begins to feel like a surveillance camera. Kolja is a type of force that ultimately indicates the frustration of the border. The abjecting mechanism cannot be perfect. Out of the eleven migrants, one made it through, a success rate just under 10 percent.

European space is ideational space liberated by the transformations of 1989 and inflected by the material-political relations of European union begun in 1992. The EU as material-political force of European union has constituted a new interior and exterior, for which the audiovisual apparatus plays a particularly important role in imagining community, precisely because this border is mobile. It is foremost ideational and compelled by a push and pull like the bridges and ruins along the Oder river. The ruins bespeak a closing off from the other side and the transformation of the river into *an abjecting limit*. The completed bridges attest to an opening to the other side, *an inclusive deterritorialization*. Those bridges were built because of a sense that on the other side there is something to be explored, someone to which a connection can be made, somebody to unite with, some common ground to be found.

The liberated mobile camera discussed in this chapter is not a guarantee of a particular position vis-à-vis the other side, but it was a technology of choice for filmmakers, who in their moment, moved into the borderlands. They understood the space as interzone and not as shatterzone, as constitutive of new potentials and not as threat to subjectivity. Schmid's work here in particular highlights the work of borders as abjecting apparatus. His film represents but does not replicate it. The film instead counters the homogenizing exercise of power, the fixing of individuals into essentialist components in order to expel them. The film offers an imaginative community based in a complex connectivity of heterogeneous individuality. It attests to the ability of the cinematic apparatus to create the ideational foundation upon which material bridges are built.

CHAPTER 5

"Outside" Europe

The last chapter considered the EU's border as mobile; its exterior can never be fixed or made permanent. Where would European culture find its limits? Does European culture end at the Urals? Or does it spread further to fill out the borders of Russia? Has Algeria, once a department of France, remained part of the Francophone world yet lost its relationship to European culture? When the Portuguese or the British describe trips to Europe, is their journey further than the voyage to or from Surinam, French Guiana, or the Cayman Islands? Which part of Canada, Australia, New Zealand, the United States, Latin America, the subcontinent, Africa, and Asia have not been directly impacted by European culture? How many countries spread across continents understand themselves as part of European culture? The last chapter also already made the point that the periphery always has the ability to pass the border and arrive inside. Clearly if it is a question of culture, the border of Europe can always expand. This is a mobile and a permeable border.

This chapter explores how the European funding of the cinematic apparatus has the potential to function much as geographic borders do, essentializing even abjecting certain spaces exterior to European values. In this chapter, we turn our attention to the "outside" of Europe and explore how *the European mode of production* outside of Europe runs the risk of instituting a cycle of Orientalism, offering European (and American) audiences tales they want to hear, actually keeping as distant strangers people who live around the corner or down the hall.[1]

Brussels's Mediterranean Shores

In 1995 a new orientation began in the EU toward a closer regional tie with neighboring countries. Especially the Mediterranean region came under closer scrutiny and in the context of the "Barcelona Process," the EU established the Euro-Mediterranean Partnership (EUROMED) with the goals of "restoring" a coherency to the entire Mediterranean region that it has had reaching back into classical antiquity.

In this perspective, there is the recognition that the territory has been historically a region of interaction and trade, fostered by ease of transportation over the sea and a history of grand empires that lined and united the shores. This state of commonality was understood as a kind of basic normalcy and that the current division between united Europe in the North and the various regions to the South and East are not natural. The initiative thus sought to create a form of interzone between the EU as a coherent body and those neighboring countries, a common territory of hospitality and privileged partnership. In the positive goals of the initiative was also a sense of solidifying the European sphere of influence in a way that was distinct from NATO and even as a free-trade zone counterbalance to the North American Free Trade Agreement signed just the year before in 1994.

The goals of the Barcelona process and the EUROMED partnership were thus threefold. First, it was to foster economic development through free-market trade. To this end, the region was promised access to the EU market through the creation of a free-trade zone, not unlike NAFTA across the Atlantic. Second, the establishment of a common security orientation aimed at bringing peace and stability to the region. To this end, a Charta for Peace and Stability was developed that proposed regular meetings and conflict management codes that would diffuse international tensions. Third, a further goal was established to foster cultural and social contact and cooperation.

If we understand the EUROMED program as aiming to establish a new transnational zone, the problem, of course, is that the development of such goals was not among equal partners. Rather, on the one side is a set of states that formed a relatively unified negotiating body. Many of these states do not share a geographic border with the Mediterranean; nevertheless, most of them have some form of neocolonial presence on the other side of the Mediterranean. And on the other side, a set of states is divided into conflicted national interests. Many of them have authoritarian political structures, are wracked by poverty, and serve as sending states to Europe in patterns of labor migration and asylum. Even if we understand the regional aspirations of the EU expressed in EUROMED as benevolent and truly neighborly in their orientation, these imbalances would lead to an unequal negotiating status and an uneven form of development.

After initial successes, the results of these initiatives became mixed. Many EUROMED members responded to the partnership with the EU by participating in *economic* liberalization but not *political*. The countries in the region followed the Chinese model of allowing for free-market economics coupled with a significant degree of political repression: authoritarian force keeps economically displaced workers and farmers in check and regional elites in power. This shift toward repression combined with the failure of the Oslo Peace Initiative and the outbreak of the Iraq War actually resulted in an escalation of tension with the European North, and the developments after the Arab Spring only intensified tension further. Perhaps, however, most problematic for regional peace and security has been the contravening hardening of migration policies. The economic displacement brought by free trade led to an ongoing wave of migration to the North to which the EU responded by unilateral attempts to seal the borders. By 2005, the Euro-Mediterranean partnership had arrived at an impasse, with more attention devoted within the EU to the eastern expansion of the borders of the EU than to the relations to the South and the Islamic world as such.

It is important to focus here on the goal of common culture and cooperation, because, out of the three goals, it at first seemed to be the least likely but ultimately has proven to be the most successful and long-lasting aspect of the initiative. Central to this goal was the now famous Thessaloniki Conference in 1997, which recommended as a vision for the future and sustainability of the entire Mediterranean region a common audiovisual program. EUROMED began in 2000 and was extended in 2006 to become EUROMED Audiovisual II. Now phase III coordinates with the EU MEDIA Program as part of Outside MEDIA and MEDIA MUNDUS. Overall EUROMED Audiovisual has become a program of the European Union that follows the patterns of support in the MEDIA of fostering cooperation and coproductions. In its configuration as phase II, EUROMED Audiovisual had a budget of fifteen million euros for three years. In addition to the participation of the European Commission, twelve more countries from the region participated from the start: Algeria, Cyprus, Egypt, Israel, Jordan, Lebanon, Malta, Morocco, the Palestinian Authority, Syria, Tunisia, and Turkey.[2] Cyprus and Malta have since joined the EU, and Turkey has moved forward on its application for ascension giving them a different status.

The Audiovisual program has as its goals:

- To provide training and professional development for film and audiovisual professionals from the MEDA countries and territories

- To enhance and upskill those involved in film development, promotion, distribution and exhibition in the MEDA region
- To promote the visibility and exhibition, and maximize audiences for Mediterranean films in the MEDA region and the EU, and European films in the MEDA countries and territories
- To reinforce the capacity of the South-Mediterranean region's public authorities to improve the organisation of the audiovisual sector and adopt measures to deal with new developments and new threats such as piracy.[3]

To accomplish these goals, EUROMED has set up offices throughout the Mediterranean but with emphasis on Israel, Turkey, Morocco, and multiple sites in Europe.

The benefit for Europe is not benign. To be sure, EUROMED coproductions have bolstered Mediterranean film production, but this proves financially profitable for European participants. If homegrown productions are down in North Africa and Middle East, nevertheless, they maintain a very important market share. Nabil Ayouch, director of the EUROMED initiated the MEDA Film program housed in Morocco, estimated that in 2005 and 2006 fourteen films in Israel achieved 9 percent market share, twenty-eight Moroccan films achieved 18 percent market share, thirty-four Turkish films achieved 52 percent, and thirty-five Egyptian films achieved 80 percent.[4] Thus, European investment in film production from these regions represents a good economic investment. Although little interest may exist for a German or a Dutch film in Egypt, a coproduction that circulates as an Egyptian national film draws audiences; even though this draw is ultimately to a European-funded film that appears as a national film. This form of film funding codifies routes of distribution as circling between Europe and funded countries. This film funding importantly does hold open screening venues and keeps indigenous film industries alive at the same time it also guarantees that European film is part of the exhibition mechanism.

The influence goes beyond production and exhibition. Distribution and visibility initiatives have led to the creation of film festivals, the expansion of the Europa Cinema Network, and the creation of postproduction marketing and sales support. There is in these programs an inherent direction of activity northward, to Europe. For instance, training is undertaken in Germany, Spain, and France at various institutions from classical film schools, through more flexible workshops, to large-scale conferences such as the Berlin Talent Campus that has taken place regularly since 2004 at the Berlin film festival.

The Berlin Talent Campus invites three hundred and fifty to five hundred young professionals from over ninety countries to attend a gathering alongside the Berlin Film Festival. This conjunction with the Berlinale allows for the Talent Campus to tap into industry professionals in attendance, who can then share with the next generation insights based on their expertise. At least thirty of the participants are selected from the Mediterranean countries and are brought together in specially designated workshops in the Talent Campus. The goal is, as Dorothée Wenner and Lior Geller presented, for them "to build a network of contacts with established EU industry professionals and [provide] assistance to international co-productions."[5] In 2007, the Talent Campus received more than thirty-six hundred applications from one hundred and twenty-one countries, including two hundred and sixty-two applications from all ten MEDA countries.[6]

At the Talent Campus, participants learn about the World Cinema Fund (WCF) and are encouraged to apply. The WCF is not directly connected to EUROMED; rather, it is a project of the *Kulturstiftung des Bundes*, a central German state mechanism for the funding of art and culture. The *Kulturstiftung* orients itself in particular to programs that operate in an international context. The WCF is thus typical of this activity. However, we discover a close cooperation between the WCF and EUROMED. Founded in 2004, the WCF operates like the Talent Campus within the purview of the Berlin Film Festival. And like EUROMED Audiovisual, the guidelines of the WCF state that it is there "to support films from regions whose film cultures are endangered by political or economic crises. The WCF is intended to help provide a higher profile and increased accessibility for these films in Germany and to enable their presentation to an international audience. Projects eligible for funding should deal with the cultural identity of their regions and should contribute to the development of the local film industry."[7] Central to the activity of the WCF is the development of film projects that require support because instability in the directors' home regions make it impossible for the film to be made and secondly is to develop the film industry outside of Europe.

With the EUROMED and the WCF presence at the Talent Campus we have something of an example of subsidiarity: how at the local level the Berlinale provides the foundation for decisions that enter into networks with local but distant partners. It is certainly a good example of how the local, the national, and the European initiatives create synergies. Yet the decisions taken here are not the same as those taken vis-à-vis inner-European partners. Such programs certainly prove beneficial to the participants; yet we should return to the point made earlier about the EUROMED project in general. Such programs do not take place as relations among equals. The programs began with an imbalance in capital, both economic and social. And when the WCF and Berlinale Talent Campus understandably praise the effect their work has had by noting how many once-apprentice filmmaker participants have come back to the Berlinale as full contributors, we may want to consider that the interzone established here has a bias in the way the products, profits, and people flow.

The direction of cultural transfer is predominately back to Northern Europe. The number of projects that establish relations across the southern rim of the Mediterranean are significantly less than those that establish relations to EU member states. It may be the European and local film industry that benefits more than the indigenous and external one, contrary to the stated goals of EU-ROMED. Insofar, then, as the EU subsidy systems and coproduction programs move in to support production in developing regions, these programs threaten to institute a strategy of uneven and unequal development, where film becomes another aspect of first world aid. The difference, however, from traditional forms of aid (industrial development, medical, or food supplies) is that film is a cultural product. And that becomes very problematic in the national-appearing approach that dominates the European coproduction strategy.

For instance, the first film produced under the auspices of the WCF was Hany Abu-Assad's *Paradise Now* (2005). This film proved to be a highly controversial film and may be the program's most prominent so far. The film tells the story of friends Khaled and Said who set out on a mission as suicide bombers from the occupied West Bank to Tel Aviv. The film eschewed the use of a typical musical score that would have directed the spectator's sympathies and instead relied on close-ups and response shots of the friends' faces to convey a sense of emotional depth in the characters themselves. A controversy arose around the film and the question whether it was not minimizing and even supporting suicide bombing as a tactic. Moreover, it initially was turned down for consideration by the Academy of Motion Picture Arts and Sciences for an Oscar because it was understood as a Palestinian film, and the Palestinian Authority did not have any status with the Academy. As a Palestinian film, it premiered at the Berlinale and after playing at numerous further festivals, it went on to broad distribution, eventually receiving an Oscar nomination as well as nominations at the German Film Awards. This film also won a Golden Globe award and a European Film Award.

Certainly this is a film set in a conflict-ridden region about a topic that could not easily be addressed under the conditions of military occupation, and certainly the Palestinian film industry is in chaos at best. However, it is important to note that Hany Abu-Assad is a Dutch-Palestinian who began his filmmaking career creating documentaries about the West Bank for primarily British and Dutch media. *Paradise Now* was cowritten and developed by Assad's friend and colleague, the Dutch producer Bero Beyer. And it premiered at the Berlinale as a result of the WCF support it received. Revisiting the second point of the WCF's stated intention, we can note that the WCF sets up a particular relationship to

Europe. The guidelines for funding go on to require that projects have a German- or EU-based production company, or a subsidiary of a German- or EU-based production company. *Paradise Now* is thus a German, French, Dutch, Israeli coproduction telling a Palestinian tale. Development and postproduction took place outside of the territories. This *national-appearing* approach effaces these important distinctions and makes it appear as if essentially cultural interests located in the occupied territories generate it.

Financially, it is clear that such funding assures that the resuscitation of the film industries takes place attached to the drip of European monies while ensuring that a portion of the profit from development projects returns to Europe. That in itself is certainly not unreasonable; however, we should note that part of the initial reason for the dismal conditions of indigenous productions, especially in the Mediterranean, derives from free-trade agreements forced on those countries by the European Union, the World Bank, and the IMF. For instance, enforcement of free-market agreements undermined the Algerian government's subsidy system so that an industry that produced roughly thirty-three films per year in the 1970s dwindled to two or three films a year by 1995. A film industry that once offered the world some of the most insightful images into the process of decolonization and postcoloniality, now must undertake coproductions with French partners. The free-market conditions forced on Algeria are precisely the kinds of conditions against which the French government and audiovisual industry has struggled for years with relative success. These programs thus institute a strategy of uneven and unequal development, where film becomes another aspect of first world aid. The difference, however, from traditional forms of aid—i.e., industrial development, medical, or food supplies—is that film is a cultural product. Thus, that these coproductions generally rely on the strategy of narration that allows them to appear as national films—or as culturally essentializing narratives about, for instance, French and Algerian, German and Turkish, or Dutch and Moroccan communities—should raise concerns.

A roundtable on the conditions of film production in Africa took place at the 2002 bATik film festival in Perugia, Italy, a festival devoted in particular to independent international film, especially African.[8] Participants of the roundtable, African filmmakers and producers, noted invariably the dependence of African films on funding from Europe: without European funds African film production would not exist. While clearly pleased about the support, the filmmakers in particular noted certain effects of the situation, not the least significant of which is an aesthetic and narrative orientation toward European tastes. Tunisian director Mahamoud ben Mahamoud noted, "It occasionally happens that in order to satisfy a French or Italian audience, an African director is forced never to address the issues that really happen in Africa."[9] African film critic Ferid Boughedir described the condition more pointedly:

> There is an urgent need to solve another huge problem created by our dependence on European cash. Many African countries do not have an internal film market. As a result, a paradoxical situation is created whereby African films are seen abroad but not at home. It is almost as though an African who looks at himself in the mirror, sees a European looking back at him.[10]

Such critical assessments continued in *Cahiers EUROMED*, a media initiative from the Middle East in 2005. In the publication a number of filmmakers were asked to respond to their work within the coproduction structure of the program. The editors of *Cahiers* asked them to respond to the nature of the dialogue established between the North and South of the Mediterranean. The assessments offered by high-profile successful filmmakers, most of whom had worked in coproduction with German companies, proved more critical and not entirely positive. The works of critically acclaimed Egyptian director Yousry Nasrallah include the French German Egyptian coproduction *Genenet al Asmak* [*The Aquarium*] (2008), which premiered at the 2008 Berlinale. Nasrallah offers a cautiously positive assessment of the program:

> Artistic co-productions that are granted European support could be considered tools for reinforcing Arab-European dialogue. Deprived of their freedom of expression by Saudi backers, producers find in these co-productions a tool for expression. Thus, they promote interior dialogue in their societies; something pretty much needed and appreciated. Intra-Arab dialogue is the first step that will help build a dialogue with others, so that an international cultural dialogue can be launched afterwards.[11]

Nasrallah identifies positively the openings made possible. Reflecting on these developments before the Arab Spring, Nasrallah seems to suggest that through such projects the public sphere opens to debates that serve first the Middle East and then in turn prepare the Arab world for a dialogue with Europe or the rest of the world. The Syrian activist and documentarist Omar Amiralay approached this dynamic more cautiously. He recognizes the restrictions on media and civil society in countries like Syria but sees an imbalance in the relation that develops with Europe:

> Since Arab national institutions are unable to fulfill their mission, one should recognize the crucial role played by Europe in assisting innovation in the Arab

> world. However, a fruitful and well-adjusted dialogue is not conceivable as long as one of the parties is still in need of the other. It is difficult to ignore the policies and the orientations of backers such as European funds. Concerning the norms in the market, it can completely diverge from one European country to another, or even from a Northern European Scandinavian country to a Southern European country.[12]

Hany abu-Assad's colleague Elia Suleiman, Palestinian filmmaker, best known for *Divine Intervention* (2002) a German French coproduction and winner of the Jury Prize at Cannes but likewise turned down by the Academy of Motion Pictures, assesses the dynamic more negatively:

> It is true that the financial aspect is important; still it is hard for me to believe that it can generate a real dialogue. On the contrary, I think that only the quality of work is capable of promoting an exchange. Funding is a trap especially that backers are, in general, former colonialist countries, supporting today projects in their old colonies. If the producer chooses to finance this or that project, the director can consciously or unconsciously choose to reflect a reality or a fiction that producers may find attractive. A cultural dialogue is a real duet: why not [present] the work of European filmmakers in our countries? I fear that we should wait much longer before learning how to sing as a duo.[13]

Suleiman's invocation of a colonial relationship is startling. His identification of a form of selection and self-censorship in the funding dynamic may be a result of the fact that the European success of *Divine Intervention*, a film that relies on surrealist motives to tell a love story set against the Israeli occupation, was received with some skepticism in the Arab world. While Suleiman has a history as a complex experimental filmmaker, the use of surrealism to depict the tragedies of life under occupation, struck many as submission to the sensibilities of the European audience.

The commercial Lebanese filmmaker Jean-Claude Codsi extends this negative assessment, noting that the programs available have been helpful for the industry financially:

> The fact remains that European institutions are the ones who decide if a Lebanese movie is going to be made or not. These movies must thus correspond to their demands, which are essentially conditioned by two choices: social (to tackle problems of our societies) or aesthetic (the search of cinematographic language which is our own one). The exclusiveness of these choices leads to a production of movies difficult to understand most of the time, hence, the total rupture between Lebanese movies and their public and the absence of internal dialogue.[14]

To be sure as a filmmaker of popular films and commercials, Codsi's orientation is not toward arthouse strategies, like those found in Suleiman's work. His observations, however, underscore that the intervention in the public sphere that the EUROMED initiatives foster takes place within a circle of educated elites, often people who received their training in Europe, like Codsi. Arthouse films are distant from the mass orientation of popular cinema, and popular media development is subjected to other free-market logics, which we will explore in the next section.

This focus on support for arthouse production has ramifications for a small film country like Lebanon. In 2009, the Lebanese Film Festival in Beirut was able to screen only one full-length feature film, a French production, *Falling from Earth* (2007), by a Lebanese diasporic filmmaker Chadi Zeneddine. The film is a beautiful poetic reflection on the history of conflicts that have racked the region. It has had some success screening at festivals and being broadcast on Lebanese television. The film uses stunning visuals to show flashbacks from the point of view of the wise fool Youssef living in a bombed-out building. But here Codsi's observations can lead us to wonder if for the long-term health of Lebanese cinema, with its conflicted civil society and fraught international relations, perhaps the creation of a united public through a popular orientation could prove more important than challenging film language oriented toward the post–New Wave expectations of (European) cineastes.

The critical assessment continued; at the 2007 Berlin film festival a panel discussion took place, addressing the activities of the EUROMED program. And again, significant among the panel's comments was the realization of a "paradox" in which filmmakers turn to Europe to develop their films, yet in doing so expose themselves to a "neo-colonialism."[15] To be sure, the Arab Spring has fundamentally transformed the conditions of the public sphere in certain countries. Moreover, the rapid spread of satellite news and social media has resulted in dramatic shifts strengthening the media against the apparatus of repressive regimes. However, this critique still obtains because, although these shifts have fostered a rethinking of relations with the countries of the Middle East, they have not necessitated a transformation of European funding structures. It is not the policy of engagement that is being criticized but rather the strategy of intervention. If the EUROMED policy was initially to restore an integrity to the Mediterranean, as long as one-half of the Mediterranean world is positioned on the other side of an ideational and material border, that project obviously cannot succeed.

Counter to stated goals, it appears that aid does not establish a self-sustaining media industry; rather, the production system and the market are maintained as extensions of the European market. It is erroneous to accept the typical film-festival narrative that highlights the unknown cinema of a particular country. Festivals and exhibitors market the national-appearing films as independent productions that they are discovering and bringing into the European market. Such a narrative belies the fact that the films are produced as subsidiaries of the European market in which the concerns of the local, regional, and national are kept ultimately subordinated to the cultural, political, and market interests of Europe.

The fundamental problem with coproduction support of films that rely on a strategy of national appearance is how it intervenes in the public sphere. A Turkish or Algerian audience approaches a film set in California, Paris, or Berlin differently from one set in Istanbul or Algiers. Debates around cultural imperialism have centered on the omnipresence of Hollywood productions on the screens of a country, but the film that displays its conditions of production does not represent the same form of "threat" as a film that masks those conditions. A Hollywood, Bollywood, or Hong Kong film on the screen enables the spectator to take up a resistant relationship to the images, to decode them as indirect address. In effect, it enables processes of hybridization and customization. When the images present themselves as autochthonous, the mechanism of disbelief takes a different form.

Berlin on the Bosporus, Ankara on the Spree

Turkey has a special status on this border of Europe. Of the Mediterranean partners, Turkey has received the secondmost support from the EU after Israel, even more so than Cyprus and Malta. The support for Turkey through EUROMED shifted in 1999 when Turkey officially was accepted to ascension. At that point, it assumed the same condition vis-à-vis the European border that Poland and the other Central European states once had. For Turkey, in terms of the audiovisual apparatus, as a result of ascension it entered into a more direct relationship with MEDIA and Eurimages. (Like EUROMED, Eurimages provided funding to a primary Turkish coproduction for the first time in 1995 as well.) With the other countries of the Mediterranean, Turkey remains imbedded in the EUROMED structures, housing important meetings and participating in established networks like the EUROMED Cinemas.[16] But as an ascendant state, it also participates directly in the Europa Cinemas Network. Thus, the Turkish film industry has available to it support from preproduction through postproduction, distribution, and exhibition. This assistance has had an important effect on not just the Turkish audiovisual industry.

To be sure, Turkey's media industry is much stronger than most of the other countries in the Mediterranean region and certainly more open than most of the Arab Mediterranean. The 1980 coup did, however, have a devastating effect with long-term consequences. Censorship and trade agreements offered an almost deadly blow to the once mighty *Yeşilçam* (Green Pine, Turkey's answer to Hollywood). The annual production of films during the years after the coup dropped from the height in the 1970s of over three hundred productions per year to down below twenty films per year up to 2003.

Since 1988, sixty Turkish coproductions have been arranged with European partners through the Eurimages program.[17] Typically, fifteen applications are submitted and three selected each year. Three films might not seem like much, but for years this number amounted to about 10 percent of annual production. Furthermore, once these relationships are established, they do not simply disappear. Sinan Çetin has developed strong connections to Germany after the success of his Turkish German coproduction, *Berlin in Berlin* (1993). Although his film *Romantik* (2007) was produced with Eurimages support, much of his work and the work of his production company, Plato Film, takes place through independent networks. Thus, there is a hidden factor that makes the estimated statistics for German engagement much higher. And this active engagement has had a positive effect. Indeed, we can note a recovery over the last years with successes in Eurimages coproductions such as the prizes for Nuri Bilge Ceylan and Yeşim Ustaoğlu bringing international attention and the local production rising to over forty films a year with a tendency to steady market growth.

European programs have been instrumental in helping Turkish film production recover not just in terms of production. There are twenty-three film theaters in Turkey that are supported by either EUROMED or European Cinemas Network so that the films that are not the typical popular mass-oriented fare produced in Turkey also have a screening space. With twenty-three cinemas, Turkey has more than many EU member states, including Austria, Belgium, Bulgaria, and Greece. It should be underscored that the screening spaces are also devoted to productions from Europe and work to limit big-budget Hollywood. This space of exhibition acts in effect as a European alternative.

Established in 2006, twenty-eight countries participate in the EUROMED cinemas with a total of seventy cinemas. The EUROMED program suggests that they exhibit reciprocally films from the Mediterranean and EU countries at a rate of two to one. However, this description requires closer precision. At first glance, the list of eighteen films exhibited in the network in Turkey seems to include only one German film, the Turkish-German gangster film *Chiko* (Yıldırım, 2007) [DE]. However, on closer inspection we can note that almost all of the films are coproductions and upon closer examination we identify German participation in four more films.[18] And, of the nine films screened in Germany, seven were solely European coproductions. The point of inspecting the dynamic of coproduction is that it becomes clear that inasmuch as these networks support local film industries and indigenous production, they are establishing circles of distribution and exhibition in which European money funds the production of films for European interests.

Being a service-providing site is not a central problem here, but we need to underscore that the relationships with Turkey, as with the rest of the Mediterranean, are ones that establish an interzone of more complicated interactions than an acultural studio site in a depoliticized market. Mine Gencel Bek extends the critical analysis of the Arab filmmakers, noting the specificity of the Turkish situation. Unlike Morocco, Algeria, Egypt, or even Israel, Turkey has applied for EU membership. The notion of belonging to Europe that compels such an application results in a very different relationship than the "neighbor" status of the colleagues in the Fertile Crescent and North Africa. Bek argues that the relationship to the EU has had a bifurcated effect on the Turkish media in general.[19] On a political level, the EU has pushed forward a democratizing agenda, which Bek assesses positively. On the other hand, the entry into the European free market has brought new market pressures to bear on the industry.

The attempts to enter into the European Union resulted in reforms that enabled private broadcasters in Turkey; Turkish Radio and Television (TRT) lost its monopoly over broadcasting. The EU forced competition and these measures resulted immediately in a development not just of new media in Turkey but of new connections between Turkey and Germany. Ayşe Çağlar notes that the first private broadcaster in Turkey was Magic Box, broadcasting by Satellite from Ludwigshafen.[20] The stations Kanal D, Kanal 7, ATV, and Show TV began broadcasting later per satellite and over cable in the mid-1990s. The measures also opened Turkish media to outside ownership, exemplified by the investment of the German Springer press in the *Doğan* group. The publishing group behind Germany's largest circulating daily, *Bild*, bought into the *Hürriyet*, Turkey's largest daily newspaper. Bek assesses that in this process "commercialization is being prioritized over communication."[21] While we might question the nostalgia for state media monopoly that lingers behind this assessment, or the security of the public sphere especially during the years of the coup, for Bek the Turkish public sphere is being recreated as a consumer society of products. It becomes a culture industry financed from a Europe to which Turkey nevertheless remains outside.

In truth, this example of an expanded Turkish-German interzone is not restricted to the media industry. Much of the contemporary Turkish economy does not have roots in a national-economic past but rather emerged directly in conjunction with globalization. Turkey does not parallel the conditions in Western Europe where globalization affects existing industries; rather, much of Turkey's current economic growth derives from its direct entry into global processes. Hence, even though Turkey tends to be assessed as a highly nationalistic country, it is not easy to discuss its economic development solely in relation to national interests.

Turkey does interact within the high-cultural arthouse circuits of production and distribution, represented by the films that are produced within the MEDIA-Eurimages circuits. But it also has an increasingly significant popular film orientation for a mass entertainment audience that developed in conjunction with the free market. These productions are not financed by MEDIA or Eurimages; nevertheless, as noted above they arise as a result and within the interzonal relations that have been developed. There are approximately 2.5 million German Turks and some 500,000 families whose entertainment needs were primarily answered by satellite and home video. Slowly in the 1990s, a number of people in the German and Turkish film industry began to consider the German and European Turks in general as a group with interests that go beyond the private sphere and might actually be in search of new types of entertainment venues, precisely like cinemas. The fact that this awareness of the Turkish community outside of Turkey developed simultaneously with an increase in Turkish media productions in Turkey is not simple serendipity. As with Magic Box, there are European components at work here. Maxximum Distribution is a German company founded in 2001 by Nermin Tutal and A. Anil Sahin with the marketing plan to bring Turkish mainstream productions to Western Europe.[22] It quickly became one of the most successful distributors in Germany, winning the Box Office Germany Award six times for creative programming. Part of the success was precisely the limited number of venues versus the motivated audience allowing Maxximum to arrive at extremely high spectator-per-copy statistics.[23] In the first two years Maxximum was able to bring thirteen films successfully into German cinemas. Maxximum has been able to expand its operations into Switzerland, France, Belgium, Denmark, and the Netherlands. Moreover, Maxximum also turned increasingly to producing its own projects in Turkey, with the goal of developing films that specifically appeal to diasporic Turks living in Western Europe. Maxximum learned from the business model developed by Warner Brothers and became a producer-distributor unit, fostering to completion Turkish films on more moderate budgets.

Sahin is particularly critical of German-Turkish film, including the work of Fatih Akın.[24] Sahin expresses his interest in overcoming maudlin tales of immigration and suffering. He wants to offer a form of "normalized" entertainment, not a continual replaying of Turkish tragedy in Germany. Sahin is interested in urban action and comedy films that capture the positive quality of life in Istanbul and in Germany, portraying along with that an urban young successful lifestyle and not "clichés of headscarves and honor killings."[25]

In these two directions, the European coproductions represent a very different form of production than that produced by Turkey's popular filmmakers. *Kurtlar Vadisi: Irak* [*Valley of the Wolves: Iraq*] (Akar, 2006) or *Yahşı Batı* [*The Ottoman Cowboys*] (Sorak, 2007) distributed with great success by Maxximum rely on narratives of masculine bravado, *Yahşı Batı* satirical and comedic, *Vadisi* nationalistic and stirring. The work of Yeşim Ustaoğlu stands out in contradistinction. Her films *Günese Yolculuk* [*Journey to the Sun*] (1999), *Bulutlari Beklerken* [*Waiting for the Clouds*] (2003), and *Pandora'nın Kutusu* [*Pandora's Box*] (2008), funded by Eurimages, take on topics such as the violent suppression of the Kurdish population in Turkey during the 1980s, the historic destruction of the Greek Ottoman population, or the decline of the Turkish family in confrontation with an elderly woman's dementia. Her films premier at and are invited to international film festivals while Maxximum films premier at the local Cineplex.

Deniz Göktürk notes that work like Ustaoğlu's might actually serve a positive, liberalizing function. Göktürk has discussed how "Eurimages and other transnational funding schemes engender critiques of 'peripheral' nation-states and enable subnational minority politics," citing specifically *Journey to the Sun*.[26] To be sure, she distinguishes this film from domestic popular production. And in terms of its function she observed that this film questioned segregationist views on Turkish and Kurdish identities, [and] . . . was awarded the Peace Prize at the Berlin Film Festival, at a time when Kurds were demonstrating against the arrest of Abdullah Ocalan in the streets of Berlin."[27] While I agree with her, I would question the assumption here that the primary address of Ustaoğlu's films is the Turkish public sphere. The films seem rather to address an international audience, and primarily a European audience where they appear as Turkish films in festivals and arthouse cinemas. Meanwhile, nationalist propaganda and low-brow humor prove popular with the Turkish domestic and diasporic audiences. Although subtitled, the latter set of films remains largely ignored by mainstream German spectators. However, it is more likely in multiplex releases addressing the Kurdish question, like *Nefes* [*Breath*] (Semerci, 2009) or *Günesi Gördüm* [*I Saw the Sun*] (Kırmızıgül, 2009), that we can identify an effect on mass audience understanding of "subnational" politics, certainly more so than in *Journey to the Sun*. Such are the ideational complexities of interzonal production.

Clearly, the Eurimages support for films and filmmakers goes to those who are in line with European cultural-political agendas. I would not contest the value of opening up for discussion the atrocities committed by military and dictatorial regimes. My concern here is not one of national sovereignty; I am not interested in supporting a reactionary nationalism that would indeed align itself with popular culture in these countries and regions. Nor am I particularly concerned with the domestic population being fooled by this cultural production. What does concern me is how national-appearing films appear and are received by critics in Europe and North America.

That this is a relationship of unequals has an important effect. This is not a process in which two sides enter into a discussion on equal terms. Certainly the goal of EUROMED is not to create the Mediterranean as an integrated region to compete with Northern Europe. EUROMED fosters integration with Europe but not within the region itself; rather, it keeps the neighboring countries in a relational condition as periphery to a European center. The countries should be strengthened not to compete with but to be integrated into a European agenda. Sari Hanafi discusses how the EU determines the nature of the "joint projects" by "selecting the participants and by setting the agenda of international conferences and meetings."[28] The selection process listens to voices that reflect what European partners want to hear and not the full diversity of positions that can be found in the society. The selection thus results in one position being given increased resources at the expense of others.

Media mediate the social configuration in which they participate. A media system can be used to foster civil society or it can be used to stabilize existing conditions and pacify tensions. The question for us then is, what do the coproductions established within the European programs reveal to us—not so much about the places they represent but about Europe itself? It is important to ask this question because we are looking at films that are in effect commissioned by European interests. While, for instance, it may be the case that it is admirable to promote a discussion of honor killings in Turkey as does the Eurimages Turkish Greek coproduction *Mutluluk* [*Bliss*] (Oguz, 2007), nevertheless when this film plays primarily in European and North American film festivals, and then without a comparison to domestic violence in those countries, the national-appearing film runs the risk of speaking for an entire culture. If discussions of honor killings in Turkey or in migrant communities in Germany were coupled with the information that 25 percent of women in Germany between ages sixteen to eighty-five have experienced some form of domestic violence, and 4–6 percent of them have experienced extreme violent abuse, the discussion would be very different.[29] If it were noted that the question of domestic violence is being addressed in Turkish media and treated with silence in the German, the discussion would be very different. Such an approach would not isolate the problem to a particular culture or might allow for a better understanding of the role of culture in fostering or hindering domestic violence. Bek notes in particular that Turkey is exposed to an essentializing cultural approach on the part of strong currents in the EU.[30] It is a values approach in which, in spite of the closest economic ties, Turkey is understood as essentially infused with cultural values that make it an unfit partner for other ties, i.e., political. Hanafi extends this observation to the rest of the Mediterranean. He argues that the attempts to build up a public sphere and civil society within these projects "represent an agenda of civil society institutionalisation, largely determined by the European side."[31]

Looking more broadly we can recognize that the establishment of forums often takes place according to a notion of equity that does not represent local senses of balance, for example, the requirements of Israeli presence as a partner in funding for Palestinian initiatives. Resources, which are earmarked to support Palestinian autonomy but are established within these parameters, come not only from an outside but risk-perpetuating occupation. As another example, Annette Jünemann has noted that the EUROMED program does not engage with Islamic organizations and as a result, she argues, it creates conditions in which the institutions it establishes can simply not represent the complexity of the interests and needs of the region.[32] These interventions do not foster civil society or a public sphere based on debate; rather, they threaten to excise important voices and discredit them as representing nonlocal interests and issues.

This imbalance in the marketing of coproductions—that is, the representation of them as national productions—actually hampers the full potential of the interzone in that it does not allow for connectivity to become an aspect of the spectator's relationship to the image. The coproductions derive from a lively form of interaction and travel. They belong to and establish lasting networks of production and postproduction. They are artifacts of a very real cultural activity and a very new active culture of production. But because this does not appear on the screen, and is in fact masked from the screen, the spectators are led to understand these films as deriving from an essential different cultural context. While within Europe the cinematic apparatus produces an increasing complexity of social configurations, outside Europe the ideational possibility of the interzone is effaced by a national imaginary. This is not a national configuration representing itself, but rather a European cinematic apparatus that represents a national configuration as alterior to Europe's transnationalism.

What is complex is made simple, what is heterogeneous is homogenized. What is actually proximate is kept distant. Under the guise of authentic images, the films establish a textual screen that prevents apprehension of the complexly lived reality of people in not-too-distant parts of the world. A key aspect of the insights offered by Edward Said's foundational work on Orientalism is that an elaborate set of textual references had developed in Europe by which that which was fundamentally proximate is kept distant. Madrid is closer to Rabat than to Berlin; Rome is closer to Istanbul than to London. Yet these cities are worlds apart. The ideational distance derives not from a foreclosure of physical access and engagement but rather through the intervention and mediation of a set of cultural texts that speak the truth of the other on behalf of that other.

To draw this discussion to a conclusion, I want to focus on one particular formation in which this dynamic appears clearly. The German Bundeszentrale für politische Bildung [Federal Agency for Civic Education] (BPB) was established in 1952 as a means to facilitate denazification and to promote democratic political principles for the young Bonn Republic. The activity of the agency has changed in the fifty-five years of its history. It now

> centres on promoting awareness for democracy and participation in politics. It takes up topical and historical subjects by issuing publications, by organising seminars, events, study trips, exhibitions and competitions, by providing extension training for journalists and by offering films and on-line products. The broad range of educational activities provided by the bpb is designed to motivate people and enable them to give critical thought to political and social issues and play an active part in political life.[33]

The BPB undertakes these goals by preparing educational material to address a number of topics: domestic politics, international affairs, history, economics, and cultural questions, among others. These materials seek to allow citizens to inform themselves, and hence they attempt to avoid political bias; yet, of course, immediately they orient themselves to a German citizen's view of the world. The German historical legacy does establish a frame for the topics; they exhibit a commitment to informing about the Third Reich, intervening in controversies around that past, and further opposing fascism and extremism in general. The BPB is thus pro-state, pro-capital, and in its explorations of religious extremism it focuses on Islam and does not consider Bavarian Catholics or Protestant fundamentalism.

A significant aspect of its current activities revolves around the preparation and dissemination of *Filmhefte*: glossy pamphlets for sale or online downloading that discuss specific films. They range between sixteen and twenty-four pages; offer background, history, and aesthetic discussion; analyze content, figures and themes; and provide detailed shot and sequence analyses. The pamphlets lend themselves to lesson plans and pedagogical settings, film discussions, and so forth. They remind one of the pressbooks studios and distribution companies release, except that they do not foreground marketing or advertising. If the pressbook predominantly addresses the entertainment value of a film, these pamphlets address its cultural and political value.

Such pamphlets do cover a number of German films, generally dealing with questions of the Nazi past, but also youth culture and some minority questions, especially gay films.[34] They also discuss a number of international films.[35] A pamphlet on *Bend It like Beckham* addresses a film from Britain, while others discuss *Esmas' Secret: Grbavica* (Zbanic, 2006), *Zulu Love Letter* (Suleman, 2004), *Moolaade* (Sembene, 2004), *Turtles Can Fly* (Ghobadi, 2004), *Atash* [*Thirst*] (Abu Wael, 2004), *Secret Ballot* (Payami, 2001), *Hejar* (Ipekçi, 2001), *Lumumba* (Peck, 2000), *Propaganda* (Çetin, 1999), *Buud Yam* (Kaboré, 1997), and *Sankofa* (Gerima, 1993). This partial list covers films from Southern Europe, Iran, North Africa, the Middle East, and sub-Saharan Africa. All these films could bear the titles of national film and of art film. Yet all are coproductions with European partners. (*Bend It* is a British-German coproduction.) All these films circulated in the Europa Cinemas system and many premiered at the Berlinale or other European film festivals. The pamphlets overlook these facts: rather, they discuss the films as national productions—Iranian, Senegalese, South African, Turkish, and so on.

Through the pamphlets, all the films serve a pedagogical function but those pedagogical functions differ significantly, depending on where the film was produced. Thus a German-produced film like *Das Leben der Anderen* [*The Lives of Others*] (Henkel von Donnersmark, 2007) is situated in a network of materials around the history of the GDR and GDR State Security Apparatus. But films shot outside Germany and especially outside Europe, once drawn into this educational setting acquire an ethnographic weight, appearing as vehicles whereby one gains insight and access to foreign cultures and lifestyles. A film like Sinan Çetin's *Propaganda* (1999) is offered as an example of everyday life "under the sign of Islam." This film is never identified as a German Turkish coproduction, nor is it made explicit that its director's previous film *Berlin in Berlin* was filmed in Germany. It is set in the 1940s in an Anatolian village on the Syrian border and tells the tale of a petty bureaucrat whose insistence on enforcing a border that no one ever had experienced before leads to any number of farcical and tragic circumstances. Furthermore, a central theme of the narrative relies on motifs from *Romeo and Juliet*. Film critic Silvia Hallensleben observed of the film, "Not only in Germany do we find duty obsessed civil servants."[36] What amused her and served as a sign of "what she learned" about Turkey should come as no surprise; Çetin through his time spent in Germany should have been all too familiar with the pettiness of bureaucrats there, and he should well have known how to make a film that would appeal to Turkish *and* German audiences. What should sadden us, however, is that Hallensleben, an excellent and savvy critic of film read the film as revealing a truth about Turkey in a way that *Breaking the Waves* (von Trier, 1996) would never offer for Scotland.

Hallensleben was duped by the artifice of a narrative strategy that represents and markets the film explicitly as a national film. She read the film in a literal manner, isolating its images to Turkey and effacing the way that Çetin participates in global cultural traditions well beyond "Asia Minor." Still Hallensleben "falling for it" should not surprise either. Let me be clear: it is conceivable that a spectator of *Breaking the Waves* would prove less interested in the horrible guilt that psychically crushes Bess, and that the spectator might be interested as a tourist in the Scottish coastal town and oil based economy. The point is that something happens in films and in the institutions of promotion and criticism to establish a (cultural) distance between the viewer and viewed, to establish a differential on one side of which the story is about another culture through which I learn (*Propaganda*) versus on the other side a story that is presumed to appeal universally (*Romeo and Juliet*). Under this condition of filmmaking, whenever there is an intercultural dialogue configured in the films, it generally takes place as a bridge of communication between two essentially different cultures. Such dialogue then extends to the postfilmic space in which the films are required to serve as insight-offering artifacts of a distant, distinct, and incommensurate culture. Thus the fact that the films are produced as coproductions is denied, along with any sense of the fundamental contact and commensurability of the partners as well as the material and ideational exchange facilitated through the filmic apparatus. For films produced as coproductions to appear as distant objects and not as transcultural products, some work has to be done at the level of narrative and in the visuals. Cultural distance is not natural, it must be constructed.

The transnational coproduction strategies are not limited to Germany but, as should be clear by now, are a fundamental mechanism of the audiovisual sector throughout Europe. Because the funding arrangements are not just between European partners, Europe has become one of the prime funding sources for film funding for North Africa, the Middle East, and Central Asia. As such, it is responsible for some of the most successful films from those regions circulating through film festivals and into broader distribution today.

Yet this funding comes at a price. As a conclusion, we can distill four characteristics of the Orientalism operating in this dynamic: 1) European funding as development aid moves into areas where there is a crisis in the local film industry. 2) The ensuing appropriation of culture is a novelty in the policies of development. 3) These films offer a critique of local culture that local films otherwise would not. However, 4) this European funding promotes and produces difference, ideational division, rather than regional union. Fundamentally, the coproduced films must offer stories that appeal to European and North American audiences.

Coda: The Empire Cashes In

Starting in 2002, the German state of Hessen attended the FRAMES conference of the Indian film industry, trying to attract Indian film productions to shoot in Hessen and to take up coproductions with Hessian film companies. No one less than the governor of the state, Roland Koch, fostered the initiative. He hoped that successful competition would not only strengthen the local media industry but draw in tourism as well. The idea was not as far-fetched as it might first appear. Bollywood films have become increasingly popular in Europe, Indian film has begun to address and incorporate stories and images from the diaspora—Deepa Mheta's *Water* is the most well-known example—and Bollywood productions had already been filmed in Europe. To be sure, those productions had been in Switzerland, where producers and directors had found ample images for the popular mountain film genre. Hessen's landscape could not compete on this level, but it certainly could out-compete the expensive Swiss franc. Moreover since 1986 the German national film board [*Filmförderungsanstalt*] (FFA) had set out on a path to foster coproductions of various forms.

At that time, the FFA had reformulated the definition of a German film to facilitate the involvement of German filmmakers in the global film market. A film qualified as German if only the film script author or a leading actor is a German citizen and if the film premiers in German in the territory of the FFA or if it premiers in an A-level film festival as a German entry.[37]

Thus, a film with a full Indian cast and crew but one German actor could qualify for funding and be listed as a German film. The various states as part of the federal quality of the German republic had followed suit in the 1990s, setting up public-private joint ventures to foster local and regional filmmaking. The regions of North Rhine–Westphalia, Bavaria, and Berlin-Brandenburg had experienced important successes with European and Hollywood coproductions. And it now was time for Hessen to capitalize as well by looking further ahead and farther afield.

The Hessen Agentur, an office of the state's investment bank, attended FRAMES promoting the convenience of the Frankfurt Airport, the quaint historical quality of the architecture, and the friendly locals—as well as the possibility of coproduction monies. In the summer of 2005, the town of Heppenheim was the first city to welcome a Bollywood production. Vinod Kumar Singh began work there on a grandiose project, *Humraah* [*The Traitor*], which included local celebrities like the Wine, Asparagus, and Pickle Queens, as well as the mayor, who had a small bit part as a knight. Projecting that *The Traitor* would attract at least one million spectators in India, V. K. Singh opened up a production office and signed a deal to produce twenty more films in Hessen.

The Frankfurter Allgemeine Zeitung (FAZ) reported on the project, describing the exotic barefoot dancing that actress Astrid Jäger in her role as Sahira had to undertake. "Astrid Jäger is called Sahira, glittering earrings hang from her ears, over her small hands jingle silver bracelets, black circles around her eyes and the nails of her little feet are painted red. Sahira dances barefoot, that's how one dances in India." The FAZ reporter also noted the difference in work styles of the Bollywood crew, the lack of cameras, the provisional quality of the shooting, the speed of the takes, and the fact that the catering was rice and peas from the Indian restaurant at the train station. But Germany was in "Bollywood Fever" and such cultural peculiarities and non-German working conditions were overlooked.

Then came the premier. Reports of the premier describe a film that would not have qualified for a good home video or a bad piece of pornography. V. K. Singh, however, dressed in a velvet Nehru jacket with gold adornment accepted the polite applause as a sign of a great success and welcomed the guests at the reception. It is still unclear how much money Singh received from Hessen for the film, but it was suggested that he made off with at least sixty thousand euros although some have estimated six hundred thousand. German Indian bloggers discussing the event and film estimated that a DVD was worth ten euros for no other reason than to wave it in the face of orientalizing bureaucrats who got what they deserve.

This story of small town naïveté and exotic fantasies, of civic financial flaunting and petty criminal conning has itself the making of a good film scenario. What interests me here is how this incident displays some of the transformations that national, especially European, film industries have gone through. It also indicates some interesting problems of the global film industry, not so much that the Hessians were taken, but that the coproductions that increasingly structure the contemporary European film industry are not just financial transactions but excursions that are fueled by scripts and scenarios that lead people across cultures. They call forth images that circulate in the public sphere, offer up the "truths" of others for perusal, and can incite larger debates. Such excursions can be the sites of an orientalizing vision that has much worse consequences than the bilkings of one flimflam man. Just as V. K. Singh was able to offer a tale of exotic success and domestic audiences ranging in the millions, the coproduced films must offer to European and North American audiences tales they already want to hear.

CHAPTER 6

Interzone Xperimental

Migration and Moving Images

Interzone: Contact, Communication, and Avant-garde

To describe the interzone as communicative space, much as a communicating door unites two rooms, points to an experience of contact. It makes sense to scour our immediate borders for places where people cross and come into contact with those on the other side. Yet the border between states is only a single and limited example of the possibilities of communication. Indeed, as Derrida's discussion of communication reminded us, the propensity of communication is to reach across space and time with a certain infinite grasp.[1] And in his sublation of the difference between spoken and written communication, Derrida also pointed obliquely to the fact that communication always takes place within a structure or apparatus. Luhmann's systems theory focused solely on the structure or apparatus and suggested that communication functions exactly like communicating rooms.[2] It was a focus on the structure and not the iteration of communication. Communication, however, is not just communication "somehow"; rather, communication is always communication of "something," and it is a communication of that something to "somewhere" and "someone." Communication takes place because the communicator can imagine a communicant. This act of imagination calls forth the apparatus, builds it, and elaborates it, and in turn the apparatus expands the possibilities and calls forth new imaginative potentials. The apparatus of communication exists inasmuch as it does not just make ready but actually sends across, shares, imparts, informs, joins, unites, and literally makes common. The interzone exists inasmuch as it is that space into which the imagination reaches out and seeks contact.

Either there are various apparatuses of communication or the apparatus of communication takes on various shapes. If the border between states is an apparatus of communication that divides out and imparts information discriminately in a particular location, the cinematic apparatus is more casual, heedless, mingling, and indiscriminate, promiscuous in its potential contacts. The communication of the cinematic apparatus is not bound to forms of physical contiguity, as is a border drawn in geographic space or as in a building where communicating rooms exist in immediate proximity. Indeed, cinema as a medium of communication can diffuse contact in all directions. Cinema as an apparatus of communication can do so both in its representations—its projections or its moving images—and in its technology as well—its material organization and systematic treatment, its *tekhnē*, its art and skill. Editing, jump cuts, montage, collage, and so forth can bring into contact the distant in time and space just as production or broadcast networks, recording media, and display devices can also enable contact across physically discontinuous and noncontiguous expanses. Why not? Human beings themselves can move across great geographic distances and enter into contact with other people. Moreover, they have the capacity to experience ideational connection regardless of their own physical position. Why shouldn't their means of communication be able to reflect and even elaborate the propensity of complex connectivity that is a very human quality?

Humans experiment with communication. In his discussion of communication, Derrida ruptured the distinction between written and spoken word and opened up an understanding that communication has always been an experimentation with contact, a reaching out, an utterance carried beyond to excess. But why limit our considerations of communication to the spoken and the written word? There is what we might describe always as the avant-garde of communication, a vanguard of human contact, that advanced group that reaches out in new ways. The avant-garde of communication shifts the colonial contact zone to interzone.

In 1895, a truly radical new potential in communication began with the introduction of film. What made it avant-garde though was not just the invention of a new technology but the new arts of communication it made possible, the new imaginings of contact it called forth. Avant-garde is simultaneously the experimentation with new *tekhnē*, an aesthetic enhancement in the system of signification *and* an immanent social communion.[3] This chapter considers the avant-garde of communication, the moments in which there have been new and radical leaps in the potential of communication. By radical leaps, I do not mean simply the quantitative expansion of communication, for instance, the speed of communication associated with globalization. I mean more specifically qualitative shifts: e.g., the invention of telephony or the development of visual communication through the moving image.

In 1906, recognizing new expressive potentials in visual language that broke with long traditions of pictorial realism, Ernst Ludwig Kirchner announced *Die Brücke*, proclaiming, "Believing in development and in a new generation both of those who create and those who enjoy, we call upon the young to come together, as young people, who will bear the future, who want freedom in our work and in our lives, independence from older, established forces. Anyone who conveys directly and without falsification the powers that compel him to create is one of us."[4] This manifesto for *Die Brücke* became a central document of the historic avant-garde, and I draw on it programmatically as an explicit understanding of an interzone. It placed a freedom of movement and expression as core to avant-garde art, calling for a youthful transformation of entrenched cultural conventions. *Die Brücke* came together as a group under the name "the bridge" seeking not just to cross but to span shores.

Taking this manifesto as its orientation, this chapter explores a number of significant experiments with the moving image that opened up new forms of contact. It will focus on the period from the 1990s to the present as a period in which the apparatus of cinema underwent rapid technological transformations. The term *expanded cinema* arose in the 1960s designating a propensity of the moving image to be deployed in other strategies than the black box of the movie theater.[5] But since the 1990s, cinema has expanded so dramatically and the media that carry the moving image have expanded to the point where the moving image has fully ruptured the walls and technologies of historic recording and projection systems. Art Historian and critic Juliane Rebentisch has described such work collectively as "cinematographic installation," that is, the expansion of narrative and representational strategies into new presentational modes.[6] "Filmmakers" such as Ursula Biemann, Michael Brynntrup, Harun Farocki, Christoph Giardet, Agnus Hegedüs, Birgit Hein, Bjørn Melhus, Matthias Müller, Pipilotti Rist, Roman Signer, Volker Schreiner, Maria Vedder, and Peter Weiz, to name only a few, have left the movie theater, taking their images into gallery and performance spaces, televising or projecting them onto corners, ceilings, sidewalks, and cyberspace. And beyond cinematographic installation, a strategy of web-based work has arisen that does not aim to "cinematize" an environment in the same way.[7] Digital web-based work has a presence and breadth of production that site-specific projects could never have.[8] In the decade of the 1990s, the home computer went from a device for calculation and document preparation to a multimedia center offering the user an interface into a synesthetic world beyond what Hans Richter or Viking Eggeling ever imagined possible. The advance of tablets and smart phones makes the moving image now all the more movable: Janet Cardiff and George Bures Miller have specialized in creating site-specific projects that rely on moving images moving in space. The new digital technologies thus return to the moving image something of the early period of cinema, creating an open field of aesthetic experimentation and a dynamic exploration of new forms of signification and dissemination.

The shift during the 1990s from analog to digital, from black box and projected image to graphical user interface and streaming image, has revolutionized the cinematic apparatus. It has ruptured the walls of the black-box screening space and filled our lifeworld with personal and impersonal visual devices, from handheld to giant building-sized. We are at a point where it makes little sense to speak of film, filmmaking, and filmmakers and more to speak of visual artists or artists of the moving image. The proliferation of technology does not, however, automatically mean a transformation in visual language nor a qualitative transformation in communication. As discussed earlier, Giorgio Agamben certainly perceives these transformations as leading to a debasement of communication. I take exception to this position. Communication has not been debased; rather, the changes to the technology of communication have gone hand in hand with changes in access. Access to experimental technology once marked the privilege of the artist; for example, the access to early video recording technology that *Tape Recording* magazine gave to Andy Warhol ensured that banality be perceived as high cultural practice. With a ubiquity of digital technology, this condition has given way to a ubiquity of access for the utterance of banality. We are surrounded by people using advanced technology to say common things, request milk from the store, and send kisses good night. But this does not mean that artistic practice is over. Refusing to follow Agamben on his descent into cultural pessimism, this chapter focuses on moments in which the art and skill of new *tekhnē* have opened up potential communication and established new interzones.

Moving Artists of the Moving Image

It bears remembering that the history of the historical avant-garde of the 1920s–1930s is largely a history of artists on the move, forced out onto new terrains and required to take up new forms of communication. This period is filled with migrant and exilic filmmakers. For instance, we can think of László Maholy-

Nagy who came to Germany after the collapse of the Hungarian Soviet Republic, took up a leading role in the Bauhaus, and eventually fled Nazi Germany and made his way laboriously to Chicago via Paris, Amsterdam, and London. Or Hans Richter who left Berlin in 1916 to participate in Zurich's seminal Dada movement, returned to Berlin until 1933, and then via Holland and Switzerland made his way to New York. Generally, in consideration of the history of German experimental film, it is often forgotten that both pre- and postwar artists like Hans Richter, Oskar Fischinger, Peter Weiss, Jean-Marie Straub/Danièle Huillet, Vlado Kristl, among others, lived as migrants and exiles. That forgetting derives in part from the fact that their work did not make migration a central thematic concern.

Much of prewar migration, of course, resulted from totalitarian regimes forcing artists to flee. Connections established through forced migration took on a different quality in the postwar era. What we could describe as a modernist diaspora continued to expand, especially within the neo–avant-garde of the 1960s. Modernist groups like Fluxus or supporters of abstract minimalism promoted a rejection of domestic, local, or state orientations for an international style and cosmopolitan common language of aesthetic concerns.[9] Not an ethnic diaspora, the neo–avant-garde thrived through significant and heated exchanges taking place between New York, London, Paris, Cologne, Vienna, Prague, Cairo, Tokyo, and so forth.[10] Regular exhibitions like the documenta in Kassel or the Biennale in Venice offered overviews. And for film in particular, meeting places like Knokke Exprmntl in Belgium, or XSCREEN in Cologne proved important for developing a global communication network among artists of the moving image.[11] Knokke hosted works from eighteen countries reaching from the United States to Japan, including now-classics by Kenneth Anger, Birgit and Wilhelm Hein, Vlado Kristl, Takahiko Limura, Jonas Mekas, Yoko Ono, Pim de la Pava, Peter Schamoni, Jack Smith, Andy Warhol, and Peter Weiss.[12] But on a much more mundane level, spare bedrooms and open invitations likewise allow us to speak of the neo–avant-garde as a shared community of interests that reached across state boundaries.

Contemporary artists of the moving image travel. They travel in new circuits, training in film schools and art academies in countries distant from their points of origin, availing themselves of funding from institutions in remote locales, and exhibiting their work before juries in countries they have not yet visited. In this terrain the spaces of exhibition have now also proliferated exponentially, dotting the map and calendar with events throughout the year, constituting a festival circuit. And most importantly, the possibilities of cyberspace and web-based networking allow collaborations to take place that overcome geographic restrictions. It enables a transnational and globalized form of development and production. There are, of course, differences in how and why people travel in these routes

Birgit Hein Abroad

Birgit Hein is one of the most significant experimental artists of the moving image. She has been at the center of Germany and Europe's experimental and underground film production since the 1960s. Her work has consistently entailed an exploration of the technology of film production, pushing at its possibilities. But the pushing at the possibilities has also been a question of expanding the expressions of visual language.

Hein was born in 1942 and studied theater at the University of Cologne. In 1964 she met Wilhelm Hein and began a decades-long intense collaboration with him. In the aftermath of the catastrophe of the Third Reich and in the midst of the radical transformations of the 1960s, they sought to recall and restore the legacy of the historical avant-garde. Their first engagements with film are considered to be some of the most significant contributions to the postwar Structural Film movement. For example, in *Rohfilm* [*Raw Film*] (1968) the detritus for film, the scraps normally found on the cutting floor, are strung together and played back at different speeds. Negatives, perforation holes, framelines, the material aspects of film that normally are invisible in a projection are put on display. Out of boundless inquiries and engagements with film as film, Birgit and Wilhelm moved to the center of Europe's experimental and underground film scene. The venue XSCREEN in Cologne mentioned earlier was started by the Heins.

Hein distinguished herself early through theoretical critical work, publishing extensively on critical and historical topics related to film and the visual arts more generally. She undertook a number of important curatorial projects, including the groundbreaking film section at the documenta VI in 1977. She also began teaching, eventually finding promotion to professorship at the University of the Arts in Braunschweig in 1990. Her workshop provided a formative experience for some of the most acclaimed contemporary visual artists. At this time she also separated from Wilhelm and began her own film production. *Die Unheimlichen Frauen* [*The Uncanny Women*] (1992) was her first independent film and it immediately garnered a number of prizes, including the German Film Critics Association award for Best Experimental Film. The successes of *Baby I Will Make You Sweat* (1994) and *La Moderna Poesia* (2000) solidified her standing as an individual artist. In 2007, Birgit Hein was inducted into the Academy of the Arts, in the section Bildende Künste [Fine Arts], where she was one of seven women among fifty men.[13]

We could describe Hein's films, *Baby* and *Poesia* as her Caribbean films. *Baby* derives from a series of trips to Jamaica that Hein undertook at the start of the 1990s.[14] *Poesia* records ensuing journeys to Cuba. These works take up questions of travel and belonging, subjectivity and cultural contact. The films call on many of the classic tropes of autobiographical film, relating a life story on a journey; but in good underground tradition, that voice-over narrator compels a confrontation with numerous taboo subjects, including aging women's bodies, menopause, female sexual desire, interracial relationships, intergenerational sex, sex tourism, the end of Communism, or the cult of the leader.

These films reveal the traveling subject as a subject in the interzone. *Baby* and *Poesia* appeared precisely at the point of transition between analog and digital image. They are experimental travelogues, interconnected in practice but distinct. Although lyrical, these are not *cinepoëms*. Both of Hein's films entail a voice-over narrator that relates specifics of these journeys and recalls and remarks on interior emotional states. And that voice stands in relationship to a complex set of images that have been exposed to various abstracting processes. These films are thus in many ways a continuation of the visual practice of the film diary *Love Stinks* (1982), which Birgit and Wilhelm recorded during an extended period as artists in residence in New York. Further, *Love*, *Baby*, and *Poesia* stand in connection to Jonas Mekas's visual diaries, although Birgit Hein's independent films distinguish themselves through the voice-over and such narration is absent from Mekas's work. Thus *Baby* and *Poesia* also reveal connections to Chris Marker's travelogue/essay films. *Poesia* cites directly Marker's 1977 *Le fond de l'air est rouge* [*The Base of the Air Is Red*/A Grin without a Cat] and clearly *Sans Soleil* (1982) provides a further influence. But unlike Marker's work, in these films the subject is not fictional. It is an observing documentary eye/I.

A great deal of the experimental quality of the films derives from the fact that she relied on a compact digital video camera to record these trips. Here, the mobile camera appears in a way that parallels the discussion in Chapter 4. However, Hein then transferred the images to film in a process that led to an aesthetic abstraction. For *Baby*, she enlarged and recorded the projected image off a screen onto 16 mm, leading to a graininess and fading that often makes the recorded image not immediately recognizable. Additionally, she often slows down the speed, moving particular shots into a flicker effect. This is especially common during sex scenes. In *Poesia*, the images are also alienated through the abstracting and aestheticizing art practice. Hein relied on the freedom of the digital camera to record for great periods of time and the lightness of the camera to move in space. The images are not tourist images of travel but images frequently abstracted by the movement of the camera in space. The editing has long takes that linger on scenes often of seeming banality or even kitsch, e.g., from within a basement room the camera looks out an open window frame watching inquisitive puppies poke their heads into the room. The shot lasts just long enough that we drift from the immediate sense of cuteness to take in the larger predicament of decaying building and stray dogs. Without explanation, we move on to the next shot. The film lacks establishing shots and refuses to offer any clear spatial orientation. The edits turn out to be jump cuts to discontinuous places. While there may be many long takes, the lack of continuity means the images pass in rapid succession. Before the spectators understand where they are, the film has moved on to the next shot.

In both films, the voice-over draws the images into meaning. This voice speaks dispassionately about provocational events. The combination recalls the quest of the historic avant-garde to shock bourgeois morality, but here it is more personal, directed toward opening a new subjective space. From the moment when the voice-over narrator begins the film by asking "so long alone, so long without sex, how long can I go on like this," the film offers a potential to shock and provoke. It is a voice that in even sonorous tones moves back and forth between intimate personal detail and explicit graphic sexual description. It is filled with graphic statements like "I am pierced, penetrated, run through, pumped out." The subject of and in *Poesia* is on a journey similar to that in *Baby*. The narrator traveling to Cuba, states early on, "I just wanted to take part in life again."

The films produce a female self in self-conscious conflict with social taboos vis-à-vis the female body. Through the voice-over, *Baby* and *Poesia* appear as directed personal filmmaking, a camera in the hands of a filmmaker subject, a recording eye/I.[15] And the films visually underscore this point. *Baby*, for example, begins pointedly with a mirror shot of Birgit Hein. Yet this is not a stabilizing act of mimesis; rather, here the filmic act of reflection creates a tenuous subject. The filmic subject appears before the eye of the camera, but it is a fleeting shot that quickly gives way to scenes of traveling: sky from an airplane and an animated plane on a route map, and then the camera moves on train tracks past a countryside filled with snow. This is intensified in *Poesia*; we are not easily given direct reflections. Hein's reflection appears in shiny surfaces, windows, glass cases, or reflected off a television screen through a CNN logo. Yet the filmmaker acts as central subject, controlling and guiding the frame, even as in the films the filmmaker as object or image remains elusive.

Travel disrupts the stabilizing mirror scenes; furthermore, the film does not take up a mnemonic autobiographical strategy typical for the travel genre and popularized in works like *Out of Africa*. Hein's voice-over does not locate us at a point in the future present looking back on a past life, i.e., I remember taking a trip to Jamaica. It evidences rather what Andrea Staskowski described as the turn to a hermeneutics of experience in women's autobiographical film.[16] The experiences of living precede the I. In *Baby*, we first hear the voice of the narrator describing the need for sex: "so long alone." The use of the first person pronoun, "I" comes pointedly at the end of a chain of phrases: "so long alone, so long without sex, how long can I go on like this?" And this continues on throughout the film; the enunciated "I" emerges just as the visual subject, only at times. As the first opening mirror shot of Birgit gives way, so too the spoken "I" remains unstable and gives way.

We should thus be very careful to recognize that the filmmaker is not the same as the subjective image in front of the camera. The images are a subject effect. The images of Birgit that do appear in the film are distanciated images taken through a mirror. And as if to underscore this point, the first image of *Baby*, Birgit in front of the mirror, reappears at the end but is extended so that instead of just seeing Birgit in the mirror, we actually see Birgit the filmmaker holding a camera, recording the image in the mirror. This repeat of the shot at the end is a visual call to rethink the evidentiary status of the images shown, to rethink the presumed recalling and documenting relationship of voice and image. It is not a coy undermining of a rather full-on assault of taboos around female sexuality. Rather, it makes clear that the film does not offer stabilized subject-object relations.

This trope of travel, the move to the south as a step out of the quotidian society and back into life, is at least three hundred years old. And at least since Goethe's *Italienische Reise* the traveler-artist sets out in order to come into contact with new others and thereby ultimately with an unknown self. In *Baby*, the opening traveling shot through the snowy landscape gives way to scenes of green foliage but then returns to the traveling shot in the snowy landscape. The journey to Jamaica represented here is incomplete, marked already in the departure by a return to snowy Europe. The historical trope of travel to the south from the cold north or out of the *scientifica sexualis* of the Anglo-European world into the *ars erotica* of the developing world is made explicit here. The statement of longing appears in the frame alongside a contrasting lush verdant greenery. However, what could be described as *the arrival shot* in Jamaica is not a shot of the lush paradise but rather something cryptic, a shot that will return later. It is of black men standing in smoke, possibly a scene of a clearing of land or a burning of trash. There is a certain element of destruction and danger alluded to in this shot. Then the camera introduces us to the Holiday Inn at Montego Bay and the beach there, where intercut with the sand, we are given one last shot of snow. The desire that motivated the trip is still connected to a snowy "back there." But the environment into which it has arrived is a disappointing globalized standard that can be found in any Holiday Inn type hotel anywhere.

The tourist enclave presents only a reified version of what is already known. In both films, arrival in Jamaica and Cuba means the opposite of settling in. Birgit becomes a flaneur in her travels, going further. She decides her journey as it develops. She meets her companions in cabs or on the street. In Cuba, her companion remains nameless; he approaches her and they travel together. It is this stance as flaneur that opens to her a difference that had not yet appeared but was present on a horizon of expectations. Moving away from Varadero, "the paradise for tourists," she comes in contact with "Cuban life." In places where it is illegal for her to be, she meets Cubans motivated not by Che but by Coke, brand name clothing, American commercials, and Santeria rituals. In this move arises a recognition of an other form of difference. She gets the idea to see the rest of the island guided by the museums of the revolution and the Che image outside of Havana. And they set out.

The films eschew any easy identification of place *and* time. Not only is there the practice of abstraction, but editing ruptures principles of continuity. The films lack establishing shots and refuse to offer any clear spatial orientation. The edits turn out to be jump cuts to discontinuous places. Without explanation we move on to the next shot. And even though there may be many long takes, the lack of continuity means the images pass in rapid succession. Before the spectators understand where they are, the film has moved on to the next shot. Immediately, the shift from Frankfurt to Jamaica or Cuba takes place without any consideration of continuity editing. In the film's editing strategy beyond continuity of place, there is a further disruption of the continuity of time. Typically, cuts come in the middle of action. In *Poesia*, the announcement comes that the plane for Havana is ready for boarding, and then we are in Havana watching a TV, and then on the beach being looked at. A man on a train is pouring a rum at a quiet moment in the journey and as he tries to hand it left, the train lurches, but before he can complete the action the film cuts away.

The blurring and abstracting of the lover in *Baby*, his exclusion in *Poesia*, destabilizes the primary Other for the film. In *Baby*, the lover appears with a certain regularity, but these shots are not made clear or explicit. The viewer has to attend to reappearance of jewelry, a gold chain or a particular watch, that decorates Joe or Ron, to recognize that this is not just one trip and not just one lover. There are sequences of intimate sexual shots. However, during these sequences, the camera is typically in extreme close-up. The angles are such that black skin and white skin meet at a diagonal across the frame. Typically, the voice-over lapses during these sequences, or even talks about something highly politically charged.

For instance, in the middle of rather turgid descriptions of the sexual encounters with Joe, which are typically set to scenes of the interior of his "hut," a sequence appears describing a local party. While attending the party Joe learns of the death of a friend who had gone to Canada. He becomes outraged over the events that led to his friend's death. And at this point Hein inserts a number of brief images of militarism, of violence, a decaying black soldier. These images come from the mondo gore racist documentary *Africa Addios* (Jacopetti and Prosperi, 1966) and from the U.S. Army "educational" film *Army Medicine in Vietnam* (1970). The latter proved so horrifying in its graphic details of the wounded that it undermined its intent to educate incoming recruits about the quality of medical care awaiting them. It is from this film that Hein extracted an image of an African American soldier being treated for burn wounds. The brief clip of black skin being peeled away to reveal "healthy" white skin, appears here in this decontextualized context as a skin-whitening experiment. These images have a different quality to the footage Hein recorded and testify to the repertoire of racist images and violence perpetrated on black bodies.

In Cuba a different condition arises; the Cubans prove not simply willing to be filmed but prepared to stare back into the camera, to hold the gaze of the lens, until at times it seems that the filmmaker becomes intimidated, flinches, looks away. That they look back means that there is a subject who appears to them; to look back means that each recognizes the other. It is a subject at once immersed and simultaneously absent as an object from sight. What do we make of Hein's unstable presence in front of the camera, her ghostly presence as transparent reflected image? Robin Curtis has noted in the German context of autobiographical film, the film tends to emphasize the bios over the autos, the "life as it is lived" over the "self that is contained as a morpheme."[17] We can recognize in these films, in their investigations of the space of Jamaica and Cuba, how the subject comes into being through what Curtis has discussed as a *Selbstverortung*, "a localization specifically with regards to the self." This strategy highlights, as Curtis says, "the spatiality of our being, the relevance that our placement in space and time has for our 'situation,' in every sense of the word." Certainly, this localization is a central aspect of the films, these journeys to "life." It is a central mechanism by which the films establish an interzone.

Migrant Artists

We can think of other forms of migration in the post–World War II era. During that time in Europe, there was less migration and it was more predominately through the development of new subsectors in the labor force. Migrants were less in exile and more part of new large ethnic enclaves in Europe's urban centers. To be sure, many people continue to leave their homes as a result of political exile and asylum, but the presence of populations of labor migrants marks those migrants ethnically. This new set of migrants has brought forth artists who directly contend with these experiences out of those milieus.[18] While there are many migrants working in the film industry, those who belong to a contemporary avant-garde as "artists of the moving image" are limited. We can think of immigrant, diasporic, and ethnic filmmakers in Britain Mona Hatoum, Lina Khatib, Tamara Krikorian, Prathiba Parmar, and the members of the Sankofa Collective, and, in the United States, Trin T. Minh-ha, Hisham Bizri, and Haile Gerima (or even Jonas Mekas). In Australia, we find visual artists Anna Kannava, David Perry, and Dirk de Bruyn. The migrant communities in Germany and Austria have proven especially rich in developing experimental visual artists, in particular because of the density of schools, festivals, and exhibition venues. Kutlug Ataman, Aysun Bademsoy, Neco Çelik, Natascha Sadr Haghighian, Angela Melitopoulos, Hito Steyerl, Andrei Ujica, and the Kanak-TV productions have achieved international recognition. And younger generation artists are rapidly gaining notoriety and awards, e.g., Rita Bakacs, Ascan Breuer, Oliver Husain, and Masayo Kajimura.

There are differences to the modernist diaspora; these artists attempt to contend with the experiences of ethnic diaspora, migration, diversity, or difference. They are often troubled by an experience of domestic, local, and/or state exclusion based on their background. These experiences give rise less to abstraction and more to subjective and representational production. Thus they do not typically contribute to structural or material film experiments. Rather than experiment with the material of film and formalist aspects of representation, they have sought to negotiate between technological considerations and what Peter Wollen described as "contentism."[19] Their films tend to have "content," i.e., are closer to narrative, often aiming to make a didactic point, or to convey an experience of what it is like to be in exile or to be a member of an ethnic minority living in diaspora. In modes of representation that recall early models of the filmic avant-garde, they combine experimentation in form with personal, identitarian, or radical political interests in order to contend with the experience and politics of migration. Yet their visual art evidences a textual richness that is not easily reduced to tendentious political concerns.[20]

Ayşe Polat: Lyricism and Estrangement

Ayşe Polat offers an interesting case study. An award-winning filmmaker, she is better known for her narrative films, especially *En Garde* (2004) which won the Silver Leopard at Locarno. Polat is an autodidact. Born in 1970, she is in the same generation as Sadie Benning and Polat; like Benning, she also began experimenting with filmmaking at an early age. Where Benning used her Fisher-Price Pixelvision camera, Polat relied on Super 8 and video cameras. Benning focused on her adolescence and experiences as a lesbian teenager. Polat's work also derives from a critical adolescence but Polat's investigations focused more on questions of ethnicity and cultural displacement. Polat belongs to one of the most significant postwar migrant populations in Germany. Polat was born in Turkey to a Kurdish family and they moved to Germany when she was eight.[21] As a Turkish Kurdish Muslim from Germany, Polat belongs to a minority in a minority in a minority, a position that entails direct experience of multiple forms of exclusion and complex inclusion. Her films frequently take up themes of travel and displacement, alienation and estrangement.

From an early age, Polat engaged with the history of arthouse film, was inspired by Agnes Varda and Jim Jarmusch. Her work considers sociopolitical relations and aligns with various aspects of Natascha Sadr Haghighian, Angela Melitopoulos, or Hito Steyerl's work, although she does not share their tendency toward essayistic filmmaking and, especially in her early work, pursued a lyrical poetic style. At age twenty-one, her first film *Entfremdet* [*Estranged*] (1991) and *Fremdennacht* [*Stranger Nights*] (1992) were both short films relying on a minimalist aesthetic. *Entfremdet* is about four days at the end of a dysfunctional relationship between two lovers. They are no longer communicating with each other and on the third day, the woman leaves. *Fremdennacht* was a retelling of the last days of the Turkish asylum seeker Cemal Altun, who rather than be deported back to Turkey and face certain torture chose to throw himself out of the window of the courtroom where his case was being heard. *Entfremdet* won a federal "Youth and Video" prize and with the funding from this award and the recognition gained from both films she was able to produce *Ein Fest für Beyhan* (*A Party for Beyhan*) on a substantial budget. *Beyhan* represents a breakthrough for her. It premiered in 1993 and quickly garnered her further awards. The twenty-five-minute short was supported by, among others, the production company of Boje Buck, which is typically oriented toward feature entertainment films. In addition, the film received financing from the film funds of Hamburg, Niedersachsen, and Brandenburg. With the higher budget, it was shot on 35 mm film under the guidance of cinematographer Uli Fischer. Berivan Kaya, herself a respected actress with a Kurdish-German background, plays the adult main character Beyhan (and Sabina Köse the child role). Its cast includes Otto Sander, Füsun Demirel, Ipek Göle, and Tranh Duc Ha. Kaya and Demirel have both played on the stage and screen. Otto Sander counts as one of the most established and perennial favorites among German actors.

Although Polat worked at the cusp of the transition from film to video, this is not a film that experiments with new technological possibilities; rather, it represents an engagement and expansion of the language and aesthetics of film to contend with the experience of diaspora and exclusion. In its connection to the historical avant-garde, this work recalls the cinepoëm and archetypal film of the first half of the twentieth century, forms through which artists like Maya Deren and Germaine Dulac attempted to break with the dominance of narrative film and create a new visual language equivalent to poetry. Like Deren and Dulac's work, it contains surreal cuts and encounters with archetypal characters, e.g., *the Traveler*. As in Deren's *Meshes of the Afternoon* (USA, 1943) or *At Land* (USA, 1944), continuity editing is undermined by shifts in location and enigmatic character behavior. Furthermore, Polat relies similarly on doubling and repetition of motives. As with Deren, portals serve to transition characters between incommensurate spaces.

After this work Polat turned to more straightforward narrative film, although in her feature films we can still recognize motifs of migration, displacement, estrangement, family, and melancholy. Furthermore, in her feature films *Auslandstournee* [*Tour Abroad*] (1999) and *En Garde* (2003) we find a development of the resistance to reductive homogeneity.[22] The strategy of lyrical symbolic and archetypal representation in *Beyhan* appears in dream sequences in those films.

Beyhan begins with a far shot of a landscape, the horizon of which cuts across midscreen. Two characters occupy the center of the frame, seated on the ground under a clothesline with laundry hanging on it. In spite of the washing, the setting appears to be in the middle of nowhere. A tracking shot follows that passes over the clothes hanging out to dry, while the sound of water and periodic sighs fill the soundtrack. As the child Beyhan and her mother come into frame, seated low on the ground around a tub in which they are washing clothes, the camera stops and moves in toward them. Suddenly after a close-up of the wash, the mother's sole reflection is accompanied by the mother frantically calling out Beyhan's name. At this point, the film cuts back to a long shot to reveal a new figure in the foreground watching, observing the action of the anxious woman in the background. This new figure is the adult Beyhan. Wearing a backpack, she turns and walks away without saying a word. This shot sequence then begins a visual journey, with the camera continually moving, tracking, and panning to replicate Beyhan's own unceasing movement.

In the next shot, the frame takes up the perspective of a traveler on a train, passing through various rural landscapes, presumably taking her away from her family. A sudden and enigmatic cut reveals Beyhan seated oddly and inconveniently on a stairway in a busy modern train station. Travelers pass by, almost stumbling over her. It becomes quickly clear that train stations serve as a central and recurring motif in the film. In one environment, an orientalist facade occupies an empty landscape of warm brown-toned hues. Written on this building in big letters is the German word for train station, *Hauptbahnhof*. People, travelers, come out of and go into the building. Yet given the edits, this facade seems a portal whose interior is in Hamburg, filled again with travelers and starkly lit. Beyhan passes repeatedly through both environments, often walking across the foreground across action moving perpendicularly into the background.

In surrealistically constructed scenes, the film imagines the space of an interzone, the space of communication and contact. At one point, Beyhan seems suddenly to be in the waiting room of the Hamburg side. There she is greeted by a stranger, an Asian character uttering lines of a haiku by the seventeenth-century Japanese poet Basho, "journeying through the world, to and fro, to and fro, harrowing the small field." This haiku connects easily to a central scene that seems to hold the key to much of the symbolism and to Beyhan's own internal conflict. Beyhan sits in a train compartment with Otto Sander, identified in the credits as *the Traveler*. He asks her if she is going away or arriving someplace, and she replies "neither, nor, and both." He praises the experience of travel contradicting her protestations that it is exhausting. "Arrival is exhausting," he claims, but for him traveling, being between places, in the train is where he is happiest. She inquires about what it means to return to the place from which one left and he responds by describing such an arrival as a failure. Beyhan pensively agrees that such a journey to return is a failure. He leaves then, while Beyhan gets up to look out of the window.

In the final scene the oriental *Hauptbahnhof* is now empty. No one is on the square in front of it except for Beyhan who is now doubled as an adult and child self. The child comes to greet the adult, informing her that everyone is waiting. They walk hand in hand into a scene where a party is being celebrated at a large table set up outside in the middle of a field. The child runs into the background as the adult Beyhan stands in the foreground, her back to the camera, observing the festivities. Her mother comes out to invite her to join, identifying it as her party, but Beyhan turns and continues walking, once again at a perpendicular angle off into the expansive horizon. The final cut opens up a pan shot to the left across a warm-hued countryside while the poet recites the haiku, one more time.

The film, like Polat's other films from this period, is a lyrical exploration of migration and displacement. It lacks linear narrative, developing this technique of *flash out of frame* to interrupt linearity. These are similar techniques to Hein's work deployed to offer a complex understanding of motives of travel, social conflict, doubling, and complicated timeframes. Polat's film does so to represent an experience of marginalized and minoritized migrancy in a globalized condition. The film simultaneously represents two primary localities that fail to fix or stabilize the subject. In its lyrical associative qualities, it eludes didacticism and instead seeks to instill in the spectator an empathetic understanding of the difficulty for the migrant to cognitively map social space.

Leslie Adelson has importantly critiqued how dominant discourse has historically located migrants in a condition between two places. Adelson describes this in-betweenism as a counterproductive approach to the Turkish-German who is kept by such discourse in a status as foreign, outsider, and between two cultures and therefore belonging to none—especially not to that of the liberal Germans who express sympathy for the state.[23] Adelson encourages us to look beyond "between." This is an important critical point for considerations of the interzone. The betweenism that Adelson identifies is typically associated with an essentializing gesture: an often sympathetic and well-intended liberal gesture that understands that Turks are in-between because they are Turks. The essentialism fails to attend to the exclusionary and limiting qualities of German social and political structures. Hence, Turkish-Germans are not between; rather, it is the ethnicized German cultural setting that excludes people from belonging to the German polity.

Polat's work takes up such in-betweenism but does not relegate it to ethnic or Turkish-German essentialism. Polat is, of course, a Turkish Kurdish German, making her well aware of the insufficiency of ethnic essentialization. Beyhan's argument with Gül or a beautiful and cryptic sequence with her Kurdish grandmother helps counter an easy reduction of Beyhan to representative of a homogeneous *Turkish* culture or population. Moreover, in its own term, *traveling*, the film relies especially on the space of the train and train station. These spaces denote a space of people from varied backgrounds on the move—not just Turks or the minoritized ethnic. As with Hein's work, we can discover here a *selbstverortung* in which the traveling figure Beyhan is defined by a relationship to her surrounding and, in the end having accepted her mobility, she seems to achieve a form of liberation.

The "More Than" of the Interzone

Interestingly, as different as the works discussed here are, they do share certain commonalities. The motivation to the films is a certain quest for liberation from social conventions, cultural determinations, and subjective restrictions.

The figures in Hein's films are marked by social expectations of women and women's bodies, moreover of mature bodies. They resist gender essentialism *and* ageist expectations. The figures in Polat's films likewise resist gender but also ethnic essentialism and the social restrictions that seek to limit the mobility of the migrant woman.

It is important that the films do not establish a sense of belonging or recognition in their places. None of them offer sedentariness as a state to be striven for. The characters are repeatedly in motion, travelers: "flaneuses," moving in space and time. The *Selbstverortung* that takes place in the films is an uneasy localization in an unstable space of movement. At the same time, the characters all also explore what this means for the subjectivity of the traveler. Although Polat relies on specific and clear figures, in contrast to Hein, the autobiographical quality in *Beyhan* is also tangential and ultimately more about the instability and transformation of "bios" than about the stability of a self-referential "auto." Hein's strategy means there is an absence of clear attachment of the shots to a point of view. Because she does not appear in the frame, the person filming does not establish an equivalency to a filmed image. He/she radicalizes the principles of the traveler film we discussed with Voigt. These works find a positive identity in the traveler as a form of cultural universal. And they establish a vibrant cultural production that fundamentally attests to new forms of belonging and social *Dasein*. The space the figures and the filmmakers inhabit, as interzone, is not a deficient space. The "neither, nor, and both" of the traveler is presented as a privilege.

To be sure this is a limited exploration of the technological possibilities of film and video, but it is an important investigation of new languages of signification. This strategy of representation is one to which other women filmmakers have turned. For instance, Canan Yılmaz's *Ben Kimim* [*Who Am I*] (2003) relied on a similar experimental lyrical form. A figure spins in a room asking first "Who am I" in German and Turkish and then giving the answer, asserting a multifaceted "I" that does not allow for any easy reduction: "I am a German, a Turk, a Turkish-German, a German Turk, a Half-German," and so forth. The spinning figure changes her appearance, dressed without a headscarf and then with one, in hipster clothes with, dreadlocks and wrapped in blue silks. This short film (four minutes) intensifies the demands for a new space of social existence in Polat's film. It uses visuals and text to move well beyond cultural betweenism toward a cultural space afforded by the interzone. All these films aspire to a cultural space of "more than": more than German, more than Turkish, more than woman, more than girl, more than mature.

The New Interventionism

By the start of the new millennium the emergence of new forms of technology accelerated dramatically, as did the emergence of new forms of cultural production. Collective projects in particular began to emerge that sought to undertake new forms of interventionist and actionist projects in the public sphere.[24] The names of the groups are extensive and bespeak an often lighthearted creativity in their appearance that masks the seriousness of their engagements. We can think of Beige, Center for Land Use Interpretation, Critical Art Ensemble, Critical Mass, Dearraindrop, Electronic Disturbance Theater (aka Electronic Civil Disobedience), Etcetera, Forcefield, Guerilla Girls, Henry VIII's Wives, Institute for Applied Autonomy, microRevolt, Milhaus, N55, Radical Software Group, Reclaim the Streets, Royal Art Lodge, Santiago Sierra, Social Impact, Superflex, Temporary Services, The Church of Life after Shopping, The Studio for Creative Inquiry, The Yes Men, Ultra-Red, and more. Exemplary of these developments was the emergence in Germany of the collective Kanak Attak, which marked a new self-assertive consciousness in Germany's minority communities.[25] It unleashed a radicalized challenge to exclusionary national imaginings of community. Collective work has come to counter individualist presumptions of artistic genius and opened up new potentials for engaged and interventionist cultural production. Fostered by cyberspace, these groups are both global and local in their attention.

Much of the work is about fostering new types of counter-publics in which the process of the production is understood as sometimes the project itself. The boundaries between tendentious political engagement and artistic work became blurred in many instances as the artists collectives aligned themselves with Kanak Attak antiglobalization movements, environmentalist struggles, urban political conflicts, geopolitical struggles, antiwar movements, and social justice issues. This work built in the first decade of the new millennium and fed in many ways into the Occupy movement and was largely responsible for the organization and attendant cultural phenomenon.

Open process creates an alternative space in the midst of urban and authoritarian settings. These are not typically closed artists groups and they are not restrictive to particular forms of production but become polymorphous based on the collective and the accumulated potentials. Moreover, the nature of the work has called forth new forms of criticism that attend precisely not to the individual but to the new mechanisms of conception, circulation, and connection.

Social Impact *Border Rescue* and Rapidly Changing Technology

We return to the question of the border. With the start of the new millennium and the pending shift of the borders of Europe, a crisis of criminalized migration developed across the EU. In 2002, the discussion of the conditions of migration intensified such that in June of that year the European Union (EU) met in Seville to address what was identified as refugee crisis. The anxiety around migration, which drew the EU leaders to consider military actions against migrants, compelled responses from the artists and cultural producers. In addition to the intensification of criminalization of migrants, many artists sought to respond to the xenophobia and Islamophobia inspired by September 11, 2001, and to address the pending eastward expansion of the EU.

Kanak Attak and especially the Kanak-TV initiative, the *TransitMigration*, and *Kein Mensch ist illegal* [*No One Is Illegal*] turned to web-based projects: websites for the dissemination of information, announcements of "real world" activities, and the presentation of art projects. Among the collective projects of the period we can also think of those led by Christoph Schlingensief who undertook various installation performance pieces, including the Big Brother–like contain project *Ausländer raus! Bitte Liebt Österreich* [*Foreigners Leave! Please Love Austria*] from 2000.[26] In 2003, the Tate Modern in England funded a much-acclaimed new media experiment with Heath Bunting's *BorderXing* project. This piece received a great deal of publicity, in part because of the status of the sponsoring institution, but also because of the breadth of its focus. It focused on Bunting's personal border-crossings across Europe and did not have the same collective and interventionist orientation as other work of the period. Central to Bunting's website was that it shut out potential viewers from ip (Internet Protocol) addresses in first-world countries, thereby inverting and drawing attention to the typical imbalance of net access in the world. Although this initial filter was an interesting gesture, Bunting did allow for people and institutions to petition for access, and if one scrolled through the list of names of institutions with access, one recognized that from Harvard University to the Museum of Modern Art in New York, the gesture actually had the inverse effect, making the site into an object of first-world aesthetic consumption. During this time, just to the south in Austria, on the edge of the European border a new project formed within the group Social Impact.[27]

Repeatedly a shaky handheld camera pans almost 360 degrees as a form of establishing shot. The words "starting point," "route," and "landmark" appear, superimposed over the images identifying the scene as offering a sequence of landmarks. The frame then moves, going into the forest, following various paths, moving along fields. About halfway through the sequence the word "border" appears in red. There are ten videos available, each titled with a route number, and in each of the videos the border appears as a rather unremarkable spot, certainly not a matter of fences or natural barriers. There is a stream or a small path, a stand of trees. Generally, a cut here marks that the camera has crossed to the other side of the border. The sequence continues until it arrives at a point again designated in red as "final point." This sequence repeats in ten variations.

Throughout we never see a trace of the camera operator. There is neither direct address nor shadows. We do not know whether there is any form of team. The camera often moves with the motion of the operator's gait. Periodically, it zooms in on a landmark, a tree, a rock, a stream, a farmhouse. After a zoom there are cuts, in-camera editing, and the next shot begins at a point further on. The zoom seems to act as a sort of deictic element, pointing out to the spectator, "there is the way." The new shots take up a sort of vocative leader function, as if to suggest, "hey you, follow me." The cuts, however, because they are not done according to patterns of continuity, have the effect of actually disorienting the movement, rupturing the orientation of the spectator. Periodic pan shots do not easily restore the sense of position or offer clear points of reference.

These ten sequences belong to a 2002 project entitled *Border Rescue.* As video, they are artistically uninteresting, exhibiting an amateurish quality. Indeed, when displayed in 2004 as a single channel loop on a small monitor in the context of "Born in Europe—New Identities" at the Martin-Gropius-Bau in Berlin these videos faded into the background of the other pieces on display. Most viewers would be surprised to hear the videos identified as a significant example of avant-garde art. In the larger context of its production and goals, however, here the moving image has left the historic spaces of projection and even broadcast. Where the previous projects discussed entailed the transition from film to video, from analog to early digital, this project comes a bit later and bridged the move both to installation and to web-based streaming video—all as a conscious part of a larger political interventionist project.

Border Rescue was developed by the activist art collective Social Impact. founded by Harald Schmutzhard in Linz in 1997.[28] The group developed as a loose collaboration of interdisciplinary teams, the shape of which depends on the theme addressed. Schmutzhard, as central organizer, draws artists together with social workers, architects, sociologists, and whatever form of expert that might be germane to a project. Social Impact projects have focused on topics from prostitution, trafficking, prison conditions, and urban sprawl, to migration. This group is a flexible group motivated first by socialpolitical and aesthetic considerations and then formed by consideration of the most appropriate technologies available. Schmutzhard has dubbed this New Genre Public Art (NGPA).

NGPA is not unlike the strategy of phorschung undertaken by Anschlaege.de (see chapter 1). Overall, NGPA intensifies interventionist attention to contemporary situations of urgent social and political conflict. Each project begins conceptually through sociological and historical research of the conditions of the conflict. Social impact describes NGPA as an orientation toward an "expansive audience," not necessarily a mass or popular audience, but certainly not toward a cultural or intellectual elite. The projects thus address first the participants. The planners and organizers seek to learn from each other and become involved in the lives of those affected by the particular conditions: in the case of *Border Rescue*, the migrants and the politicians. Each work of art here, as collective project, first creates a new form of community. They then address the "casual audience," bystanders who might become engaged in the art piece. These are not pieces performed for spectators; rather, they invite some form of direct engagement and participation. The third and final orientation is to the art community but in an attenuated relationship. With NGPA, the conception of interventionist social processes takes priority over the accomplishment of a marketable aesthetic product.[29] NGPA seeks to establish new modes of social organization rather than commodities or museum pieces.

Schlingensief's container installation and parody of reality TV offered inspiration to *Border Rescue*, although the latter does not rely on the kind of irony and satire at the core of Schlingensief's actionism. After the preparation of the videos and the development of the website, *Border Rescue* actually went public with a press conference in Linz on June 12, 2002. Schmutzhard announced the project and the intent of the group to undertake their research of the Austrian Czech border from June 14–21. The launching of the website was thus timed to coincide with the European Commission's conference on migration and asylum in Seville taking place at the same time. After the announcement, Social Impact then displayed the website as an interactive installation at the 23rd Ars Electronica Festival.

Border Rescue represented their most advanced new media piece at the time. *Border Rescue's* web presence begins with an animated flash intro. Text moves against a blurred background of hooded figures, presumably trying to sneak across the border. It forms a sort of animated collage, informing the spectator that between 1993 and 2003 at least 3,777 deaths have been recorded of individuals trying to cross the borders into Europe illegally. They question what number would identify the unrecorded deaths. The webpage that then opens up describes the project and its intentions. It offers an informational section under the link, "death list/facts." With these links, the site evidences its relation to net activist communities, treating the web as a vehicle for information dissemination and political community building. The quality of provocation in these images and statistics allows us to draw a connection here to both Dada and didactic agit-prop strategies in the historic avant-garde.

Most provocative, though, is the section entitled "Routes." Here the link opens up to an interactive map that shows the Upper Austrian border with the Czech Republic. The stated goal is to assist illegal migrants to enter Austria and the EU safely. Additionally, the page offers a sheet filled with tips about how to cross the border, what to wear, how to behave, and how to negotiate the authorities. On the map, eight yellow interactive dots mark points on the border that the Social Impact group researched. They crossed at these points multiple times using GPS devices, creating maps, and the videos of the crossing points. The yellow dots open up to the maps and videos so that a potential migrant can actually study the route, view the videos, and print out the maps.

Social Impact's provocation seeks confrontation with the political authorities. They deploy the visual apparatus against the state in this work. They draw politicians and police out onto the unfamiliar terrain of Culture in order to raise awareness about a social condition. This strategy proved provocative enough to the authorities that Schmutzhard received a subpoena from the Austrian Attorney General after the Bundeskriminalamt (BKA), their version of the FBI, cited Schmutzhard for trafficking. Moreover, then Austrian Chancellor Wolfgang Schüssel, while visiting the Ars Electronica Festival, had to respond to questions about *Border Rescue*. Art here infused life as a defense against inhuman institutions.

Focusing on the quality of the moving image, it is in conjunction with the text that the videos come to make sense. The maps contain a set of instructions that address the sequences of each video. The limitations of the new technology returned the visual language to earlier forms and these texts recall the text of the *monstrator* from the early days of cinema; indeed, the performance of the camera in general, the motion of the frame is one of *monstration*, an action of showing and revealing.[30] As then, the text here trains the viewer's perceptions and orients them vis-à-vis the images presented. This is a form of art intervention that is oriented toward a place of state control. In the neoliberal era of globalization, one of the primary functions of the state is the monitoring and regulation of the free flow of goods and the restricted flow of persons. The neoliberal state makes sure that the border is as porous to goods and services but as fine a filter as possible to people. Yet the camera of *Border Rescue* shows not only that such total control by the all-pervasive surveillance apparatus of the state is impossible. By revealing the topographically indistinct character of the border, the same camera also implicitly contests its significance as a marker of fundamental or essential difference.

It must be said that it is unlikely that the website did indeed assist anyone in crossing the border. It presumed a fluency in English and especially a level of net access that illegal immigrants were unlikely to have. The project clearly oriented its information to the Austrian public sphere. It constructed a media event to draw attention to conditions caused by the Austrian state. It incited Austrian citizens to inform themselves and encouraged them to see draconian and totalitarian police actions as ineffectual vis-à-vis the flow of people across the borders of the EU. And it did have an effect insofar as placing the question of border control squarely and noisily in the public sphere. But it also succeeded in surviving the legal threat that resulted from this public success, because the attorney general ultimately had to drop his charges against Schmutzhard.

The Interzone of Tendentious Art

It is clear that for the most part none of the collectives are concerned with the obsolescence of their projects. Kanak Attak's actionism or Schmutzhard's notion of New Genre Public Art, in their interventionist strategy, choice of media, and disregard for the commodifiable art form has little to do with the old genre of public art that dots the landscape and decorates the walls of institutions and urban environments. The focus on intervention in a specific historical moment through specific technological means, localizes events and limits their duration. The interventionist projects contain thus a built-in obsolescence, or a use-value that leaves little surplus. In the case of many of these projects as with *Border Rescue*, the websites were never intended as an object of contemplation, and the information they offered became dated. *Border Rescue* was passé at the moment that Social Impact ceased updating it. And two years later, in 2004 the eastern expansion of the EU displaced the conditions of the Austrian border that had compelled the art project. In the second decade of the new Millennium the Mediterranean became the primary border to cross for people seeking unsanctioned entry into Europe. And the EUROMED security measures discussed in the previous chapter have turned that border into a watery grave for many.

This built-in obsolescence of interventionist art recalls Marx's distinction of tendentious art (*Tendenzkunst*) *from* art with lasting human value.[31] Marx understood tendentious art as that type of art produced in the service of a political movement. Slogans, poems, pamphlets, posters, chants, were important for political activity, but after the event they lost their value. Although it does not make it impossible, the simple ephemeral quality of the internet as site of distribution and exhibition limits the realization of enduring qualities and pushes web-based art into the realm of tendentious art. But these projects are typically political *events* constituted through aesthetic means. In such tendentiousness, art ceases to become a simple aesthetic ancillary to politics; it is constitutive. This is a radical historical transformation of the role of the aesthetic. Far from confirming Benjamin's famous warning about the aestheticization of politics, projects like those organized by Social Impact rather politicize aesthetics, and precisely in doing so they enliven the public sphere and compel social debate. That art becomes "tendentious" in the process is to be expected, but it is not art in the service of political activity being carried out by a vanguard party; rather, tendentious art here itself creates the political issue or alters the parameters of the arena where it is debated.

Tendency/Autonomy/Event

Events are everywhere. Wherever one turns, one is afforded "a great event." Event planning represents a career choice and event management companies have formed to supply a market in need of full-service event organization. Such prominence of events is not limited to North America. *Eventkultur* has become a ubiquitous term in German. The potential participant-spectator is attracted with promise of an event, a great event, the greatest event. The event in this sense can designate a concert, a visit to the museum, a shopping experience. Event culture adds to the possibilities whereby individuals can fill their free time; moreover, it represents something greater than simple amusement. It offers an experience. Event, in this sense is akin to the German word, *Erlebnis*. The term is translated into English as *experience*, but an experience of the type that leaves a strong and lasting impression on a person: i.e., it was a grand, beautiful, impressive, exceptional experience. Indeed one can talk interchangeably of *Event-culture* or *Erlebniskultur*. This experience derives from the encountering of new situations and conditions—experience as a remarkable encounter with the unknown.

German, as is well known, distinguishes another form of experience, *Erfahrung*. That word for experience designates recognition and insight drawn from repeated observation: i.e., long years of experience taught her. It is an accomplishment rather than a process. This experience affects the subject because the subject derives knowledge from it. The contemporary event, however, relies on a form of uniqueness that does not lend itself to repeated observation. It is marketed as a one-time thing. The event in this sense would seem to withhold the potential for rational development, recognition, and insight afforded by

Erfahrung. Walter Benjamin famously identified *Erfahrung* as the dynamic of the avant-garde.[32] The accelerated pace of modernity offered experiences at such a rate that they ceased to affect the subject; nevertheless, avant-garde art, literature in particular, through its strategies of observation and narration presented the possibility of restoring a depth of *Erfahrung* to the events of modernity.[33] Benjamin would most likely ascribe to contemporary event culture a continued acceleration of the process he noted at the start of the last century.

Certainly, contemporary experiential culture as it is marketed lends itself to Frankfurt School inspired critique and not just because, in many forms, event culture actively seeks to open elite institutions of cultural production—museums, universities, even government offices—accomplishing a mass orientation and thereby undermining high cultural autonomy. It transforms art and its institutions, blurring borders between entertainment and education, art objects and commodity culture, museums and event spaces. For these reasons Peter Bürger rejected one of the central forms of art-as-event, the "happening," perceiving it as antithetical to autonomous art. This is why he lectured his contemporaries in the movements of the 1960s that he downgraded to neo–avant-garde:

> All art that is more recent than the historical avant-garde movements must come to terms with this fact in bourgeois society. It can either resign itself to its autonomous status or "organize happenings" to break through that status. But without surrendering its claim to truth, art cannot simply deny the autonomy status and pretend that it has a direct effect.[34]

Yet, we need to rethink the fundamental rejection of the Event that is evident here, and reflect more deeply on the experience it offers. For "the event" is in fact central to the history of the avant-garde. The Dadaists of Zurich bear significant responsibility for introducing the event as a site of culture; further to the left one can consider agit-prop as a form of mass-oriented interventionist event; and even further to the left one could consider the Soviet avant-garde's work as trying to link to the Russian Revolution as event. And while Benjamin may be correct that the nineteenth-century aestheticist elitism of Stefan George and Charles Baudelaire sought insulation from the growing mass culture, nevertheless their quest for an autonomous space of art descends from the salons of the eighteenth century and the quest for a (revolutionary) expansion of bourgeois influence. In the reverse, we can trace connections through postwar *Aktionismus*, happenings, and installation art of the 1960s and '70s, through 1980s performance art to the present. The event as art, it would seem, has a long avant-garde and revolutionary pedigree. The event as site of *Erlebnis* seems indeed to require an assaying of its positive and negative potentials.

Tangential to avant-garde aesthetics, philosophical considerations of the event in itself have a long history of their own tracing back to Aristotle's *Metaphysics*. In such considerations, the event is neither material thing nor substance but rather an occurrence in time. This occurrence brings substance and force together arranging them for a period. Considering time, the event holds qualities both of a punctual moment and a process or duration. For Heidegger, the event [*Ereignis*] is part of becoming [*das seiende*] or the process of formation in the right now. He discusses it as the happening whereby human and being are brought into agreement.[35] The event is an opening in time in which something is shown and can be interpreted. What makes an event such is that it is not stable or permanent but unfolding in time.

Derrida, in his early foundational essay "Signature Event Context," attended to this processable aspect, or how the event opens up new possibilities. In that essay the "event" is part of discourse. It is the contextualization of a sign that places quotation marks around it, but the event as context also compels an infinite web of intertextuality: "put between quotation marks . . . [the sign] can break with every given context and engender infinitely new contexts in an absolutely nonsaturable fashion."[36] The event, noted and cited, generates new events. Unlike in the case of Heidegger, the event here is such because it establishes the possibility of other events.

More recently, shortly before his death, Derrida in attending to the event returned to considerations of the subject akin to Heidegger's *Ereignis* as opening in time. In *Philosophy in a Time of Terror*, Habermas and Derrida considered how the event overtakes the subject. In the event the subject becomes aware of a lack of understanding; I am confronted with an awareness of something I do not understand. I am aware of it and aware of my lack of understanding.[37] The event in this sense is akin to the Kantian subject's confrontation with the sublime that momentarily rattles the bounds of subjectivity. In the event, as Derrida considers it, reason does not offer a restoration of comprehension to the subject, unlike the confrontation with the Kantian sublime.

We are left, therefore, with having to go back again to Aristotle as we seek to resolve this apparent tension between pleasure and reason in the experiencing of the event. In his *Metaphysics*, Aristotle distinguished between *Energia* and *Kinesis*, a distinction driven in effect by the consideration of the event and of particular interest to considerations of the moving image. *Energia* is expressed as part of a state of being, e.g., visiting a friend, reading a book, or watching a movie. *Kinesis*, that word denoting movement from which we draw our word *cinema*, describes a process that changes being. The kinetic transformation of the subject is an event that comes to an end upon the accomplishment of the goal. Historically, to watch a particular movie was like taking a trip from A to B; the kinetic event took place until the credits rolled or the passenger arrived in B. The kinetic event transforms the subject over time, until the goal of the event is accomplished. Events can have a purpose other than a reproduction of reified relations.

Janet Cardiff and Georges Bures Miller: Audiovisual Walking

Janet Cardiff (1957) and Georges Bures Miller (1960) are modern migrant artists, both born in Canada and now both living between Berlin and Gindrod in British Columbia. Both are installation artists who deploy sound and image in new ways and settings so that the received and commonplace of the cinematic apparatus is disrupted into new audiovisual experiences. They rely on technological innovation; yet, importantly for the argument here, they do not fetishize the new technology but rather explore the possibilities for new cognitive experiences and the new methods of signification it makes possible. Their work deploys new technologies to actualize kinesis, a transformation not just of the act of spectating but a transformation of the audience as such.

They began their collaborative work in the mid-1990s and quickly gained notoriety, leading to the award-winning work, *Paradise Institute*, at the Venice Biennale in 2001. The work took place in the traditional space of the black-box movie theater where they projected a film with quasigeneric qualities including mystery and sci-fi elements. But the cinema was a space in which perspective itself had been distorted so that although it held only sixteen seats, the spectators confronted an illusion that they were in the balcony row of a grand old cinema. Furthermore, along with the disruption of the visual and simultaneous to the screening, the spectators, wearing headphones, are exposed to an audio "disruption." In the audio experience the "audience" begins to move to the foreground of the experience. Broadcast as surround sound, the spectator experiences how the "audience's" cell phones ring, how a nonexistent companion asks if you've turned the stove off, and they hear banging noises from the "outside" of the "cinema." In the course of the film, the spectators in the sixteen-seat theater became incorporated into a real-life happening in which the images of the film and the experiences of the space come to meld together in new ways.

The use of sound to alter environments, the deployment of the audio to transform the visual, is part of the earliest practice in their work. In the 1990s, Cardiff and Bures Miller developed a series of audio walks in which individuals were guided through a space by a voice that interacted with the listener. Here, the voice changed the relationship to the surroundings. As would be deployed in *Paradise Institute*, these walks incorporated a prerecorded soundscape. The listener not only heard the voice but the footsteps of the companion and of passersby who were not there. Also, the listener heard sounds of nature that were not there, a nature that frequently belonged to a different season than the one of the moment of listening such that the sounds could not be there. Meanwhile the "real" ambient sounds of the people and world about were clouded out and dulled by the headphones and the recording itself.

In 2005, Cardiff and Bures Miller premiered a new piece, *Ghost Machine*, as a site-specific piece for the Hebbel am Ufer Theater (HAU 1) in Berlin. This piece drew together the principles of the earlier projects. It was inspired after Matthias Lilienthal, the artistic director and manager of the theater recognized a strong similarity between the space imagined in *Paradise Institute* and the real space of the restored *Jugendstil* HAU 1. For its premier in 2005, Cardiff and Bures Miller relied on the view screens of digital cameras in which a prerecorded audiovideo walk played back. For a new installation of the work in 2010 they transferred the piece to new ipad technology.

The spectator receives a playback device, camera or ipad, and a headset. In regular intervals, the audience to the piece is allowed to begin the guided walk. As individuals, they walk at a set pace through the corridors and stages of HAU 1, guided by the voice in the headset. This spacing allows for a situation in which the audience consists of singular individuals moving collectively through the rooms and stages, halls and back corridors of the theater, crossing each other's paths but caught up in their own moment within the story. The walk begins with the voice saying, "I'd like you to walk with me. . . . Swivel the camera in this direction, follow the picture so that we can stay together." This is a moment of technological direction that establishes the spectating scenario for the walk and binds the participant in the project's timescape. It is also a moment that again recalls the earliest days of the moving image and the work of the monstrator. It appears that each new technological invention returns to and restores, if only briefly, some of the aspects of all the technological past as if in the transformations of the avant-garde a technological ontogeny must recapitulate aesthetic phylogeny.

The participant-spectators have an image that parallels the material space in which they move. The recording was done in that space. It is edited but yet appears to the spectator-walker as one long take on the screen. But it is an *audio*visual experience and the audio component for the film was recorded using a Kunstkopfmikrofon, a microphone developed for the RIAS, the radio broadcast of the American Armed Forces in Berlin. The device allowed for in effect a 3D spatial experience, a surround sound long before Dolby. The soundscape then contains not just the voice but the noise of a plastic sheeting that was on the floor of a room under renovation—a sheeting no longer there in the moment of the particular audience member. People walk by in the recording, talking and filling the space now empty; or vice versa, the spectator moves past people who are not in the recording. There is a mystery playing through the walk; the voice describes a visit in the past to see a man in his apartment. The past of the recording is thereby given a further past so that the audience member moves not just in a present time but in two layers of added past time, the past present of recording and a "*plusquam*-past" of the recording itself. This past has a mystery, even murder mystery, quality to it, bringing in a level of generic story to the directing voice. The voice combines narration and monstration.

The *Alter Bahnhof Video Walk* takes the principle of *plusquam*-past and intensifies it via the local specificity of the piece. This walk was prepared for the 13th Documenta and on display in 2012 in the old train station of Kassel, also known as the Kulturbahnhof/Cultural Train Station.[38] This cultural center plays a multiuse role in Kassel as both a spot of transportation and as venue for the recurring *documenta*. Here, the history of the train station becomes a part of the walk in which the memory of the space, in the Third Reich comes to play a role. The voice takes us on a walk through the space, passing first through a musical performance that has a certain surreal quality to it, appearing out of nowhere as a certain interruption in the reality of the moment. But then, taking a corner, the spectator passes a man discussing the bombing of Kassel and the carnage of incendiary bombs. The work then moves the audience to Horst Hoheisel's *Thought/Stone/Collection*, a permanent work in the train station that commemorates the deported Jews who left from the station's track 13, most of them to their death in Nazi concentration camps. The progress of the walk eventually moves to track 13 before returning along the same route and into new spaces of the station. The voice reflects on various questions of spectating, drawing on ideas from Plato's cave metaphor. At one time, the screen shows us an image of the voice; she identifies a figure as herself on a visit in the past. At another time, the voice leads the audience to a spot from which they look down at the participants who are at that moment being initiated into the project and who themselves are being told to look up. The audience becomes incorporated here and in effect sees itself, positioned in its own past spectating. Here, then, the past has added layers, that of the distant historical past, that of the past to the narrative, that of the recording moment, and that of the audience itself.

In these pieces, the images do not mimic the human eye, moving about with speed; rather, they are recorded cinematically, slowly relying, in effect, on a new form of continuity editing. Whereas in classical cinema, continuity editing was developed to foster a sense of illusion for the spectator, a set of conventions that left the spectators feeling that they were in the room; here, the continuity editing is deployed to establish an intimate relationship to multiple levels of space and time. The image here is not mummified; rather, it is released and activated in the present. The environment, the space of the recording, remains the same space as the experience. The recording even draws in shifts, noting that renovations are done or that garbage cans have moved, thereby alluding to a future of its own moment, the present of the spectator.

Even if it is scripted, each time it is called forth, it is set in new experiences. The *noeme* "that has been" ascribed to the photograph is sublated here into a clear "that is now." In the end of *Alter Bahnhof* the audience arrives in the large entry hall and observes a dance piece on the screen that was recorded in that space. Here the layers come together so that the performance located in a past moment is no longer past. It lasts long enough that a number of audience members gather in that space, each watching the performance from a unique position and each also able, as they observe the space of the moment, to observe each other as well. The experience of the black box, being seated and fixed in a particular point in a dark room, is transformed here into a collective individual experience, mobile and infused with a new set of subjective experiences.

Even if these walks are patterned so that they pass through the same space, each audience member takes up that path each time in a particular way, passing through that space in a particular network of associations. The image, then, is like a memory, transformed and renewed by each act of remembering. Memories are not static qualities frozen, mummified in the past, *punctum* that have the potential to sting in the present; they are active events, each transformed by the repetition, no repetition ever the same.

Returning us to the considerations of the avant-garde, Bürger developed his rejection of the event as happening out of a flawed understanding of revolution and the revolutionary claims of the avant-garde manifestos. Bürger took at face value the claims found there that the avant-garde would infuse life with art, breaking its autonomous status. Because the historic avant-garde could not accomplish this radical transformation of life, Bürger deemed the project failed. Yet it was forgotten that art cannot be more revolutionary than the era in which it exists. Artists can revolutionize their form and strategies of production, but art cannot accomplish a revolution that is social in character. This recognition need not mean that the avant-garde project is over, especially if we understand it as adaptive and imaginative. As the ongoing reification of lifeworlds expands globally, the avant-garde continues to be driven by an underlying ambition to offer humanity a world of dreams that surpass or at least respond to reification. The shape of autonomy, the form of intervention, the stuff of the dreams may have changed, but the avant-garde continues. My argument here is that this is so precisely because art's revolutionary potential resides in its ability to constitute *events* in an interzone, opening up socially transformative potentials.

To be sure, art can never be more revolutionary than the era in which it exists. No film or painting can replace human activity. No poem or video installation can transcend a collectively determined alienation. However, art that pushes at the limits of representation, that draws on possibilities afforded by new technologies, art that calls new forms of signification into being, such art performs freedom—as long as we recognize that freedom is neither a condition nor even a right. Rather, it is an experience apprehended in actions of liberation. Art is the means whereby in totally administered conditions we catch a glimpse of other possibilities. In reified conditions that foment suspicion and anxiety, the work of art can facilitate a recognition of our mutual interdependence. Instead of fear and existential *Geworfenheit*, individual abandonment in a hostile world, we can move out onto a new terrain, an interzone where we may find our greatest resource in each other.

Conclusion

It is a point of consideration, in the current moment when transnationalism as a term is very *en vogue*, how odd it is that the majority of research on culture that invokes the term transpires nevertheless within rather rigid national parameters. Studies of "transnational" German, Japanese, or Brazilian literatures or cinemas create for themselves a conundrum that cannot be properly studied within their own parameters: if it is transnational, it cannot be assessed within national parameters. Therefore, this book has been all over the place, and that is the point.

To recognize the relationship of the cinematic apparatus to the social configuration unfolding in Europe and beyond currently, the study has necessitated a broad comparative and historical approach. At the same time, to invoke the term *transnational* here is itself misleading. This study set out to correct and revise my own research on transnationalism by rejecting the neo-Hegelian assumption that informs much of the work on transnationalism in Europe.

Overcoming the Neo-Hegelian Impasse

Hegel's model of consciousness (*Geist*) developed from the individual in the family unit through concentric circles expanding dialectically outward, to the local, regional, and national. This model of *Geist* haunts the understanding of European transnationalism in which it is generally assumed that Europe, or

European identification, is the next in the expanded circles of political cultural unity and that Europe is the sublation of the nation-state into some greater union. This model of thinking presumes an entity Europe that stands as a union above the locales, regions, and nations of Europe.

Jürgen Habermas, for instance, advocated for a constitutional legitimation process in order to accomplish a European public sphere. Habermas sees transnational communication as the key here because precisely new forms of communication fostered the emergence of the first modern form of social integration: the nation. He does note that the nation was once an artificial form of civic solidarity, and hence the current artificiality of the transnational need not be taken as a sign of the impossibility of transnational union. He is careful to acknowledge that the new European public sphere need not be a replication of the national onto the European, yet precisely in that opposition, national/European, he evidences the neo-Hegelian perspective. He advocates, then, for higher order supranational political bodies legitimated through a constitution and democratic procedure as well as a new, albeit multilingual, public sphere of debate and consensus building, of civic solidarity that over time would cease to be artificial and become key to a truly European culture.

Habermas's model points upward and outward. Habermas's model of *Öffentlichkeit* was always an idealist proposition that had some material form in bourgeois coffeehouse culture of the Enlightenment. Retaining that model now ignores the reality of the EU: that the political, economic, and cultural union has developed its own form through systems of subsidiarity, harmonization, synergy, and so forth. This study has not shied away from the terms *public sphere* or *civil society*, but it has sought to attend to the public sphere as it now emerges and even does exist in Europe. In this dynamic, the nature of solidarity, association, communication does not flow upward and outward from key nations and linguistic communities to a meta and European level. Communication is diffused and dispersed in multiple directions, drawing together interlocutors with varying interests, in locations that need not be proximate. In fact, it is frequently the case that communication across space and in compressed time is easier in this new Europe than communication with the most immediate neighbor—who may simply not be "at home." European solidarity does not develop upward and outward but across, through, from below, sideways, crisscrossing terrains, potentially via urban centers, and equally likely via regional resistance to metropolitan control.

The interzone describes both the moments in which such communication begins and the fact that a move to union, i.e., an emergence of new forms of solidarity, is indeed often "artificial," hesitant, and tentative. Imaginative communities develop now more frequently not as metacommunities but as subcultures, micropolitical associations, ethnic migrant identities, midlevel economic partnering, sexual communities, and other "lower order" distinctive societies. Europe develops not through grand schemes of social and cultural reconciliation, as once took place in the development of national solidarities out of the spirit of regional and ethnic conflict. Europe develops in smaller forms of conciliation, alignment, and approximation. It develops more through a network of cheap seat flights across the continent that convey party youth, traveling businessmen, and migrant laborers than it does through quests for a constitution. It develops more through audiovisual production than it does through uninspiring lists of bureaucratic decisions that are generated out of Brussels. Cinema, this study has argued—that is, the moving image in its transforming forms, or better stated, the audiovisual apparatus—plays a key role in generating the interzones on which the imaginative communities of the new Europe meet themselves for the first time.

The neo-Hegelianism in this approach takes on the form of a *political idealism*. There is another form we might describe as a *cultural idealism*, more attentive to questions of values and culture. Political idealism as with Habermas represents a proscriptive approach in which certain standards of political organization are set as criteria with which to assess critically the progress toward particular goals, particularly a liberal democratic bias. The approach based on cultural idealism, on the other hand, is ascriptive, based on making a distinction between Europe and the European Union, where the former is the cultural ideal of the latter. Here, Europe becomes a matter of ethics in the same way that Hegel defined *Sittlichkeit*, mores, as foundation of the national community. Cultural idealism presumes that there is an integrity to European culture that precedes union. It follows a logic along the lines of Willy Brandt's famous quote from the point of German unification: "now what belongs together will grow together."

It might surprise if I suggest that Jacques Derrida serves as an emblematic representative of this trend. In his final discussions of Europe, Derrida developed a values approach to Europe. In his political writings, especially *The Other Heading*, Derrida came to identify a *devoir*, a duty and a possibility of Europeanness, in that Europeans must be hospitable to that which never will be European.[1] Derrida defines Europeans, then, as a people who welcome their others. To be sure, this is a positive definition that appears at first to be based in action and not essence; hospitality is good and we all applaud the actions of those who give food to the hungry and drink to the thirsty, who welcome strangers and give them rest.

Yet this particular quality, hospitality, which is defining of Europe for Derrida cannot actually be understood as either inherent or exclusive to Europe. In an interesting essay on this matter, Serhan Mersin and Pinar Yıldız have sought to sidestep the Eurocentrism of Derrida's understanding of hospitality.[2] Such a gesture is itself generous and even hospitable but unnecessary and perhaps counterproductive. It is important to recognize that hospitality is an action available to all and not defined by territory or bound to a particular space. But to ascribe it as Derrida does as proper to Europe, a quality of Europeanness, problematically establishes a nonspace akin to Adelson's considerations of in-betweenness.[3] Europe is hospitable to that which is not European::that which is not European is not hospitable::the outside of Europe is an unneighborly, unsociable space. Europe is hospitable and the non-European is therefore hostile.

Furthermore, in defining a particular class of people as the hospitable ones, this value of hospitality retains for the class of the hospitable a right permanently to be host. Through hospitality, that group thereby claims a permanent ability as a group to say to an Other, you have entered as a stranger onto "our" shores. This value of European hospitality may have been imagined in relationship to a group of asylum seekers coming to the shores of Europe. It may imagine the Europeans as more welcoming of the asylum seeker than King Thoas was of Orestes. Whether Derrida was calling for such a stance of welcome or believed it as already characteristic of European asylum laws will remain unexamined here. About European asylum laws, I refer back to the discussion in Chapter 5 of the policy transformation that took place in the EUROMED program after September 11, 2001. This law has turned people into uncounted unnamed masses, turned them out into the desert without provisions, and watched from a distance as they called for help from sinking boats in the Mediterranean.

Here, I would point to how the distinction of hospitality that appeared as a positive attribute, the propriety of Europeans, actually affronts truly those who are not strangers at all. Derrida grants his Europeans a *devoir* to extend hospitality to those who, in effect, have been living and working for generations and generations in European metropoles and European colonies; who were educated in European schools; and who speak, read, and write in European tongues. If these people are still strangers to whom one extends hospitality, it is only because they are imagined not to subscribe to something called "European values." If they are still strangers, then hospitality to them, which is all they are going to get, becomes a defining privilege, which only those who are imagined to belong already to Europe may extend.

Neither of these approaches, proscriptive or ascriptive, offers mechanisms to apprehend the material, political, or cultural potentials of Europeanization. They proscribe how such should be or ascribe how such is to an ideal type, arriving at a form of exclusionary essentialism. To consider the interzone, by contrast, allows us to move away from the neo-Hegelian impasse that lies behind proscriptive and ascriptive approaches. That is because the analysis of the interzone does not begin from a hierarchical structure or a priori propositions of categories. Belonging is not a matter of essential connections made on the ground of European identity. If there is any ideational component to European union, that component derives from the imagining of community. Nothing belongs together or everything potentially does; only the ability to imagine community limits belonging. The analysis of the interzone begins not from what should be linked but from the assumption that we live in a culture of linkages. The analysis of the interzone seeks to recognize the emergence of particular material conditions that result in new realities—out of which general descriptions and overarching concepts may or may not result.

Germany, Poland, Turkey

The examples of this study have come primarily from three countries: Germany, Poland, and Turkey. These three countries reveal interzonal processes, potentials, and limitations. Exploring their histories revealed their role in the projects of imperial modernization and postimperial nation-building. Considering their contemporary form revealed how they are caught up in second modernity transformations of political, economic, and cultural boundaries. All three play important roles within the contemporary processes of Europeanization.

Germany is the political and cultural space in which the knots of modernity have been frequently tied, cut, and retied. The end of World War II compelled many people, among them many Germans, to seek to unravel some of those knots. The move toward European union arose initially out of the postwar desire to contain Germany. The modern European idea has come indeed to contain Germany. Germany is the motor of Europe. German unification in 1990 was important for Germany *and* Europe, a reconciliation of divisions and conclusion to past conflicts: 1990 was a union that resolved the legacies of the past; 1992 was a union of the future, setting forward processes that are still unfolding.

If Germany is the motor of Europe, Poland is its heart. For centuries, the Polish idea sustained a sense of community in the absence of an autonomous apparatus of governance. For centuries, Polish communal imagining looked past occupying forces toward an ideal of Europe as a space of emancipation. And indeed the restoration of Polish autonomy was a triumph of European civility. The two-plus-four agreement that regulated the union of Germany was predicated on the possibility of accord between Germany and Poland and their union eventually in Europe.

Turkey is in a space at the borders of the EU. The Ottoman Empire and the Turkish State were historically understood as part of Europe. The discourse of a people as bridge between Europe and Asia, which is oriented toward contemporary Turks, once actually identified the ethnic Germans whose settlements reached out past the borders of the Prussian and Austrian Empires down into the Ottoman and out into the Russian. The Danube-Swabians, the Banat Germans, the Black Sea Germans, and, of course, the Volga Germans bore the function of establishing an ethnic interzone. In the nineteenth and early twentieth centuries, Turkish-German designated settlers in Macedonia and West Anatolia.[4] This bridge function is now inverted. Turkey is the limit of the EU. If Turkey is in a space at the borders of the EU, nevertheless the Turkish population is intimately interconnected with the European collectivity. Turkey has been a migrant-sending country primarily to Europe. Germany has the largest number of Turkish residents outside Turkey. This migrant population has a special status because Turkey, unlike the countries of origin of most of Europe's migrants, is moving toward admission to the EU. If Turkey joins the EU, it would transform dramatically the political status and social conditions of the German Turks. As an applicant country, the resolution of the status of Turkey would result in a further transformation of the European ideal. This historical transformation and the contemporary potential of Turkey generate multiple interzones.

State Apparatus and Cinematic Apparatus

The varying relationships—Germany, Poland, and Turkey—rely on the production and reproduction of imaginative communities. The central portion of this study has focused on the varying, aligning, and competing roles of state and cinematic apparatus in producing and reproducing the imaginative communities. Key to that discussion has been a reinvigoration of apparatus theory. Those already engaged with the history of apparatus theory may have been surprised that Louis Althusser has not played much of a role to this point. Althusser's ideological state apparatus (ISA) was an intellectual dead end with negative consequences for apparatus theory. In that work, the state took on a vague and ill-defined form. The state had neither capitalist nor communist, democratic nor totalitarian form. And further in his distinction of repressive and ideological state apparatus, only the former had specific institutional form (religion, schools, the family, and so forth). The latter, the ISA, became all-encompassing. If in his earlier work he had drawn the historic Marxist distinction between scientific knowledge and ideology, in his work on the ISA, ideology became all-encompassing, synonymous with the unconscious. Althusser literally transposed Freud's language that the unconscious is eternal onto ideology: ideology is eternal. He further transposed Lacan's understanding of the psyche onto the discussion of ideology: "Ideology represents the imaginary relationship of individuals to their real conditions of existence."[5] The discussion allowed for no outside. Although he was open to a history of particular ideologies, ideology became transhistorical in this analysis.

Contradictions and deficiencies arise immediately. Where there is no outside, the very ability to describe ideology would be impossible. If we accept as true that Althusser could describe a function called "ideology," this meant, in effect, that one could achieve an insight that was itself not ideological. Suggesting that all cats are gray in the dark does not allow for distinctions between and among cats, and similarly suggesting that we are all immersed in an ideological fog necessarily eviscerates the activity of philosophical theoretical investigation. Fundamentally, where ideology is everywhere, always, and everything, it is unfortunately nothing. It can describe nothing except the state of being in a fog.

For cinematic apparatus theory, especially as formulated by Jean-Louis Baudry, the problem of ideology as the representation of imaginary relationships to real conditions forms a key impasse in the further development. The spectator, like the citizen individual, is trapped in imaginary relationships. The representations of cinema, the illusory world of the moving image, stand in for the inability of the individual to view *real* conditions directly. Theorists of apparatus theory fell into a deeply skeptical position vis-à-vis the very object they were studying. They become infused with a quasipuritanical fear of cinematic pleasures and pleasure in general. For many of them the hope of an outside to the imaginary relationship created by ideology arose out of adopting a counter-cinematic antipleasure posture. The hope for a recognition of the real conditions of existence is placed in images that offer no enjoyment. It was a bleak worldview that understood the real material world as one without enjoyment. It was an impossible project for the nascent discipline of film studies that immediately positioned the object to be studied as a degraded object.

The potential of apparatus theory arises when we begin to look for the gaps and ruptures in an apparatus or the way that apparatuses align and distinguish themselves. Reconsidering the state apparatus, we can note a difference in state forms. Even if we accept a dominance of state regulation, we can note a difference in modes of governance that also entail nonstate forms. We can note that individuals may live in a state but only on specific occasions experience that condition and otherwise consider their lives distinct from, and even in opposition to, a state form. Various state apparatuses do indeed contend with these gaps, but with varying levels of success. Likewise, we can consider that the apparatuses of production—whether cultural, material, physical, mental, or so forth—may align themselves with the state apparatus or resist that apparatus as a fetter on production. In this study, paradigmatic for this conflict has been the way that film not only can draw together audiences but the way that production costs continually compel film production to aim at the broadest audience potential, to seek new audiences, new forms of spectator experience, new combinations of interests. This quest pushes the cinematic apparatus up against the state apparatus as a fetter. Certainly, at various times Hollywood production has served as advocate of the United States, especially providing propaganda for war efforts. French cinema benefits from important trade barriers that make the French market a safe haven for an indigenous production. Yet Hollywood has become largely synonymous with production that seeks global interest; it establishes world markets for the moving image, it breaks down national barriers flooding media systems with its products, and this Hollywood mode of production cannot be directly aligned with the U.S. state apparatus in any easy way. Moreover, French cinema does not designate any mode of production that is inherently counter-cinematic oppositional to Hollywood or a model form of alternative production. Indeed, there is nothing about the French cinematic apparatus that should lead us to believe that in an inverted situation, the French film producers would refrain from seeking to attract world interest and dominating global audiovisual markets. An exploration of Chinese cinema is beyond the scope of this conclusion, but it is clear that the confrontation of the Chinese state and cinematic apparatuses is an example of these potentials in the clearest form in the contemporary moment.

Rather than hold the objects of film studies in contempt or fear the pleasures they afford, we can approach them as artifacts of labor, products of real material relations organized in contradictory and competing apparatuses. We can shed old models of ideology that held individuals as trapped in imaginary relationships. The cinematic apparatus can be understood as an apparatus that produces imaginative communities. *In the productions of imaginative representation, individuals enter into a relationship with their real conditions of existence. This relationship is not ideological but one of the primary means whereby individuals engage with the systems of production and reproduction that organize human society.*

The exploration of the European cinematic apparatus was undertaken here not just with the goals of reinvigorating apparatus theory but also to reveal a unique quality of contemporary European film production. The flexibility of the European apparatus to reach beyond the borders of the EU and organize the production of cinema on a global basis develops according to a model that serves as alternative to the Hollywood cinematic apparatus. The European cinematic apparatus develops via a weak alignment of state and cinematic apparatus. Indeed, the condition here is one in which the apparatus of governance is organized according to principles of synergy, harmonization, subsidiarity, and so forth, which align the local, regional, national, and transnational. This form of weak governance does not require state ideological production from the cinematic apparatus. There are no films that heroicize Brussels or celebrate the bureaucratic "victories" of Jean Monnet and Robert Schuman.[6]

What it does require is an uneasy distinction from the representations that appear on the screen between an inside and outside of the EU, inside and outside to Europe. In spite of the fact that the European cinematic apparatus collects and bundles, and synergizes and harmonizes local, regional, and national means of production into a common mode across the globe, that cinematic apparatus retains a national non-European appearance for productions "outside." The European cinematic apparatus produces films from Bavaria, Flanders, Portugal, France, Germany, Ghana, Columbia, Turkey, North Africa, and Scandinavia, equally. Yet the films "of" Peru, Paraguay, and Pakistan circulate differently within that apparatus than the films of Portugal. The European cinematic apparatus organizes world production but in a condition of differentials that establish a difference of inside and outside to a European space.

The cinematic apparatus organizes production yet restricts the appearance of that apparatus. This point is essential for the revision of apparatus theory. There is no means whereby we can identify a clear determination of the moving image by the means of production short of clear instances of ideological state censorship, especially of the kind that was common in the old East Block. Yet this does not mean that the imaginary relationships, the imaginative communities produced within the cinematic apparatus must necessarily entrap spectators in a condition divorced from real material conditions. This study itself proves that we have the ability to explore the complexity of the apparatus and reveal exactly the moments of contradiction. It proves that we have the ability to distinguish between imaginary representations and real conditions, and that we know how also to use our apparatus of representation to produce new forms of real human community. The process to that community takes place via interzones.

Notes

Introduction. The Idea of Bridges and the Image of Roads: Culture and Space

1. Adelson, "Against Between"; Adelson, *Turkish Turn*.
2. Beck, *What Is Globalization*, 67.
3. You are weary at last of this ancient world
   Shepherdess O Eiffel tower whose flock of bridges bleats at the morning
   You have lived long enough with Greek and Roman antiquity
   Here even automobiles look old
   Only religion stays news religion
   As simple as hangars at the airfield
   Alone in Europe you Christianity are not antique
   The one modern European is you Pope Pius X
   And you whom windows watch what shame keeps you
   From entering a church and confessing your sins this morning
   Handbills catalogues advertisements that sing overhead
   Furnish your morning's poetry for prose there are newspapers
   Dime detective novels packed with adventure
   Biographies of great men a thousand and one titles
   This morning I saw a fine street whose name slips my mind.
   [. . .]
   Apollinaire, *Alcools*, 2.
4. Jauss, "1912," 39.

5. Berry and Epstein, *Transcultural Experiments*, 225.
6. Bakhtin, *Dialogic Imagination*, 345.
7. Pratt, *Imperial Eyes*, 6.
8. Ibid.
9. Petty, *Contact Zones*, 1.
10. Ong, *Flexible Citizenship*, 7.
11. Burroughs, *Interzone*.
12. See, for example, Tarrow, *New Transnational Activism*; Radhakrishnan, "Between Living or Telling"; Jameson, *Geopolitical Aesthetic*; Verdery, "Transnationalism, Nationalism, Citizenship, and Property."
13. Sbragia, *Euro-politics*; Marks et al., *Governance in the European Union*; Leibfried, Pierson, and Streeck, *Standort Europa*.
14. Sieg, *Choreographing the Global*.
15. Higson and Maltby, *"Film Europe" and "Film America."*
16. Everett, *European Identity in Cinema*; Forbes and Street, *European Cinema*; Ezra, *European Cinema*; Wood, *Contemporary European Cinema*.
17. Wayne, *Politics of Contemporary European Cinema*.
18. Jäckel, *European Film Industries*.
19. Betz, "Name above the (sub)Title."
20. Betz, *Beyond the Subtitle*.
21. Galt and Schoonover, *Global Art Cinema*.
22. Sieg, *Choreographing the Global*.
23. Everett and Goodbody, *Revisiting Space*; Barber, *Projected Cities*; Konstantarakos, *Spaces in European Cinema*.
24. Halle, *German Film after Germany*.
25. Paterson, "European Policy-making."
26. Katzenstein, *Tamed Power*, 33.
27. Sbragia, *Euro-politics*, 4.
28. Galt, *New European Cinema*.
29. His first film, *Berlin Is in Germany* (2001), chronicled the life of an ex-con who spent the decade of the 1990s in prison. Upon his release, he entered into a post–Wall world in which the state into which he had been born no longer exists and the foundation of his world is radically altered.

Chapter 1. The Film Apparatus

1. Lauretis and Heath, *Cinematic Apparatus*; Rosen, *Narrative, Apparatus, Ideology*.
2. Initial inspiration came from the work in *For Marx*, but as the discussions continued, debates followed Althusser's own developments in the consideration of ideology, especially ideological state apparatuses. See Althusser, *For Marx*; Althusser, *Lenin and Philosophy, and Other Essays*.
3. Bordwell and Carroll, *Post-theory*.
4. Comolli, "Machines of the Visible."

5. Ibid., 121.

6. Halle, *Queer Social Philosophy*.

7. All statistics are taken from Council of Europe, *European Audiovisual Observatory*.

8. Green and Paterson, *Governance in Contemporary Germany*; Paterson, "European Policy-making"; Katzenstein, *Tamed Power*.

9. Sbragia, *Euro-politics*; Marks et al., *Governance in the European Union*; Leibfried, Pierson, and Streeck, *Standort Europa*; Katzenstein, *Tamed Power*.

10. Terms of the character test are at www.kulturstaatsminister.de and www.ffa.de (accessed October 15, 2013).

11. "Red Carpet for International Film Productions," 6.

12. Agamben, *"What Is an Apparatus?" and Other Essays*.

13. Foucault, "Confessions of the Flesh."

14. Agamben, *"What Is an Apparatus?" and Other Essays*, 2.

15. Ibid., 14.

16. Ibid., 13.

17. Ibid., 14.

18. Riesinger, *Der kinematographische Apparat*.

19. Stemmrich, *Kunst/Kino*.

20. Tinsobin, *Das Kino als Apparat*.

21. Zielinski, *Variantology*; Zielinski, *Audiovisionen*; Matzker and Zielinski, *Fiktion als Fakt*; Kittler, *Optische Medien*; Kittler, *Grammophon, Film, Typewriter*; Kittler and Ofak, *Medien vor den Medien*.

22. Friedberg, *Virtual Window*.

23. Winkler, *Diskursökonomie*; Winkler, *Der filmische Raum und der Zuschauer*.

24. Comolli, "Machines of the Visible," 121.

25. Closs, Lange, and Westcott, *Public Funding for Film*.

26. Berghahn, *Hollywood Behind the Wall*.

27. Wayne, *Politics of Contemporary European Cinema*.

28. Imre, *Identity Games*; Skrodzka, *Magic Realist Cinema*.

29. Kornatowska, "Polish Cinema"; Haltof, "Fistful of Dollars"; Halle, *German Film after Germany*.

30. Halle, "'Happy Ends' to Crises of Heterosexual Desire."

31. Iordanova, *Cinema of the Other Europe*, 27.

32. Sosnowski, "Cinema in Transition," 12.

33. Kornatowska, "Polish Cinema," 47.

34. Jäckel, "Cooperation between East and West in Europe," 56.

35. Iordanova, *Cinema of the Other Europe*, 160.

Chapter 2. Interzone History

1. Jäckel, *European Film Industries*; Jäckel, "Cooperation between East and West in Europe"; Jäckel, "Inter/Nationalism of French Film Policy"; Jäckel, "Film Policy and Practice"; Everett, *European Identity in Cinema*; Everett and Wagstaff, *Cultures of Exile*.

2. Betz, *Beyond the Subtitle*.

3. Bergfelder, *International Adventures*; Bergfelder, Harris, and Street, *Film Architecture and the Transnational Imagination*; Bergfelder, "Exotic Thrills and Bedroom Manuals"; Bergfelder, "Nation Vanishes."

4. Higson and Maltby, *"Film Europe" and "Film America."*

5. http://ec.europa.eu/avpolicy/docs/reg/tvwf/eu_works/bilateral_coprod.pdf (accessed October 15, 2013).

6. Bamyeh, *Ends of Globalization*.

7. Tilse, *Transnationalism in the Prussian East*.

8. Thum, *Traumland Osten*; Thum, *Die fremde Stadt*; Sammartino, *The Impossible Border*; Bartov and Weitz, *Shatterzone of Empires*.

9. Vitali and Willemen, *Theorising National Cinema*.

10. Abel, Bertellini, and King, *Early Cinema and the "National."*

11. Gunning, "Early Cinema as Global Cinema," 11.

12. Abel, *Red Rooster Scare*.

13. Musser, "At the Beginning," 25.

14. Castan, *Max Skladanowsky*; Althen, "Ein Jahrmarktskind"; Elsaesser and Wedel, *Kino der Kaiserzeit*.

15. Fürstenau, *Max Skladanowsky*; Castan, *Max Skladanowsky*; Narath, *Max Skladanowsky*; Althen, "Ein Jahrmarktskind"; Barber, "Skladanowsky Brothers."

16. Castan, *Max Skladanowsky*, 20.

17. Haltof, *Polish National Cinema*, 1.

18. Skaff, *Law of the Looking Glass*, 63.

19. Skaff, *Law of the Looking Glass*, "Early Cinema and 'the Polish Question.'"

20. Haltof, *Polish National Cinema*, 4.

21. Condee, *Imperial Trace*.

22. Pommerin and Uhlmann, *Quellen zu den Deutsch-polnischen Beziehungen*.

23. The Deutscher Ostmarkenverein [German Society of the Eastern Marches] founded in 1894 in Posen took as its stated goal the fostering of *Deutschtum*, quickly developing into a movement to undermine *Polentum*. As a cultural propagandistic movement, the German Society deployed all methods of new media including regular film screenings. These efforts, however, had limited success in Germanifying the Polish majority population. Grabowski, *Deutscher und polnischer Nationalismus*, 6.

24. Elsaesser and Wedel, *Second Life*.

25. Hendrykowska and Hendrykowski, *Film w Poznaniu*.

26. Ibid., 37.

27. Ibid., 64.

28. Evren, *Sigmund Weinberg*; Erdoğan and Göktürk, "Turkish Cinema"; Evren, *Türk Sineması*.

29. Arslan, *Cinema in Turkey*, 33.

30. Ibid., 37.

31. Ibid., 44.

32. Ibid., 48.
33. Loiperdinger, "Kaiser's Cinema."
34. Balan, "Wondrous Pictures in Istanbul," 173.
35. Özön, *Karagözden sinemaya*; Özön, *Türk Sinema Tarihi.*
36. Evren, *Sigmund Weinberg.*
37. Arslan, *Cinema in Turkey*, 25.
38. Balan, "Wondrous Pictures in Istanbul," 182.
39. Evren, *Türk Sineması*; Özön, *Türk Sinema Tarihi.*
40. Balan, "Wondrous Pictures in Istanbul," 183.
41. Sammartino, *The Impossible Border.*
42. Yıldız, *Beyond the Mother Tongue.*
43. Wahl, "Babel's Business"; Wahl, *Sprachversionsfilme Aus Babelsberg*; Wahl, "Tonfilmfrieden/Tonfilmkrieg"; Wahl, *Das Sprechen des Spielfilms.*
44. Higson, "Cultural Policy and Industrial Practice," 118.
45. Quaresima, "Mehrsprachenversion/Dubbing?" 24.
46. Garncarz, "Emergence of Nationally Specific Film Cultures"; Higson and Maltby, *"Film Europe" and "Film America"*; Houcken, *International Feature Film Industry.*
47. Klimes and Zeman, "Aktualita."
48. Votruba, "Historical and National Background."
49. Szczepanik, "'Tief in Einem Deutschen Einflussbereich,'" 91.
50. Nancy Condee makes a convincing argument that the imperial condition continued to inflect Soviet and Russian cinemas to this day. See *The Imperial Trace.*
51. Quaresima, "Mehrsprachenversion/Dubbing?"
52. *A Declaration of Interdependence.*

Chapter 3. Contiguous

1. Kuszewski, *Zeitgenössischer Polnischer Film*, 8.
2. Ibid., 42.
3. Coates, *Cinema, Religion, and the Romantic Legacy*, 175ff.
4. Thum, "Mystische Landschaften," 207.
5. King, "Placing Grün Ist Die Heide (1951)."
6. Sosnowski, "Cinema in Transition," 12.
7. Kornatowska, "Polish Cinema," 47.
8. This coproduction number is actually less than the percentage of Poland's neighbor Germany, but the overall production is higher: e.g., 161 films in 2007 of which 87 were coproductions.
9. Haltof, "Fistful of Dollars," 19.
10. Ibid.
11. In a very different context, Christine Haase has made a similar argument about Tom Tykwer's global hit, *Lola Rennt* [*Run Lola, Run*] (1998). Haase, *When Heimat Meets Hollywood*; Haase, "You Can Run, but You Can't Hide."

12. Sosnowski, "Cinema in Transition." 15.
13. Falkowska, "Cinema of the Abject."
14. Ibid., 2.
15. Kittel, *Vertreibung der Vertriebenen?*; Röger, "Flucht."
16. Halle, "Re-imagining the German East."
17. Ebbrecht, "Die Große Zerstreuung."
18. The GDR official rhetoric of Socialist and Soviet friendship did not allow such an organization to form. Thus, isolated from the developments that took place in West Germany in the 1960s, where the community of the expellees confronted internal ideological developments and generational rifts, the experience in the East developed at a substate and private level, carried on as a direct family trauma. After the *Wende*, however, the BdV emerged quickly as a form of counter-public.
19. Bartetzko, "Lebensbeobachter."
20. Knoben, "Der Starke Stamm."
21. Ebbrecht, "Die Große Zerstreuung," 27.
22. "KF-Memel Bleibt Deutsch."
23. Schenk, "Fünf Brüder Aus Westpreußen."
24. Knoben, "Der Starke Stamm."
25. Schenk, "Söhne."
26. For a discussion of the brick as motif in literature see Kopp, Germany's Wild East.
27. Carter, "Mitteleuropa Und Seine Filmische Wiederkehr."
28. Ibid., 70.
29. Rüffler, "Stanislaw Mucha."
30. Brachmann, "Entschuldigung, Ich Muss so Lachen."
31. Ibid.
32. Halle, "Views from the German-Polish Border."

Chapter 4. Interzone Dis/continuous

1. In early cinema the camera occupied a slightly elevated position above eye-level to offer the spectator a privileged position vis-à-vis the action.
2. "Treaty Establishing a Constitution for Europe," Article I—3, 2.
3. I have discussed these films in the context of related work. Halle, "Die deutsch-polnische Interzone"; Halle, "Views from the German-Polish Border."
4. Cook et al., *Berlin School Glossary*.
5. Abel, "Intensifying Life.'"
6. Ibid.
7. Kopp, "Chrstoph Hochhäusler's This Very Moment," 301.
8. Abel, "Intensifying Life.'"
9. Ibid.
10. Ibid.
11. Ibid.

12. Kopp, "Chrstoph Hochhäusler's This Very Moment," 303.
13. Ibid., 302.
14. Orłowski, *"Polnische Wirtschaft."*
15. Kopp, "Chrstoph Hochhäusler's This Very Moment," 295.
16. Ibid., 305.
17. Daniel Kothenschulte, "Die Brücken am Fluss," *Frankfurter Rundschau*, July 31, 2003.
18. Falkowska, "Cinema of the Abject."
19. See Press Package: 6. Available at verlieh.polyfilm.at (accessed October 30, 2013).

Chapter 5. "Outside" Europe

1. See also Halle, "Offering Tales They Want to Hear."
2. Other organizations in EUROMED include the Anna Lindh Euro-Mediterranean Foundation for the Dialogue between Cultures, EUROMED Heritage, EUROMED Information and Communication, EUROMED Youth, and EUROMED Gender programs.
3. "EUROMED Audiovisual II."
4. Voileau, "Produce—Coproduce."
5. Wenner and Geller, "Mediterranean Professionals Training."
6. Ibid.
7. "World Cinema Fund Guidelines."
8. Montinari, "Special Report."
9. Ibid.
10. Ibid.
11. Caruso, "Enhancing the Euro-Mediterranean Audiovisual Cooperation."
12. Ibid.
13. Ibid.
14. Ibid.
15. Voileau, "Produce—Coproduce."
16. *Activity Report.*
17. Karanfil and Savk, *Imaginaries Out of Place*; Demirhan, "Eurimages Experience."
18. *Boss of It All* (Von Trier, 2006) [DK / SE / IS / IT / FR / NO / FI / DE], *Funny Games U.S.* (Haneke, 2007) [FR / DE / IT / GB], *Waltz with Bashir* (Folman, 2008) [IL / DE / FR / US], *2 Days in Paris* (Delpy, 2007) [FR / DE].
19. Bek, "Effects of the Membership Processes," 327.
20. Çağlar, "Mediascapes, Advertisement Industries and Cosmopolitan Transformations"; see also Çağlar, *Mediascapes, Advertisement Industries and Cosmopolitan Transformations.*
21. Bek, "Effects of the Membership Processes," 327.
22. For an extended discussion of Maxximum and the institutions involved, as well as an audience survey, see Halle, "German Turkish Spectator."
23. "Maxximum Film Etabliert."

24. Harders, "Jugendkultur," 130.
25. Ibid.
26. Göktürk, "Anyone at Home?" 202.
27. Ibid., 205.
28. Hanafi, "Civil Society in North-South Relations," 417.
29. Müller et al., *Lebenssituation*.
30. Bek, "Effects of the Membership Processes," 327.
31. Hanafi, "Civil Society in North-South Relations," 417; see also Jünemann, "Forum Civil Euromed: Critical Watchdog and Intercultural Mediator."
32. Jünemann, "Forum Civil Euromed"; Jünemann, "Zehn Jahre Barcelona-Prozess."
33. http://www.bpb.de/die_bpb/PE8IKY,0,0,The_Federal_Agency_for_Civic_Education.html (accessed October 30, 2013).
34. *Das Leben der Anderen, Requium, Knallhart, Kombat Sechzehn, Sophie Scholl, Alles auf Zucker, Die fetten Jahren, der neunte Tag, Sommersturm, Muxmäuschenstill, Gegen die Wand, das schreckliche Mädchen, Lichter, Das Wunder von Bern, Luther, Goodbye Lenin, Im Toten Winkel.*
35. A number of American films are discussed: *Erin Brokovich, Bowling for Columbine, Blue Eyed*, and *Ali*.
36. Hallensleben, "*Propaganda*," 47.
37. *Filmförderungsgesetz*, 14–15.

Chapter 6. Interzone Xperimental

1. Derrida, "Signature Event Context."
2. Luhmann, *Die Gesellschaft der Gesellschaft*.
3. Halle and Steingröver, *After the Avant-garde*.
4. Miall, *Kirchner*, 5. "Mit dem Glauben an Entwicklung, an eine neue Generation der Schaffenden wie der Genießenden rufen wir alle Jugend zusammen, und als Jugend, die die Zukunft trägt, wollen wir und Arm- und Lebensfreiheit verschaffen gegenüber den wohlangesessenen älteren Kräften. Jeder gehört zu uns, der unmittelbar und unverfälscht das wiedergibt, was ihn zum Schaffen drängt."
5. Youngblood, *Expanded Cinema*; Hein, *Film als Film: 1910 Bis Heute*.
6. Rebentisch, *Ästhetik der Installation*.
7. For a useful discussion, see Fleischmann and Reinhard, *Digitale Transformationen*.
8. See Shaw and Weibel, *Future Cinema*.
9. For insightful and nuanced discussions of modernist connections, see Mercer, *Cosmopolitan Modernisms*; Hansen, "Mass Production of the Senses."
10. For discussions of various aspects of the international historical and neo–avant-garde, see Bürger, *Theory of the Avant-garde*; Scheunemann, *Avante-Garde/Neo-Avant-Garde*; O'Pray, *Avant-Garde Film*; Danino and Maziáere, *Undercut Reader*; Halle and Steingröver, *After the Avant-garde*; Sitney, *Visionary Film*; Harper, "Hiroshi Teshigahara"; Kendall, "Theoretical Roots of the Literary Avant-garde."
11. Cammaer, "How EXPRMNTL Made"; Joseph et al., *X-Screen*.

12. The famous venue for European experimental film, Knokke-le-Zoute Exprmntl, began in 1947 and occurred five more times, the last in 1974.

13. For access to Hein's work contact the filmmaker directly. Her email address is available through the University of the Arts in Braunschweig: http://www.hbk-bs.de/home/ (accessed September 11, 2013). For detailed discussion of Birgit Hein's works, see Stoeber, *Birgit Hein*; Curtis, *Conscientious Viscerality*; Hein, "Interview with Filmmaker Birgit Hein"; Halle, "Visual Alterity Abroad."

14. Stoeber, *Birgit Hein*; Brauerhoch, "Stray Dogs"; Blümlinger, "Der Himmel Über Kuba."

15. Everett, "Through the I of the Camera."

16. Staskowski, *Conversations with Experience*.

17. Curtis, "From the Diary to the Webcam," 229.

18. Berghahn and Sternberg, *European Cinema in Motion*.

19. Wollen, *Readings and Writings*.

20. For a related discussion, see Halle, "Experiments in Turkish-German Filmmaking."

21. Rendi, "Kanaka Sprak?"

22. Berghahn, "From Turkish Greengrocer to Drag Queen."

23. Adelson, "Against Between"; Adelson, *Turkish Turn*.

24. McLeod and Kuenzli, *Cutting across Media*; Sholette, *Interventionists*; Lacy, *Mapping the Terrain*.

25. For a more elaborated discussion of Kanak Attak, see Halle, "Experiments in Turkish-German Film-making"; Halle, *German Film after Germany*; Heidenreich and Vukadinović, "In Your Face"; Cheesman, "Talking 'Kanak'"; Cheesman, "Akçam."

26. Langston, "Schlingensief's Peep Show."

27. For a related discussion, see Halle, "Rapidly Expanding Cinema."

28. www.border-rescue.social-impact.at (accessed September 11, 2013).

29. To be sure, their resistance to commodification of their projects, does not preclude a market engagement of their own. The 2003 project *no_milk///no_honey* involved the formation of a marketing agency that promoted antiracist consciousness-raising clothing.

30. Tom Gunning and André Gaudreault have variously discussed the role of monstration from the early days of silent film. Gaudreault and Barnard, *From Plato to Lumière*; Gunning, "Cinema of Attractions"; Gunning, "Aesthetic of Astonishment."

31. For a collection of Marx and Engels that draws together important reflections on art and especially *Tendenzkunst*, see Marx and Engels, *Marx and Engels on Literature and Art*.

32. Benjamin, "Storyteller"; Benjamin, "On Some Motifs in Baudelaire."

33. Ziarek, *Historicity of Experience*.

34. Bürger, *Theory of the Avant-garde*, 57; Bürger, *Theorie der Avantgarde*.

35. Heidegger, *Beiträge Zur Philosophie*.

36. Derrida, "Signature Event Context," 322.

37. Habermas and Derrida, *Philosophy in a Time of Terror*.

38. http://www.youtube.com/watch?v=sokqe7m31pw (accessed September 11, 2013).

Conclusion

1. Derrida, *Other Heading*.

2. Mersin and Yıldız, "Transforming Hospitality."

3. Adelson, "Against Between."

4. Fuhrmann, *Der Traum*.

5. Althusser, "Ideology and Ideological," 162.

6. The 2007 made-for-TV movie, *Nous nous sommes tant haïs* [*How Much We Hated Each Other*] (Apprederis) is an unremarkable exception that bears this point out as a rule.

Bibliography

A Declaration of Interdependence: A Crowdsourced Short Film, 2011. http://www.youtube.com/watch?v=fzZ1Gl5UfE0&feature=youtube_gdata_player (accessed October 15, 2013).

Abel, Marco. "Intensifying Life: The Cinema of the 'Berlin School.'" *Cineaste* 33, no. 4 (Fall 2008).

Abel, Richard. *The Red Rooster Scare: Making Cinema American, 1900–1910*. Berkeley: University of California Press, 1999.

Abel, Richard, Giorgio Bertellini, and Rob King, eds. *Early Cinema and the "National."* Bloomington: Indiana University Press, 2008.

Activity Report: Workshop on Co-production. Istanbul, Turkey: EUROMED, June 24, 2008. http://euromedaudiovisuel.net/p.aspx?t=general&mid=74&l=en&did=144. (accessed November 1, 2013).

Adelson, Leslie. "Against Between: A Manifesto." In *Unpacking Europe*, 244–255. Edited by Salah Hassan and Iftikhar Dadi. Rotterdam: NAi Publishers, 2002.

Adelson, Leslie A. *The Turkish Turn in Contemporary German Literature: Toward a New Critical Grammar of Migration*. New York: Palgrave Macmillan, 2005.

Agamben, Giorgio. *"What Is an Apparatus?" and Other Essays*. Stanford: Stanford University Press, 2009.

Althen, Michael. "Ein Jahrmarktskind. 'Das Wintergartenprogramm' 1895 der Gebrüder Skladanowsky." In *Deutsche Augenblicke: Eine Bilderfolge Zu Einer Typologie Des Films*, 8–9. Edited by Peter Buchka. Munich: Belleville, 1996.

Althusser, Louis. *For Marx*. Verso Classics. New York: Verso, 1996.

——. "Ideology and Ideological State Apparatuses." In *Lenin and Philosophy, and Other Essays*, 127–188. New York: Monthly Review Press, 1972.

——. *Lenin and Philosophy, and Other Essays*. New York: Monthly Review Press, 1972.

Apollinaire, Guillaume. *Alcools: Poems*. Middletown, Conn.: Wesleyan, 1995.

Arslan, Savaş. *Cinema in Turkey: A New Critical History*. New York: Oxford University Press, 2010.

Bakhtin, M. M. *The Dialogic Imagination: Four Essays*. Austin: University of Texas Press, 1982.

Balan, Canan. "Wondrous Pictures in Istanbul: From Cosmopolitanism to Nationalism." In *Early Cinema and the "National,"* 172–185. Edited by Richard Abel, Giorgio Bertellini, and Rob King. Bloomington: Indiana University Press, 2008.

Bamyeh, Mohammed A. *The Ends of Globalization*. Minneapolis: University of Minnesota Press, 2000.

Barber, Stephen. *Projected Cities: Cinema and Urban Space*. Locations. London: Reaktion, 2002.

——. "The Skladanowsky Brothers: The Devil Knows." *Senses of Cinema*, no. 56 (October 11, 2010). http://sensesofcinema.com/2010/feature-articles/the-skladanowsky-brothers-the-devil-knows/ (accessed October 15, 2013).

Bartetzko, Dieter. "Lebensbeobachter: Volker Koepp." *Frankfurter Allgemeine Zeitung*, May 17, 2005.

Bartov, Omer, and Eric D. Weitz, eds. *Shatterzone of Empires*. Bloomington: Indiana University Press, 2013.

Beck, Ulrich. *What Is Globalization*. Malden, Mass.: Polity, 2000.

Bek, Mine Gencel. "The Effects of the Membership Processes of the European Union on Media Policies in Turkey." In *Media, Democracy and European Culture*, 325–338. Edited by I. B. Bondebjerg and Peter Madsen. Lanham, Md.: Intellect Books, 2009.

Benjamin, Walter. "On Some Motifs in Baudelaire." In *Illuminations*, 155–201. New York: Schocken Books, 1969.

——. "The Storyteller." In *Illuminations*, 83–111. New York: Schocken Books, 1969.

Bergfelder, Tim. "Exotic Thrills and Bedroom Manuals: West German B-Film Production in the 1960s." In *Light Motives: German Popular Film in Perspective*, 197–218. Edited by Randall Halle and Margaret McCarthy. Contemporary Film and Television Series. Detroit: Wayne State University Press, 2003.

——. *International Adventures: German Popular Cinema and European Co-productions in the 1960s*. New York: Berghahn Books, 2005.

——. "The Nation Vanishes: European Co-Productions and Popular Genre Fomulae in the 1950s and 1960s." In *Cinema and Nation*, 139–52. Edited by Mette Hjort and Scott Mackenzie. London: Routledge, 2000.

Bergfelder, Tim, Sue Harris, and Sarah Street. *Film Architecture and the Transnational Imagination: Set Design in 1930s European Cinema*. Amsterdam: Amsterdam University Press, 2007.

Berghahn, Daniela. "From Turkish Greengrocer to Drag Queen: Reassessing Patriarchy in Recent Turkish-German Coming-of-age Films." *New Cinemas: Journal of Contemporary Film* 7, no. 1 (August 1, 2009): 55–69.

———. *Hollywood behind the Wall: The Cinema of East Germany*. Manchester: Manchester University Press, 2005.

Berghahn, Daniela, and Claudia Sternberg, eds. *European Cinema in Motion: Migrant and Diasporic Film in Contemporary Europe*. Basingstoke: Palgrave Macmillan, 2010.

Berry, Ellen E., and Mikhail N. Epstein. *Transcultural Experiments: Russian and American Models of Creative Communication*. New York: Palgrave Macmillan, 1999.

Betz, Mark. *Beyond the Subtitle: Remapping European Art Cinema*. Minneapolis: University Of Minnesota Press, 2009.

———. "The Name above the (sub)Title: Internationalism, Coproduction, and Polyglot European Art Cinema." Edited by Sharon Willis and Randall Halle. *Camera Obscura Special Issue: Marginality and Alterity in Contemporary European Cinema*, no. 46 (2001): 1–45.

Blümlinger, Christa. "Der Himmel über Kuba." *Texte zur Kunst* 42, (June 2001): 192–195.

Bordwell, David, and Noël Carroll, eds. *Post-theory: Reconstructing Film Studies*. Wisconsin Studies in Film. Madison: University of Wisconsin Press, 1996.

Brachmann, Jan. "Entschuldigung, Ich Muss so Lachen: Der polnische Filmregisseur Stanislaw Mucha über Ikea in der Westukraine, Klauen in Ostpolen und die alte Mitte Europas." *Berliner Zeitung*, April 30, 2004.

Brauerhoch, Annette. "Stray Dogs—Zu Birgit Heins Film Baby I Will Make You Sweat." *Frauen und Film* 60 (1997): 164–171.

Bürger, Peter. *Theorie der Avantgarde*, n.d.

———. *Theory of the Avant-garde*. Minneapolis: University of Minnesota Press, 1984.

Burroughs, William S. *Interzone*. Edited by James Grauerholz. New York: Penguin (Non-Classics), 1990.

Çağlar, Ayşe. "Mediascapes, Advertisement Industries and Cosmopolitan Transformations: German Turks in Germany." *New German Critique* 92, (Spring-Summer 2004): 39–61.

———. *Mediascapes, Advertisement Industries and Cosmopolitan Transformations: Turkish Immigrants in Europe*. Vol. 53. EUI Working papers/RSC. Florence: European University Institute, Robert Schuman Centre for Advanced Studies, 2002.

Cammaer, Gerda Johanna. "How EXPRMNTL Made the Small Coastal Town of Knokke the Scene for Radical Artistic New Waves and Political Sea Changes." *Camera Obscura*, no. 81 (2012): 169.

Carter, Erica. "Mitteleuropa und Seine Filmische Wiederkehr: Zu Stanislaw Muchas Die Mitte." *GFL Journal*, no. 3 (2006): 62–77.

Caruso, Valerio. "Enhancing the Euro-Mediterranean Audiovisual Cooperation." *Cahiers Euromed*. Europa Jaratouna (2005). http://www.eurojar.org/en/euromed-articles/enhancing-euro-mediterranean-audiovisual-cooperation/1076 (accessed April 26, 2010).

Castan, Joachim. *Max Skladanowsky Oder der Beginn einer deutschen Filmgeschichte*. Stuttgart: Füsslin, 1995.

Cheesman, Tom. "Akçam—Zaimoğlu—Kanak Attak': Turkish Lives and Letters in German." *German Life and Letters* 55, no. 2 (2002): 180–195.

———. "Talking 'Kanak': Zaimoğlu Contra Leitkultur." *New German Critique*, no. 92 (April 1, 2004): 82–99.

Closs, Wolfgang, André Lange, and Tim Westcott, eds. *Public Funding for Film and Audiovisual Works in Europe: A Comparative Approach*. 2 vols. Strassbourg: European Audiovisual Observatory, 2004.

Coates, Paul. *Cinema, Religion, and the Romantic Legacy*. Farnham, U.K.: Ashgate Publishing, Ltd., 2003.

Comolli, Jean-Louis. "Machines of the Visible." In *The Cinematic Apparatus*, 121–143. Edited by Teresa De Lauretis and Stephen Heath. New York: St. Martin's Press, 1980.

Condee, Nancy. *The Imperial Trace: Recent Russian Cinema*. New York: Oxford University Press, 2009.

Cook, Roger F., Lutz P. Koepnick, Kristin Kopp, and Brad Prager, eds. *Berlin School Glossary: An ABC of the New Wave in German Cinema*. Bristol: Intellect Books, 2013.

Cooke, Paul. "Supporting Contemporary German Film: How Triumphant Is the Free Market?" *Journal of Contemporary European Studies* 15, no. 1 (April 2007): 35–46.

Council of Europe. *European Audiovisual Observatory: Yearbook 2008—Film, Television and Video in Europe 2008*. 15th ed. Strassbourg: Council of Europe, 2009.

Curtis, Robin. *Conscientious Viscerality: The Autobiographical Stance in German Film and Video*. Berlin: Edition Imorde, 2006.

———. "From the Diary to the Webcam: Michael Brynntrup and the Medial Self." In *After the Avant-garde: Contemporary German and Austrian Experimental Film*. Edited by Randall Halle and Reinhild Steingröver. Rochester, N.Y.: Camden House, 2008.

Danino, Nina, and Michael Maziáere, eds. *The Undercut Reader: Critical Writings on Artists' Film and Video*. London: Wallflower Press, 2003.

Demirhan, Mehmet. "The Eurimages Experience: Case Study of a Turkish Co-production Supported by Eurimages." Presented at the EUROMED: Workshop on Co-production, Istanbul, Turkey, June 23, 2008. http://www.euromedaudiovisuel.net/Files/2008/07/10/1215713135121.pdf (accessed September 3, 2013).

Derrida, Jacques. *The Other Heading: Reflections on Today's Europe*. Studies in Continental Thought. Bloomington: Indiana University Press, 1992.

———. "Signature Event Context." In *Margins of Philosophy*, 307–330. Translated by Alan Bass. Chicago: University of Chicago Press, 1985.

Ebbrecht, Tobias. "Die Große Zerstreuung: Heimat-TV im Deutschen Geschichtsfernsehen." *Deutsch-Tschechische Nachrichten*, no. 5. Vom Münchener Diktat zur Nachkriegsordnung. Geschichte und ihre Instrumentalisierung in der aktuellen deutschen Politik (December 5, 2004): 3–32.

Elsaesser, Thomas. *European Cinema: Face to Face with Hollywood*. 1st ed. Amsterdam: Amsterdam University Press, 2005.

Elsaesser, Thomas, and Michael Wedel, eds. *A Second Life: German Cinema's First Decades*. 1st ed. Amsterdam: Amsterdam University Press, 1996.

——. *Kino der Kaiserzeit: Zwischen Tradition und Moderne*. München: Edition Text + Kritik, 2002.

Erdoğan, Nezih, and Deniz Göktürk. "Turkish Cinema." In *Companion Encyclopedia of Middle Eastern and North African Film*, 533–567. Edited by Oliver Leaman. New York: Routledge, 2001.

"EUROMED Audiovisual II—Technical Assistance—EUROMED Audiovisual II." http://www.euromedaudiovisuel.net/general.aspx?anchors=1&treeID=3&lang=en (accessed January 25, 2010).

Everett, Wendy, ed. *European Identity in Cinema*. 2nd ed. Bristol: Intellect Ltd., 2005.

——. "Through the I of the Camera: Women and Autobiography in Contemporary European Film." *Studies in European Cinema* 4, no. 2 (August 30, 2007): 125–136.

Everett, Wendy E., and Peter Wagstaff. *Cultures of Exile*. Vol. 7. Polygons. New York: Berghahn Books, 2004.

Everett, Wendy Ellen, and Axel Goodbody. *Revisiting Space: Space and Place in European Cinema*. Oxford: Peter Lang, 2005.

Evren, Burçak. *Sigmund Weinberg: Türkiye'ye Sinemayı Getiren Adam*. Istanbul: Milliyet Yayınları, 1995.

——. *Türk Sineması*. Istanbul: Türsak, 2005.

Ezra, Elizabeth, ed. *European Cinema*. New York: Oxford University Press, 2004.

Falkowska, Janina. "The Cinema of the Abject and the Cinema of Capitalist Fantasy in Poland." University of Western Ontario: unpublished, 2010.

Filmförderungsgesetz. Berlin: FFA, 1993.

Fleischmann, Monika, and Ulrike Reinhard, eds. *Digitale Transformationen: Medienkunst als Schnittstelle von Kunst, Wissenschaft, Wirtschaft und Gesellschaft*. Heidelberg: Whois, 2004.

Forbes, Jill, and Sarah Street, eds. *European Cinema: An Introduction*. New York: Palgrave Macmillan, 2001.

Foucault, Michel. "The Confessions of the Flesh." In *Power/Knowledge: Selected Interviews and Other Writings, 1972–1977*, 194–229. Edited by Colin Gordon. New York: Vintage, 1980.

Friedberg, Anne. *The Virtual Window: From Alberti to Microsoft*. Cambridge, Mass.: MIT Press, 2006.

Fuhrmann, Malte. *Der Traum vom deutschen Orient: Zwei deutsche Kolonien im osmanischen Reich 1851–1918*. Frankfurt am Main: Campus Verlag, 2006.

Fürstenau, Theodor. *Max Skladanowsky*. Wiesbaden: Deutsches Institut für Filmkunde, 1970.

Galt, Rosalind. *The New European Cinema: Redrawing the Map*. New York: Columbia University Press, 2006.

Galt, Rosalind, and Karl Schoonover, eds. *Global Art Cinema New Theories and Histories*. Oxford: Oxford University Press, 2010.

Garncarz, Joseph. "The Emergence of Nationally Specific Film Cultures in Europe." In *Early Cinema and the "National,"* 185–94. Edited by Richard Abel, Giorgio Bertellini, and Rob King. Bloomington: Indiana University Press, 2008.

Gaudreault, André, and Tim Barnard. *From Plato to Lumière: Narration and Monstration in Literature and Cinema*. Toronto: University of Toronto Press, 2009.

Giovannella Rendi, Ferrara. "Kanaka Sprak? German-Turkish Women Filmmakers." *GLF*, no. 3 (2006): 78–93.

Göktürk, Deniz. "Anyone at Home? Itinerant Identities in European Cinema of the 1990s." *Framework* Special Issue: Middle Eastern Cinema 43, no. 2 (Fall 2002): 201–212.

Grabowski, Sabine. *Deutscher und polnischer Nationalismus. Der deutsche Ostmarkenverein und die polnische Straz 1894–1914*. Marburg: Herder-Institut, 1998.

Green, Simon, and William E. Paterson, eds. *Governance in Contemporary Germany: The Semisovereign State Revisited*. Cambridge: Cambridge University Press, 2005.

Gunning, Tom. "An Aesthetic of Astonishment: Early Cinema and the (in)Credulous Spectator." *Art and Text*, no. 34 (1989): 31–45.

———. "The Cinema of Attractions: Early Film, Its Spectator and the Avant-Garde." In *Early Cinema: Space, Frame, Narrative*, 56–62. Edited by Thomas Elsaesser and Adam Barker. London: BFI, 1990.

———. "Early Cinema as Global Cinema: The Encyclopedic Ambition." In *Early Cinema and the "National,"* 11–16. Edited by Richard Abel, Giorgio Bertellini, and Rob King. Bloomington: Indiana University Press, 2008.

Haase, Christine. *When Heimat Meets Hollywood: German Filmmakers and America, 1985–2005*. Rochester, N.Y.: Camden House, 2007.

———. "You Can Run, but You Can't Hide: Transcultural Filmmaking in Run Lola Run (1998)." In *Light Motives: German Popular Film in Perspective*, 395–417. Edited by Randall Halle and Margaret McCarthy. Detroit: Wayne State University Press, 2003.

Habermas, Jürgen, and Jacques Derrida. *Philosophy in a Time of Terror: Dialogues with Jürgen Habermas and Jacques Derrida*. Chicago: University of Chicago Press, 2004.

Halle, Randall. "Die deutsch-polnische Interzone: Kino als transnationaler Apparat in der Europäischen Union." In *Kino in Bewegung: Perspektiven des deutschen Gegenwartsfilms*, 185–207. Edited by Thomas Schick and Tobias Ebbrecht. Wiesbaden: Springer DE, 2011.

———. "Experiments in Turkish-German Film-making: Ayşe Polat, Kutlu Ataman, Neco Çelik, Aysun Bademsoy and Kanak Attak." *New Cinemas: Journal of Contemporary Film* 7, no. 1 (August 1, 2009): 39–53.

———. *German Film after Germany: Toward a Transnational Aesthetic*. Urbana: University of Illinois Press, 2008.

———. "The German Turkish Spectator and Turkish Language Film Programming: Karli Kino, Maxximum Distribution, and the Interzone Cinema." In *Turkish German Cinema in the New Millennium*, 123–135. Edited by Sabine Hake and Barbara Caroline Mennel. Film Europa. New York: Berghahn Books, 2012.

———. "'Happy Ends' to Crises of Heterosexual Desire: Toward a Social Psychology of Recent German Comedies." *Camera Obscura* 15, no. 2 (2000): 1–39.

———. "Offering Tales They Want to Hear: Transnational European Film Funding as Neo-Orientalism." In *Global Art Cinema: New Theories and Histories*, 303–320. Edited by Rosalind Galt and Karl Schoonover. Oxford: Oxford University Press, 2010.

———. *Queer Social Philosophy: Critical Readings from Kant to Adorno*. Urbana: University of Illinois Press, 2004.

———. "Rapidly Expanding Cinema: On Border Rescue and the Tendentiousness of Interventionist Art." In *After the Avant-garde: Contemporary German and Austrian Experimental Film*, 157–181. Edited by Randall Halle and Reinhild Steingröver. Rochester, N.Y.: Camden House, 2008.

———. "Re-imagining the German East: Expulsion and Relocation in German Feature and Documentary Film." *German Politics and Society* (Winter 2013): n.p.

———. "Views from the German-Polish Border: The Exploration of Inter-national Space in Halbe Treppe and Lichter." *German Quarterly* 80, no. 1 (January 1, 2007): 77–96.

———. "Visual Alterity Abroad: Hegel through Birgit Hein's Baby I Will Make You Sweat and La Moderna Poesia." *Film-Philosophy* 14, no. 1 (November 14, 2009): 103–121.

Halle, Randall, and Reinhild Steingröver, eds. *After the Avant-garde: Contemporary German and Austrian Experimental Film*. Rochester, N.Y.: Camden House, 2008.

Hallensleben, Silvia. "Propaganda. BRD/Türkei 1999." *EPD Film*, no. 11 (1999): 47.

Haltof, Marek. "A Fistful of Dollars: Polish Cinema after the 1989 Freedom Shock." *Film Quarterly* XLVIII, no. 3. Extracted from FIAF—International Index to Film Periodicals (1995): 15–25.

———. *Polish National Cinema*. New York: Berghahn Books, 2002.

Hanafi, Sari. "Civil Society in North-South Relations: The Case of the Euro-Mediterranean Partnership." *Orient* 46, no. 3 (2005): 414–428.

Hansen, Miriam. "The Mass Production of the Senses: Classical Cinema as Vernacular Modernism." *Modernism/modernity* 6, no. 2 (1999): 59–77.

Harders, Antje. "Jugendkultur: Sehnsucht nach Istanbul." *Der Spiegel*, August 30, 2004.

Harper, Dan. "Hiroshi Teshigahara." *Senses of Cinema*, no. 66 (May 2003): n.p.

Heidegger, Martin. *Beiträge Zur Philosophie (Vom Ereignis) (1936–38)*. Vol. 65. Edited by Friedrich W. von Herrmann. Gesamtausgabe. Frankfurt am Main: Klostermann, 1994.

Heidenreich, Nanna, and Vojin Saša Vukadinović. "In Your Face: Activism, Agit-Prop and the Autonomy of Migration. The Case of Kanak Attak." In *After the Avant-garde: Contemporary German and Austrian Experimental Film*, 131–157. Edited by Randall Halle and Reinhild Steingröver. Rochester, N.Y.: Camden House, 2008.

Hein, Birgit. *Film als Film: 1910 Bis Heute*. Cologne: Kolnischer Kunstverein, 1977.

———. "Interview with Filmmaker Birgit Hein." In *After the Avant-garde: Contemporary German and Austrian Experimental Film*. Edited by Randall Halle and Reinhild Steingröver. Rochester, N.Y.: Camden House, 2008.

Hendrykowska, Malgorzata, and Marek Hendrykowski. *Film w Poznaniu: 1896–1945*. Poznań: Wydawn Poznańskie, 1990.

Higson, Andrew. "Cultural Policy and Industrial Practice: Film Europe and the International Film Congresses of the 1920s." In *"Film Europe" and "Film America": Cinema, Commerce and Cultural Exchange, 1920–1939*, 117–131. Edited by Andrew Higson and Richard Maltby. Exeter Studies in Film History. Exeter: University of Exeter Press, 1999.

Higson, Andrew, and Richard Maltby, eds. *"Film Europe" and "Film America": Cinema, Commerce and Cultural Exchange, 1920–1939*. Exeter Studies in Film History. Exeter: University of Exeter Press, 1999.

Houcken, Robin. *The International Feature Film Industry: National Advantage and International Strategies for European Film Companies*. 1. Aufl. 13. Potsdam: Verlag für Berlin-Brandenburg, 1999.

Imre, Anikó. *Identity Games: Globalization and the Transformation of Media Cultures in the New Europe*. Cambridge, Mass.: The MIT Press, 2009.

Iordanova, Dina. *Cinema of the Other Europe*. London: Wallflower Press, 2003.

Jäckel, Anne. "Cooperation between East and West in Europe: Film Policy and Integration, from Hope to Disenchantment?" In *Central and Eastern Europe in Transition*, 41–67. Edited by Frank H. Columbus. Commak, N.Y.: Nova Science Pub. Inc., 1998.

——. *European Film Industries*. London: British Film Institute, 2003.

——. "Film Policy and Practice in Canadian Regional Cinema: The Case of the Atlantic Provinces." *British Journal of Canadian Studies* 20, no. 1 (May 1, 2007): 25–49.

——. "The Inter/Nationalism of French Film Policy." *Modern and Contemporary France* 15, no. 1 (2007): 21–36.

Jameson, Fredric. *The Geopolitical Aesthetic: Cinema and Space in the World System*. London: British Film Institute, 1992.

Jauss, Hans-Robert. "1912: Threshold to an Epoch. Apollinaire's Zone and Lundi Rue Christine." Translated by Roger Blood. *Yale French Studies*, no. 74 (January 1, 1988): 39–66.

Joseph, Branden, Liz Kotz, Pamela Lee, and Matthias Michalka, eds. *X-Screen: Film Installations and Actions in the 1960s and 1970s*. Cologne: Walther Konig, 2004.

Jünemann, Anette. "The Forum Civil Euromed: Critical Watchdog and Intercultural Mediator." In *A New Euro-Mediterranean Cultural Identity*, 84–107. Edited by Stefania Panebianco. London: Routledge, 2003.

——. "Zehn Jahre Barcelona-Prozess: Eine Gemischte Bilanz." *Aus Politik und Zeitgeschichte* 45 (2005). http://www.bpb.de/publikationen/TGBS83.html (accessed September 3, 2013).

Kanzler, Martin, Susan Newman-Baudais, and André Lange. *The Circulation of European Co-Productions and Entirely National Films in Europe 2001 to 2007*. Report Prepared for the Council of Europe Film Policy Forum Co-organised by the Council of Europe and the Polish Film Institute Kraków, September 11–13, 2008. Strassbourg: European Audiovisual Observatory, August 2008. http://www.obs.coe.int/online_publication/expert/krakow_report.pdf (accessed September 3, 2013).

Karanfil, Gokcen, and Serkan Savk, eds. *Imaginaries out of Place: Cinema, Transnationalism and Turkey*. Newcastle upon Tyne: Cambridge Scholars Publishing, 2012.

Katzenstein, Peter J., ed. *Tamed Power: Germany in Europe*. Ithaca, N.Y.: Cornell University Press, 1997.

Kendall, Elisabeth. "The Theoretical Roots of the Literary Avant-garde in 1960s Egypt." *Edebiyat: Journal of M.E. Literatures* 14, no. 1–2 (2003): 39–56.

"KF-Memel Bleibt Deutsch." YouTube Video. *Kanal:EDELWEISSIST*. http://edelweissist.youtube.video4me.net/user/Edelweissist/play/8vwXzPwBARA/KF-Memel_bleibt_Deutsch (accessed April 21, 2013).

King, Alasdair. "Placing Grün Ist Die Heide (1951): Spatial Politics and Emergent West German Identity." In *Light Motives: German Popular Film in Perspective*, 130–147. Edited by Randall Halle and Margaret McCarthy. Contemporary Film and Television Series. Detroit: Wayne State University Press, 2003.

Kittel, Manfred. *Vertreibung der Vertriebenen? Der historische deutsche Osten in der Erinnerungskultur der Bundesrepublik (1961–1982)*. Munich: Oldenbourg, 2007.

Kittler, Friedrich A. *Grammophon, Film, Typewriter*. Berlin: Brinkmann und Bose, 1986.

——. *Optische Medien: Berliner Vorlesung 1999*. Berlin: Merve-Verlag, 2002.

Kittler, Friedrich A., and Ana Ofak, eds. *Medien vor den Medien*. Munich: Fink, 2007.

Klimes, Ivan, and Pavel Zeman. "Aktualita: Tschechoslowakische Tonbildschauen 1937–38." In *Babylon in FilmEuropa. Mehrsprachen-Versionen der 1930er Jahre*, 79–88. Edited by Jan Distelmeyer. Munich: Edition Text + Kritik, 2006.

Knoben, Martina. "Der starke Stamm: Eine deutsch-polnische Geschichte, wunderbar unaufgeregt Erzählt: Volker Koepps Film 'Söhne.'" *Süddeutsche Zeitung*, June 18, 2007.

Konstantarakos, Myrto. *Spaces in European Cinema*. Lanham, Md.: Intellect Books, 2000.

Kopp, Kristin. "Chrstoph Hochhäusler's This Very Moment: The Berlin School and the Politics of Spatial Aesthetics in the German-Polish Borderlands." In *The Collapse of the Conventional: The German Film and Its Politics at the Turn of the New Century*, 285–308. Edited by Brad Prager and Jaimey Fisher. Detroit: Wayne State University Press, 2010.

——. *Germany's Wild East: Constructing Poland as Colonial Space*. Ann Arbor: University of Michigan Press, 2012.

Kornatowska, Maria. "Polish Cinema." *Cineaste* XIX, no. 4. Extracted from FIAF—International Index to Film Periodicals (1993): 47–50.

Kuszewski, Stanisław. *Zeitgenössischer polnischer Film*. Warsaw: Verlag Interpress, 1978.

Lacy, Suzanne, ed. *Mapping the Terrain: New Genre Public Art*. San Francisco: Bay Press, 1994.

Langston, Richard. "Schlingensief's Peep Show: Post-Cinematic Spectacles and the Public Space of History." In *After the Avant-garde: Contemporary German and Austrian Experimental Film*, 204–225. Edited by Randall Halle and Reinhild Steingröver. Rochester, N.Y.: Camden House, 2008.

Lauretis, Teresa De, and Stephen Heath. *The Cinematic Apparatus*. New York: St. Martin's Press, 1980.

Leibfried, Stephan, Paul Pierson, and Sylvia Streeck, eds. *Standort Europa: Sozialpolitik zwischen Nationalstaat und europäischer Integration*. Frankfurt am Main: Suhrkamp, 1998.

Loiperdinger, Martin. "The Kaiser's Cinema: An Archeology of Attitudes and Audiences." In *A Second Life: German Cinema's First Decades*, 41–51. Edited by Thomas Elsaesser and Michael Wedel. Amsterdam: Amsterdam University Press, 1996.

Luhmann, Niklas. *Die Gesellschaft der Gesellschaft*. Frankfurt am Main: Suhrkamp, 1997.

Marks, Gary Wolfe, Fritz Scharpf, Philippe Schmitter, and Wolfgang Streeck, eds. *Governance in the European Union*. Thousand Oaks, Calif.: SAGE Publications, 1996.

Marx, Karl, and Friedrich Engels. *Marx and Engels on Literature and Art*. Vol. 1. Edited by Lee Baxandall and Stefan Morawski. Documents on Marxist Aesthetics. Milwaukee: Telos, 1973.

Matzker, Reiner, and Siegfried Zielinski, eds. *Fiktion als Fakt: "Metaphysik" der neuen Medien*. Bern: Lang, 2000.

"Maxximum Film etabliert: Türkischer Mainstream als Publikumsmagnet." *Blickpunkt: Film*, December 2, 2003. http://www.mediabiz.de/film/news/maxximum-film-etabliert-tuerkischer-mainstream-als-publikumsmagnet/145239 (accessed November 1, 2013).

McLeod, Kembrew, and Rudolf Kuenzli, eds. *Cutting across Media: Appropriation Art, Interventionist Collage, and Copyright Law*. Durham: Duke University Press Books, 2011.

Mercer, Kobena, ed. *Cosmopolitan Modernisms*. Annotating Art's Histories. London: Institute of International Visual Arts, 2005.

Mersin, Serhan, and Pınar Yıldız. "Transforming Hospitality: Forming New Transcultural Fields in Turkish Cinema." In *Imaginaries out of Place: Cinema, Transnationalism and Turkey*, 23–37. Edited by Gokcen Karanfil and Serkan Savk. Newcastle upon Tyne: Cambridge Scholars Publishing, 2012.

Miall, Nina. *Kirchner: Expressionism and the City Dresden and Berlin 1905–1918*. Exhibition Catalogue. London: Royal Academy of Arts, 2003.

Montinari, Mazzino. "Special Report: Produce—Coproduce . . . : 2002—Producing in Africa." *Cineuropa*, March 22, 2007. http://cineuropa.org/dossier.aspx?lang=en&treeID=1364&documentID=75785. (accessed April 15, 2007). See also http://kaganof.com/kagablog/2007/08/15/producing-in-africa/ (accessed October 30, 2013).

Müller, Ursula, Monika Schröttle, Sandra Glammeier, Christa Oppenheimer, Barbara Schulz, and Alexandra Münster. *Lebenssituation, Sicherheit und Gesundheit von Frauen in Deutschland: Eine repräsentative Untersuchung zu Gewalt gegen Frauen in Deutschland*. Baden-Baden: Bundesministerium für Familie, Senioren, Frauen und Jugend; Koelblin-Fortuna-Druck, 2008.

Musser, Charles. "At the Beginning: Motion Picture Production, Representation, and Ideology at the Edison and Lumière Companies." In *The Silent Cinema Reader*, 15–30. Edited by Lee Grieveson and Peter Krämer. New York: Routledge, 2004.

Narath, Albert. *Max Skladanowsky*. West Berlin: Deutsche Kinemathek, 1970.

Ong, Aihwa. *Flexible Citizenship: The Cultural Logics of Transnationality*. Durham: Duke University Press, 1999.

O'Pray, Michael. *Avant-Garde Film: Forms, Themes, and Passions*. London: Columbia University Press, 2012.

Orłowski, Hubert. *"Polnische Wirtschaft": Zum deutschen Polendiskurs der Neuzeit*. 21. Wiesbaden: Harrassowitz, 1996.

Özön, Nijat. *Karagözden sinemaya: Turk sinemasi ve sorunlari*. Ankara: Kitle Yayınları, 1995.

———. *Türk Sinema Tarihi*. Istanbul: Artist Yayınları, 1962.

Paterson, William E. "European Policy-making: Between Associated Sovereignty and Semisovereignty." In *Governance in Contemporary Germany: The Semisovereign State Revisited*, 261–283. Edited by Simon Green and William E. Paterson. Cambridge: Cambridge University Press, 2005.

Petty, Sheila. *Contact Zones: Memory, Origin and Discourses in Black Diasporic Cinema*. Contemporary Approaches to Film and Television Series. Detroit: Wayne State University Press, 2008.

Pommerin, Reiner, and Manuela Uhlmann. *Quellen zu den deutsch-polnischen Beziehungen, 1815–1991*. Vol. Bd. 10. Quellen zu den Beziehungen Deutschlands zu seinen Nachbarn im 19 und 20. Jahrhundert. Darmstadt: Wissenschaftliche Buchgesellschaft, 2001.

Pratt, Mary Louise. *Imperial Eyes: Travel Writing and Transculturation*. New York: Routledge, 1992.

Quaresima, Leonardo. "Mehrsprachenversion/Dubbing?" In *Babylon in FilmEuropa. Mehrsprachen-Versionen der 1930er Jahre*, 19–37. Edited by Jan Distelmeyer. Munich: Edition Text + Kritik, 2006.

Radhakrishnan, Rajagopalan. "Between Living or Telling: Ethnicity in the Age of Transnationalism." *ADE Bulletin*, no. 143 (Fall 2007): 18–25.

Rebentisch, Juliane. *Ästhetik der Installation*. Frankfurt am Main: Suhrkamp Verlag, 2003.

"Red Carpet for International Film Productions: Was sich die Branche vom deutschen Filmförderfonds erhofft." *MedienboardNews* 7, no. 1 (January 2007): 6–7.

Rentschler, Eric. "From New German Cinema to the Post-Wall Cinema of Consensus." In *Cinema and Nation*. 1st ed., 260–277. Edited by Mette Hjort and Scott Mackenzie. London: Routledge, 2000.

Riesinger, Robert, ed. *Der Kinematographische Apparat: Geschichte und Gegenwart Einer Interdisziplinären Debatte*. Münster: Nodus Publikationen, 2003.

Röger, Maren. "Flucht, Vertreibung und Heimatverlust der Deutschen in Film und Fernsehen Polens und Deutschlands 1945–2010." In *Deutschland und Polen: Filmische Grenzen und Nachbarschaften*, 71–88. Edited by Konrad Klejsa and Schamma Schahadat. Marburg: Schüren Verlag, 2010.

Rosen, Philip. *Narrative, Apparatus, Ideology*. New York: Columbia University Press, 1986.

Rüffler, Sarah. "Stanislaw Mucha: Filmen Gegen Brüssel." *Cafebabel.com Das Europamagazin*, May 28, 2005. http://www.cafebabel.de/article/1251/stanislaw-mucha-filmen-gegen-brussel.html (accessed November 1, 2013).

Sammartino, Annemarie. *The Impossible Border: Germany and the East 1914–1922*. Ithaca: Cornell University Press, 2010.

Sbragia, Alberta, ed. *Euro-politics: Institutions and Policymaking in the "New" European Community*. Washington, D.C.: Brookings Institution, 1992.

Schenk, Ralf. "Fünf Brüder aus Westpreußen." *Neues Deutschland*, June 31, 2007.

———. "Söhne." *Film-dienst* LX, no. 11. Extracted from FIAF—International Index to Film Periodicals (2007): 27.

Scheunemann, Dietrich, ed. *Avante-Garde/Neo-Avant-Garde*. Amsterdam: Rodopi, 2005.

Shaw, Jeffrey, and Peter Weibel, eds. *Future Cinema: The Cinematic Imaginary after Film*. Cambridge, Mass.: MIT Press, 2003.

Sholette, Gregor. *The Interventionists: Users' Manual for the Creative Disruption of Everyday Life*. 2nd ed. Edited by Nato Thompson and Gregory Sholette. Cambridge, Mass.: MIT and MASS MoCA, 2006.

Sieg, Katrin. *Choreographing the Global in European Cinema and Theater*. New York: Palgrave Macmillan, 2008.

Sitney, P. Adams. *Visionary Film: The American Avant-garde, 1943–2000*. Oxford: Oxford University Press, 2002.

Skaff, Sheila. "Early Cinema and 'the Polish Question.'" In *Early Cinema and the "National,"* 69–76. Edited by Richard Abel, Giorgio Bertellini, and Rob King. Bloomington: Indiana University Press, 2008.

———. *The Law of the Looking Glass: Cinema in Poland, 1896–1939*. Athens: Ohio University Press, 2008.

Skrodzka, Aga. *Magic Realist Cinema in East Central Europe*. Edinburgh: Edinburgh University Press, 2012.

Smith, Terry. "Contemporary Art and Contemporaneity." *Critical Inquiry* 32, no. 4 (June 1, 2006): 681–707.

———. *Contemporary Art: World Currents*. 1st ed. Old Pappan, N.J.: Pearson, 2011.

———. *What Is Contemporary Art?* Chicago: University of Chicago Press, 2009.

Smith, Terry, Okwui Enwezor, and Nancy Condee, eds. *Antinomies of Art and Culture: Modernity, Postmodernity, Contemporaneity*. Durham: Duke University Press Books, 2009.

Sosnowski, Alexandra. "Cinema in Transition." *Journal of Popular Film & Television* 24, no. 1 (Spring 1996): 10–17.

Staskowski, Andréa. *Conversations with Experience: Feminist Hermeneutics and the Autobiographical Films of German Women*. German Life and Civilization. New York: Lang, 2004.

Stemmrich, Gregor, ed. *Kunst/Kino*. Köln: Oktagon, 2001.

Stoeber, Michael. *Birgit Hein*. Kunst der Gegenwart Aus Niedersachsen 60. Hannover: Niedersächsische Lottostiftung, 2004.

Szczepanik, Petr. "'Tief in Einem Deutschen Einflussbereich': Die Aufführung und Rezeption deutschprachiger Film in der Tschechoslowakei in den frühen 1930er Jahren." In *Babylon in FilmEuropa. Mehrsprachen-Versionen der 1930er Jahre*, 89–102. Edited by Jan Distelmeyer. Munich: Edition Text + Kritik, 2006.

Tarrow, Sidney. *The New Transnational Activism*. Cambridge: Cambridge University Press, 2005.

"The Treaty Establishing a Constitution for Europe." European Union, October 29, 2004. http://www.cvce.eu/obj/the_treaty_establishing_a_constitution_for_europe-en-4eb2765d-720c-4358-a5fe-e318d06562f1.html (accessed November 1, 2013).

Thum, Gregor. *Die fremde Stadt: Breslau 1945*. Berlin: Siedler, 2003.

———. "Mystische Landschaften: Das Bild vom 'Deutschen Osten' und Die Zäsuren Des 20. Jahrhunderts." In *Traumland Osten. Deutsche Bilder Vom Östlichen Europa im 20. Jahrhundert*, 181–208. Edited by Gregor Thum. Göttingen: Vandenhoeck and Ruprecht, 2006.

——, ed. *Traumland Osten. Deutsche Bilder Vom Östlichen Europa im 20. Jahrhundert*. Göttingen: Vandenhoeck and Ruprecht, 2006.

Tilse, Mark. *Transnationalism in the Prussian East: From National Conflict to Synthesis, 1871–1914*. New York: Palgrave Macmillan, 2011.

Tinsobin, Eva. *Das Kino als Apparat: Medientheorie und Medientechnik im Spiegel der Apparatusdebatte*. 1st ed. Boizenburg: Verlag Werner Hülsbusch, 2007.

Verdery, Katherine. "Transnationalism, Nationalism, Citizenship, and Property: Eastern Europe since 1989." *American Ethnologist* 25, no. 2 (1998): 291–306.

Vitali, Valentina, and Paul Willemen, eds. *Theorising National Cinema*. London: British Film Institute, 2006.

Voileau, Frédéric. "Produce—Coproduce: The Mediterranean Countries." *Cineuropa*, March 22, 2007. http://cineuropa.org/dossier.aspx?lang=en&treeID=1364&documentID=75750 (accessed October 30, 2013).

Votruba, Martin. "Historical and National Background of Slovak Filmmaking." *KinoKultura* Special Issue, no. 3 (2005). http://www.kinokultura.com/specials/3/votruba.shtml#cz1918 (accessed September 3, 2013).

Wahl, Chris. "Babel's Business—On Ufa's Multiple Language Film Versions, 1929–1933." In *The Many Faces of Weimar Cinema: Rediscovering Germany's Filmic Legacy*, 235–248. Edited by Christian Rogowski. Rochester, N.Y.: Camden House, 2010.

——. *Das Sprechen des Spielfilms: Über die Auswirkungen von Hörbaren Dialogen Auf Produktion und Rezeption, Ästhetik und Internationalität der siebten Kunst*, 2005.

——. *Sprachversionsfilme aus Babelsberg. Die internationale Strategie der Ufa 1929–1939*. München: Edition Text + Kritik, 2009.

——. "Tonfilmfrieden/Tonfilmkrieg. Die Geschichte der Tobis vom Technik-Syndikat zum Staatskonzern / Die Tobis 1928–1945. Eine kommentierte Filmografie." *Historical Journal of Film, Radio, and Television* 25, no. 4 (October 1, 2005): 668.

Wayne, Mike. *Politics of Contemporary European Cinema*. Bristol: Intellect Ltd., 2002.

Wenner, Dorothée, and Lior Geller. "Mediterranean Professionals Training: Berlinale Talent Campus." Paper presented at the First Regional Conference: EUROMED AUDIOVISUAL II PROGRAMME, Berlin, Kalkscheune, February 10, 2007. http://www.euromedaudiovisuel.net/Files/2007/02/01/1170363872482.pdf (accessed September 3, 2013).

Winkler, Hartmut. *Der filmische Raum und der Zuschauer: "Apparatus"—Semantik—"Ideology."* Heidelberg: Carl Winter, 1992.

——. *Diskursökonomie: Versuch über die innere Ökonomie der Medien*. Frankfurt am Main: Suhrkamp, 2004.

Wollen, Peter. *Readings and Writings: Semiotic Counter-strategies*. London: NLB, 1982.

Wood, Mary P. *Contemporary European Cinema*. London: Bloomsbury Academic, 2007.

"World Cinema Fund Guidelines." World Cinema Fund, 2009. http://www.berlinale.de/de/das_festival/world_cinema_fund/richtlinien_formulare/index.html (accessed November 1, 2013).

Yıldız, Yasemin. *Beyond the Mother Tongue: The Postmonolingual Condition*. New York: Fordham University Press, 2011.

Youngblood, Gene. *Expanded Cinema*. New York: Dutton, 1970.

Ziarek, Krzysztof. *The Historicity of Experience: Modernity, the Avant-Garde, and the Event*. Evanston: Northwestern University Press, 2001.

Zielinski, Siegfried. *Audiovisionen: Kino und Fernsehen als Zwischenspiele in der Geschichte*. Reinbek b. Hamburg: Rowohlt, 1994.

———. *Variantology: On Deep Time Relations of Arts, Sciences and Technologies*. 4 vols. Cologne: König, 2005.

Index

RANDALL HALLE is the Klaus W. Jonas Professor of German and film studies at the University of Pittsburgh. He is the author of *German Film after Germany: Toward a Transnational Aesthetic*.

The University of Illinois Press
is a founding member of the
Association of American University Presses.

Composed in 10.5/13 Marat Pro
by Lisa Connery
at the University of Illinois Press
Manufactured by Sheridan Books, Inc.

University of Illinois Press
1325 South Oak Street
Champaign, IL 61820-6903
www.press.uillinois.edu